# THE
# MARMALADE
# DIARIES

**Also by Ben Aitken**

*Dear Bill Bryson: Footnotes from a Small Island*
*A Chip Shop in Poznań: My Unlikely Year in Poland*
*The Gran Tour: Travels with my Elders*

# THE
# MARMALADE
# DIARIES

## THE TRUE STORY
## OF AN ODD COUPLE

### BEN AITKEN

ICON

This edition published
in the UK and USA
in 2022 by Icon Books Ltd,
Omnibus Business Centre,
39–41 North Road, London N7 9DP
email: info@iconbooks.com
www.iconbooks.com

First published in 2022

Sold in the UK, Europe and Asia
by Faber & Faber Ltd,
Bloomsbury House,
74–77 Great Russell Street,
London WC1B 3DA or their agents

Distributed in the UK, Europe and
Asia by Grantham Book Services,
Trent Road, Grantham NG31 7XQ

Distributed in the USA
by Publishers Group West,
1700 Fourth Street, Berkeley, CA 94710

Distributed in Canada
by Publishers Group Canada,
76 Stafford Street, Unit 300
Toronto, Ontario M6J 2S1

Distributed in Australia
and New Zealand
by Allen & Unwin Pty Ltd,
PO Box 8500,
83 Alexander Street, Crows Nest,
NSW 2065

Distributed in South Africa
by Jonathan Ball, Office B4,
The District, 41 Sir Lowry Road,
Woodstock 7925

Distributed in India
by Penguin Books India,
7th Floor, Infinity Tower – C,
DLF Cyber City,
Gurgaon 122002, Haryana

ISBN: 978-178578-910-6

Typeset in Baskerville MT by Marie Doherty

Printed and bound in Great Britain
by Clays Ltd, Elcograf S.p.A.

*For Megan*

# Contents

# Prologue

This is not a book about marmalade. Marmalade features – it is the glue that supports the whole – but it is not spread lavishly all over the place. I say this to forewarn readers who want a book about marmalade, which this isn't. Marmalade is in the title because I consumed it each morning during one of the strangest years of my life.

It was one of the strangest years of my life because for the most part I spent it with a recently widowed 85 year old. I moved in with Winnie because she had a spare room and needed a hand around the house (or several, as it turned out). I needed a spare room and could lend said hand. What neither of us needed was a strict and protracted national lockdown to commence ten days after my moving in. Had I known what was around the corner, I would have stayed where I was. It was by no means my ambition to spend 96 per cent of the foreseeable future with a stranger 50 years my senior. I've got quite a flexible conception of what a good time looks like, but even I would have baulked at that.

I didn't know what was around the corner, however, and so I moved in, and over the following months Winnie and I more or less resembled a newlywed couple, minus the consent and passion. We did much of our chatting at breakfast – long, wintry, lockdown mornings. It was over marmalade that we bonded, if you'll excuse the image.

What follows is a record of our unlikely cohabitation, which lasted until it reached a natural endpoint in the summer of 2021. The record is unlikely to be treasured by posterity, or join the ranks of existing diaries of socio-cultural significance, like those of Samuel Pepys and Bridget Jones. Hey-ho.

# 1

## Under no circumstances am I to inherit the house

*21 October 2020.* I'm moving in with Winnie. She's 85 and lost her husband Henry ten months ago. Her children feel she could do with someone in the house (someone other than themselves, presumably), for a bit of security and to assist with odd jobs, including but not limited to fetching coal and removing lids. I saw the room advertised online. When I clocked how low the rent was, I wondered if there was a catch. Turns out the catch was Winnie.

Winnie's got the space. She's naturally gifted in this regard. It's a six-bedroom Victorian job. Detached. Halfway up a hill. Whopping garden. In every way opposed to any dwelling I've hitherto inhabited. I'll be lodging in a small flat at the top of the house, where the servants used to recuperate and share notes regarding the general pleasantness of their masters. I'm promised a view of Croydon.

Winnie Carter, 85, widow. That's pretty much all I know. That and she likes to garden and talk about paintings. She used to volunteer as a guide at a couple of art galleries, I'm told, illuminating the human condition via Titian and so on. Her son, Stewart, a diplomat who lives six miles away, said that I'm not to mind his mother's ways, whatever that means. He said that once I'm accustomed to her idiosyncrasies things will 'settle down'.

Of course I asked about the novel coronavirus sweeping

the globe, about whether Winnie would prefer me to keep my distance and so on. The opposite, said Stewart. She's fit and relaxed, said Stewart. Just don't snog each other, said Stewart. I can't help thinking Stewart wouldn't mind if his mum popped off early so he might inherit his old bedroom sooner.

I stand in the driveway and size up the house. Name: Windy Ridge. Windows: sash, single glazed. Brick: yellow. Door: red. Knocker: unusual. Stewart answers the door.

'Hello!'

'Stewart?'

'Ben?'

We fist bump – two modern souls in sync. I offer my fist to Winnie. She just looks at it then shuffles past me – 'I'm just going to check on the bins.' Nice to meet you too.

The next hour or so is a bit of a blur. Stewart shows me how to do the alarm, how to lock the garage door, how to lock the back door, how to lock the front door, which bottles of wine are worth more than I am, etc. – the practical stuff. Then Winnie and I sign a contract, about how under no circumstances am I to inherit the house. I'd read the contract in advance, so put my name on the line without ado. Winnie hadn't read it in advance, and doesn't intend to read it now by the look of it. She's not fussed. 'Yes, yes – give him a key.' I can't help thinking my moving in is more for the family's sake than hers. I suspect I got the nod from Winnie less because she reckons I'll be terrific company and more because I used to be a carer for a lad with cerebral palsy. Winnie's eldest son has cerebral palsy, you see, and I wouldn't be surprised if my new housemate planned to send me in his direction twice a week. Though I'd struggle to be of much use to Arthur at the moment. Apparently he's in a care home a few streets away that currently has a zero-tolerance policy to visitors. Whatever the reason Winnie's given me the nod, I'm grateful to have got it.

I climb the stairs. And then again. Up to the top – a sort of flat, with bedroom and kitchen and bathroom and study. I size up my new nest. Odd, always, to arrive at a new place. Odder still a new home. Even odder the home of a person resident for 50 years, newly widowed.

Why this move? Surely there were more likely housing options? Yes and no. Yes – at my age one should (if they are the least bit attentive to orthodoxy) be trying to buy their first home, or trying to move in with their partner(s), or trying to rent a room in a part of town not dominated by people drawing a pension (or several, as the case may be). No – I don't have the money to live where I'd like, or with whom I'd like. I would have to work for 300 years to afford this property outright. London: attractive, repulsive.

But it's not just the money. It's not just that the rent is 200 quid a month. My decision was also based on recent events. A couple of years ago I went on a series of holidays with people twice and thrice my age: all-inclusive coach holidays whereupon I played umpteen games of bingo and copped countless anecdotes about rationing and Thatcher. I wrote a book about my intergenerational travels. *The Gran Tour* was not endorsed by Richard and Judy and nor was the book in anyway a bestseller. (Unless we count a particular fifteen-minute window in a particular bookshop in Norwich when I bought four copies myself.) But it did pay a very significant dividend: it equipped me with the knowledge that an older housemate is no more likely to be unbearable than a younger one.

It doesn't take long for me to deduce that Winnie isn't a keen chef. I pick up on the idea when she says, about ten minutes after Stewart has left, 'So what's for supper?'

I play it safe and do a bolognaise, and in the process use the wrong pot or pan about a dozen times. (It's fair to say she's pedantic about kitchenware.) She takes one mouthful (still on her feet, which is a novel approach) and then declares it *amusing*, which, as far as I'm aware, isn't a condition bolognaise aspires to. I serve the pasta with some focaccia which she describes as *determined looking*. She's certainly got a way of putting things.

We eat at the dining table, which dominates one side of the sitting room, which boasts two sets of French windows that give onto the garden. There's a sofa, two boardroom-style swivel chairs, a reclining armchair, another chair made from what appears to be pinewood, several dressers and a corner cabinet (I believe the term is), wherein, for all I know, are the remains of Winnie's previous tenant. I'm not usually one for furniture – I tend to just sit on the stuff and get on with it – but I make a point of mentioning all this because it's pretty much all I'm mentioning to Winnie over dinner. My conversational tactic so far has essentially been 'say what you see'. I'll give you a taster.

'Nice lamp,' I say.

'Has a habit of blowing bulbs.'

'Garden looks nice.'

'A jolly nuisance.'

'Is there meant to be a man in it?'

'He comes once a week. I give him £30 and a can of beer.'

'For the day?'

'I wish. He does three hours. Which isn't nearly enough.'

'No?'

'In fact, I'm given to understand he's appreciative of assistance.'

'That's a nice peppermill.'

'Rather obstinate, I'm afraid.'

'What plant is that?'

'Arguably the most common houseplant in the world.'

'Ah.'

'It's a weeping fig. Or *Ficus benjamina*.'

'So it's got my name on it.'

'It might have your name on it but it shan't have your hands. I don't expect to be relieved of any possessions. I've had enough of that.'

'How do you mean?'

'Some members of my family were recently living here and they appeared hellbent on commandeering everything but the chimney.'

'The arrangement didn't work out then?'

'No. It didn't. Hence your arrival. Shall we open another bottle?'

On the whole, dinner has the nice awkwardness of a first date. When our fingers briefly touch going for the parmesan at the same time, Winnie displays reflexes that belie her years. Notwithstanding my opening gambit of itemising everything in the room, which only made Winnie worry I am pricing all her stuff, I'd say the conversation is generally OK.

But I'd also say it is generally surface level – until, that is, Winnie spills some salt on the table and something about the mishap prompts her to remember losing her elder brother when he was eighteen. (The world is strewn with cues at 85, I fancy.)

'He drowned at sea attempting a rescue,' says Winnie. 'The boat was called *Illustrious*. I remember my father taking the call. Saying, "Right you are, right you are, yes-yes," keeping a brave face, but with tears streaming down his cheeks.'

She gives this some thought – the discrepancy between what's said and what's felt – then smiles, looks at me, and says, 'Do you come with pudding?'

At the end of the day, the dishes done, news of rising cases coming through from the telly in the sitting room, she quietly sets the kitchen table for breakfast. She sets it for two – two plates, two bowls, two butter knives, two spoons, a jar of marmalade – but the second setting isn't for me. It's for Henry. You can tell by the way she's doing it – so slowly, so lovingly. She sees me seeing, goes to put one set away, then decides against it. 'Oh, there's no harm.'

**22 October.** When I come down in the morning and enter the kitchen, she's having an argument with the answerphone. She can't erase the messages, with the result that new messages aren't getting through on account of the backlog. I try to assist but the device defies me as much as it defies her. Neither of us can clear the slate. 'Just what I need. Do wonders for my social life this will.' When she offers me a piece of toast, I have to tell her I've already eaten upstairs. She gives me a look – *like that is it?* I apologise and explain that I didn't want to get under her feet. She says, 'But what are feet for if not to be got under?' and then directs me to the coal bucket, and then onward to the coal shed. She's always kept a fire and doesn't mean to pack in the habit now.

I do lamb chops for dinner. She shows me a trick: heating the red wine in the oven with the plates. She's inflexible about the plates. Reckons they simply *must* be heated, and never mind if the food gets cold in the meantime. I suggest they could be warmed in the microwave to save time, but the lady is not for turning. As with wood – the older, the less inclined to bend. When I share this insight she knocks on my head and makes a noise to suggest it's hollow. I think the kitchen might prove to be a bit of a conflict zone.

Dinner chat is initially dominated by the garden, but then a slice of baked cheesecake prompts recollections of New York. Her father was sent out to be one of the British Reps at the newly formed United Nations, with the result that Winnie was out there for the last two years of school. The family went by boat, as was common back then. Winnie remembers being upgraded to a first-class cabin on account of seasickness, which she's happy to admit wasn't entirely genuine. Winston Churchill was on board for the crossing.

Winnie sat opposite him one night at dinner. 'And what did you make of him?' 'I thought he was just another pale lump.'

Odd how one thing leads to another. 'Arthur wasn't a pale lump, that's for sure,' Winnie's saying now. 'He came out blue. I remember thinking: *babies aren't meant to be blue.* This was in the Philippines. Henry got a job out there with an oil company. They had to cut my pelvis open because he was breached. Arthur, not Henry.'

She takes a step back, or sideways, to provide a bit of context. They were newly married, in their early twenties, living in a flat on Manila Bay. After Arthur was born, Henry was immediately sent 'up country' for two weeks, which Winnie could have done without. Caring for a cerebral palsied newborn wasn't something she was accustomed to. The couple were in the Philippines for about two years, came back with all sorts of lovely furniture – plus Arthur of course.

I do the dishes then retreat upstairs, not yet confident to loiter in the sitting room. I leave Winnie in the kitchen, filling a hot-water bottle.

**23 October.** She's between courses when I come down in the morning – muesli and toast. With regards to the latter, she prefers a granary loaf. Gets it without exception from the Italian baker on Kingston Road. She does so because the baker, Mr Spinnici, used to be a racing driver and once changed Winnie's tyre without complaint or charge when she came to a halt outside his shop in 1972. She's been going twice a week ever since. Winnie says that Mr Spinnici is looking forward to making my acquaintance, which must be her way of saying I'll be fetching the bread from now on. Her marmalade looks decent, so I mention the fact. 'We're running low,' she says, and leaves it at that.

She really is quite fussy about crockery and so on. 'Oh you can't do an egg in that,' she says when I start doing an egg in that. 'You have to use the one at the back that looks like it's got a tropical disease.'[1] And she almost snaps my hand off when I go to use her favourite fork. She owns about a hundred forks but only ever uses one of them. Its middle prongs are bent and misshapen. She and Henry found it on the Portobello Road just after they were engaged in 1958, she explains, putting it away carefully.

She phones Stewart. Activates speakerphone so she can continue making tea. Before Stewart has said hello Winnie has begun vocalising a constellation of historic thoughts and present concerns. 'Stewart. It's Mum. Gloria Lamont at 46. Turns out she's got dreadlocks and is *very* slim. (This teapot's on the blink.) She reckons we've got Japanese knotweed down the bottom of the garden and it's starting to encroach. (I wouldn't do that if I were you, Ben.) Anyway, how are you?' Then, having posed the question, she's out the back door and into the garden to scatter some crumbs for the birds, leaving Stewart to deliver his answer to the kitchen. Never have I seen or heard such original use of a telephone.

Dinner is pumpkin stew. She has this to say about it: 'It was certainly *different*. But then again, I suppose some things *are*.'

---

[1] The limestone in the eggshell causes limescale to build up on the pan, so she always uses the same one to isolate the damage.

**24 October.** Along with *The Times* (which drops with a diurnal plop) a flyer lands on the mat. It's for a production of *Educating Rita* at the local theatre, recently revived after a substantial hiatus on account of coronavirus. I take the pair through to the kitchen, where Winnie's applying her marmalade. I ask her if she'd like to see the play, fancying we might spy in the drama an echo of our own situation – namely, a senior figure bringing a junior one up to scratch. She answers my question by reminding me that I didn't tend to the fire this morning. I tell her I didn't realise it was exclusively my responsibility. She says the last person that didn't realise that didn't last long. Then she points to a picture in the paper of a government minister and says, 'According to him, we're all in this together. What nonsense. We're in this *apart*.'

Winnie gives me a slow tour of the garden. Along the way, she tells me what most gives her a headache – 'that *damned* Japanese knotweed' – and what most gives her joy – the tulips and roses. At the end, she pauses for a moment to weigh it all up. 'The headache-joy ratio rather depends on the season, I'm afraid, and right now it's headache-heavy. Hey-ho.'

**25 October.** Winnie is having her hair cut in the utility room. I see her in profile, with Liz the hairdresser behind, as I'm going down the stairs. Winnie clocks me as I descend and says to Liz, 'Do him next, would you? Poor scrap can hardly see a thing.' She decides to have some colour put in at the last minute.

**26 October.** We run into an old friend of Winnie's walking up to the common. They haven't seen each other for quite some time, I infer. The impression I get is that Winnie hasn't seen many of her friends for quite some time, having fallen off the radar since Henry got ill (a series of debilitating strokes in the ten years up to his death). Valerie was clearly full of concern, but Winnie wanted to push on, didn't want to dally.

We walk a fair way on the common. Winnie knows the trees by their leaves. She looks up at one, points to the leaves at its top – the only survivors. 'They hang on up there,' she says, 'because that's where the light is.' Walking home, she says that after Henry died she went through a blank period. 'I was upside-down. Still am, to be honest.' When we get back, she spends the next hour or so clearing leaves off the pavement.

**27 October.** There's a small television on top of the fridge in the kitchen. We eat breakfast while watching a show about Francis Bacon. 'Brilliant painter, horrible paintings' is Winnie's verdict. Somewhat intimidated by the strength of this opinion, it takes some courage to nominate Lowry as one of my favourite painters, chiefly for his throwing light on things accustomed to shadow. Winnie gives my nomination some thought, then wrinkles her nose and says, 'No. Not my cup of tea, Lowry.'

To change the subject – and perhaps cheer Winnie up a bit – I tell her I got lost yesterday. Up on the common. When I went for a run. She asks whereabouts and I say there was a pond, surrounded by forest, close to the windmill. She knows where I'm on about. 'I took the children up to that pond once, and one of them – it might have been Stewart – pointed to a corner of the pond and said it was vibrating. And by George he wasn't kidding. It was a legion of frogs having a gang bang.' (I almost choke when she says 'gang bang'.)

**28 October.** A week in now and things are going *OK*. Whether Winnie's feeling any less upside-down, I can't say, but the optimist in me reckons she might have got fractionally happier as the week's gone on. Case in point: when the phone went a few minutes ago, Winnie got there before the answerphone cut in, which hasn't happened since I've been here. It was one of her grandchildren, wanting to know if Turner was a Cubist, which caused Winnie to laugh a great deal. It was nice to hear.

**30 October.** I'm getting used to Winnie's advice. Don't get up at 10 and expect a jolly reception. Don't mix mushrooms. Don't poke that or it'll smash. Don't pull that or it'll – too late, you've broken it. Don't go out wearing that unless you wish to be stared at. All of the above offered quite cheerily, I hasten to add. If she gets some trick-or-treaters tomorrow night, Winnie plans to give them a few choice words.

**31 October.** Out for a meal with my girlfriend – our fourth anniversary. Oddly, I almost asked Winnie if she wanted to come along. Walking across Trafalgar Square, we hear on the grapevine that another national lockdown will start next Thursday – on bonfire night, of all occasions. I suppose the coincidence is handy if we want to symbolically throw our liberties and optimism onto the pyre. I guess I'll be seeing more of Winnie than planned.

# 1936

*Winnie's parents were contrastingly employed at the time of their daughter's birth. Whereas Mr Lovelock was in the habit of flying planes out of Croydon airport, Mrs Lovelock mostly occupied herself with worrying acutely about whatever she could lay her hands on. (By way of example: on the eve of the 1923 UK general election – which would return a Labour government for the first time – Winnie's mother spent several painful hours fearing she'd have to learn Russian.) Yes, make no mistake, Winnie Lovelock didn't appear out of thin air. If she appeared out of anything it was the maternity ward of Greenwich Hospital in London. The first thing Winnie's mother said of her daughter – 'Look at the size of that bottom' – is thought to have been influential in the child's development. Winnie was called Winnie upon the insistence of her brothers, who were at that time enamoured of A.A. Milne's* Winnie-the-Pooh *stories. It wouldn't be long after their sister's arrival, however, that the boys would come to see that the Winnie of the stories and the Winnie sharing their bedroom were really quite different beasts indeed. The youngest of the brothers opted to express his feelings thusly: 'On this evidence, give me fiction any day.'*

# 2

# What the hell are you doing here then?

**4 November.** Day before lockdown. Up to the common to sit on a bench and self-consciously pay attention to nature. The trees are all but bare and thus true to form, true to their most basic characters. All sorts out and about. Almost a festive spirit. Someone wishes me a Happy Lockdown. When I get back home, Winnie's at the kitchen sink, gazing out at the fog. 'Season of mists and mellow fruitfulness,' she says, which I suspect might be poetry. When I ask if that was poetry she turns and spots me *in flagrante*. 'Over my dead body will you boil veg in that amount of water.'

**5 November.** First day of lockdown. Spirits a bit low at Windy Ridge to be honest. Neither of us bargained on this. Fireworks seem a tad inappropriate, given the occasion. Nonetheless, we watch them shoot up and burst and briefly shine before disappearing by degrees over South London. Dinner is some old pork casserole. I propose rice with it but she's adamant the two don't marry. She's got very strong opinions about what goes together, I've noticed, which doesn't bode well.

**6 November.** I've started to linger in the sitting room after dinner. Less inclined to retreat, to seek privacy. I ask if she wants to watch *University Challenge*. 'Is it Paxman?' 'Yeah.' 'Then no.' She sits down in any case, watches twenty minutes or so before calling it a night. She touches me on the shoulder when she goes off to bed. First time that's happened.

I switch chairs: to the electric recliner that was bought for Henry after his first stroke. He had a series of them, I understand. He'd had enough by the end. Couldn't stand the incapacity. It wasn't his idea of life. His death unhinged her more than she expected. She feels like she's lost everything. Henry and Arthur were the pillars holding up her life, giving it sense and structure and integrity. Now Henry's dead and Arthur's locked up. That's how she sees it, how she feels it. She used to meet up with various friends at a keep-fit class at the YMCA down the road, but that's been cancelled. She's been told to get on Zoom. While she agrees that Zoom doesn't sound like an altogether bad platform for a keep-fit class, she's not sure it's for her. So these days she does her exercises sat on the end of the bed in the morning, listening to news of soaring reproduction rates. She told me all of the above during the final third of *University Challenge*, meaning I was unable to comprehend any of the questions, which gave her the confidence to ask me at the end of the programme if I was fibbing when I said I went to university.

**7 November.** There's an issue with her windscreen wipers. She couldn't get them to do the back window and now she can't get them to stop. She tells me to get in the car and then drives us to the Skoda garage in Tooting to get the man there to have a look. When Winnie practically reverses into his showroom, the man there probably gets more of a look than he would like.

We go to the farmers' market after. Winnie has a word with all the vendors while I buy guinea fowl, pork belly, and a dozen lamb and rosemary sausages, which causes Winnie to ask if I'm pregnant. I buy the two of us a coffee. She's so appalled by the cost that she has to turn her back when I pay. She says her flat white tastes of cardboard.

She drives home the long way, to show me a few things. It's telling what she points out – the children's first school, the expensive dentist, the less expensive but potentially ille-gitimate dentist, a spot where there used to be an apple orchard. The latter prompts a memory of the first time she got drunk. She was at the indoor market in Oxford, eighteen or nineteen. She was given half a pint of cider by a jolly vendor, didn't know how strong it was, thought it tasted of apple juice. At the drop of a hat, she couldn't walk her bike between the stalls anymore, knocked over a load of pars-nips. Then she threw up twenty minutes later riding along Queen Street.

She does eggs for dinner. When she asked me what my ambi-tions were in the way of cooking an evening meal, I said I had no ideas. She said in that case she'd boil two eggs (to discourage me from running out of ideas again, presumably). She shows me how to test for stinkers by seeing if they sink or float. I say, 'That's a nice trick.' She says, 'I'm not as green as I'm cabbage looking.' When she gets an egg that floats – a stinker – she cracks it open just to check. Can't stand the idea of throwing one out mistakenly. She threw one out once – a floater – and couldn't sleep that night for fear she'd made a mistake, so got up and went out into the garden in her nightie and found it in the compost.

Her brother Jacob died in his forties of cancer. She tells me as we watch someone having two tumours cut out of their liver on the telly. In other news, I've stopped worrying about the occasional whiff of cigarette smoke on my clothes since she said she lost her sense of smell in 2016.

**9 November.** Winnie gets *The Times* each morning. She'll have a look stood up at the kitchen table, eating her toast with marmalade. She doesn't mind a joke at the expense of our elected members, that's for sure, and she often knows the people popping up in the obituaries, if that's not an inappropriate way of putting it. She's started hooking out the crossword for me so I don't have to wait until she's done with the paper, which is nice of her. I ask for help with a clue – small finch, six letters. She says she'll have a quick look. I think she's going to Google it, but instead she spends half an hour going through an anthology of birds. She says the old method is better than Google *because* of its deficiencies. The task of locating the anthology and then flicking through the pages ensures you find things along the way. She says her bank wants her to go online, but she's not comfortable with the idea. 'Do as you wish, not as you're told,' I say. She nods briefly in agreement and then says, 'But don't go around thinking the same applies to you.'

She remembers an Italian carer who she wishes had done less what she wished and more what she was told. 'She was a funny girl. We got her from the agency. On her first day she came up to me and said, "I am Italian. I am lesbian. I look after Mister only. Capito?" She stormed out one evening when she realised I'd put herbs in the bolognaise. Never came back. Reckoned it was sacrilegious. They weren't all bad though. The carers. Ron was a good one. He was here for nearly ten years. South African. Or Zimbabwean. He was very good with Henry. But he got *too* involved. Couldn't help it. I used to say to him, "Don't get too close. It won't do you any good." Cried his eyes out at the end. Was more upset about Henry's death than Henry was as far as I could tell.'

A letter hits the mat from Gloria Lamont at 46, re an overhanging branch. Winnie gets straight on the phone to Stewart, who doesn't prove as helpful as Winnie would like when it comes to getting four quotes from local tree surgeons within the hour. 'Would you like me to quit my job and come and do it myself?' asks Stewart. 'Well I dare say you've had worse ideas than that,' says Winnie.

**10 November.** Up at 7 in case the tree surgeons come early – a favour for Winnie. Get the fire going easily enough: coal in, ash out, etc. Tree surgeons don't come until 9, in the event. Winnie watches them at it from the bottom of the ladder, doubtless offering a few pointers. Then she comes into the sitting room and watches from here. I've never seen her look so content. She could be watching a favourite film. You can almost see the serotonin gushing around her body, if that's what serotonin does. The sight of the tree surgeons has obviously got her in the mood, because next she invites me to clean the downstairs loo and spectates from the doorway, arms crossed and smiling.

Because we're getting on so well today, Winnie wants to introduce me to the freezer in the basement. It's absolutely loaded. Winnie could survive an apocalypse comfortably. And maybe that's the point. She all but climbs in and emerges with a leg of lamb that she tosses to me quite recklessly. 'See what you can do with that,' she says, and laughs. Another little flourish of bonhomie – good to see. Incidence rate of such sneaking up I feel.

She tells me about the time she, another girl from school and the other girl's sister drove from New York to Texas in a Jeep. Her mother allowed her to go on the understanding the other girl's sister was responsible, which she most assuredly wasn't. Texas made an impression on Winnie – and how! This was in the 1950s, you have to remember. When black people were segregated. Winnie couldn't bring herself to look. So she drank cocktails instead, which was a rather shameful approach to the matter now that she thinks about it.

Anyway, when she got back to England, having sailed from New York to Southampton, she remembers getting the train to Oxford, and seeing a green sports car bombing along the country lanes and thinking, 'I wouldn't mind matching up with someone who's got one of those.' So imagine her excitement when she met Henry for the first time, in his digs at Oxford, where she discovered him putting a sports car together in his sitting room. 'What colour was it?' I say. 'Grey,' she says.

She looks at her cup of tea, realises it's gone cold, tips it into the sink, then looks at the washing on the line and says, 'It was rather passionate, really. We had time to ourselves. His parents had split, and mine were still in New York. I told him – I'm not going to muck about, Henry; if you don't marry me then I'm off.' She turns to me and asks, 'So how long have you and yours been at it?' I tell her we've been at it four years. 'Then just what the hell are you doing here then?' she says. I confess to having asked myself the same question.

**11 November.** 'The gardener's got bowel cancer,' she says, passing me the marmalade. 'Henry got that one. When they pulled it out they said it was the biggest they'd seen. Henry was rather proud, which gives you an idea how competitive he was.'

**12 November.** I didn't suffer much of a lockdown last time (March to May 2020). I was in Australia – stuck there somewhat, living in a caravan, having gone for a wedding. The most biting restriction was having to take your coffee away. I can't say I'm suffering at the hands of lockdown 2.0 – not acutely, not painfully – but nor can I say it's enriching my life. In so many ways there's been a depletion. Not one to moan about, granted, but a wide and significant depletion nevertheless. Put one way, I've substituted a significant chunk of culture and recreation and wellbeing for a collection of bad habits and Winnie. That's the crude analysis. Am I lonely? No. Not really. (Maybe a bit.) I've been out for walks. I've spoken to cashiers and vendors. I've met a couple of friends outdoors.

And Winnie's here of course, which is a clear and countable good. And yet, and yet, and yet … It's a matter of attitude of course. And so far my attitude has had a mind of its own.

Up to the common with Winnie to have a walk in the woods. She says she used to come up most days with the children or the dogs. She'd avoid paths that were 'too organised', preferring the smaller hidden trails where you stood a chance of twisting your ankle. 'You'd have a chance of seeing birds that way. Birds don't hang around near gangs of people.' She points to a spot along the bridleway and says she was attacked there once. Aged 40. He got her on the floor and had his hands where they had no right to be. Bilbo (her border terrier) started licking the assailant's face and Winnie yanked his finger back, which did the trick nicely. She gave Bilbo two dinners that night. She tries to take a photo of a group of tall slim trees. She's not happy with the result. 'When you try and capture it, the light is never right, is it? It's never the same. Which makes me think you're better off just looking.' At its end, she thanks me for the walk. She says one isn't inclined to do it alone, rightly or wrongly.

**13 November.** Winnie's granddaughter visits. Tells Winnie she's got a boyfriend in Milan. 'Crikey,' says Winnie, 'talk about socially distanced.' When Abigail leaves, Winnie sets about cleaning Arthur's electric razor, which she does at length with a toothbrush. I ask if she's able to see Arthur when she nips round to drop stuff off. 'Through the window. If I'm lucky.'

**14 November.** Breakfast with Winnie. A beginner's guide. She always starts standing up. She'll be stood for her muesli, and perhaps the first pages of the newspaper, as if ready to dash off somewhere at any moment. Only when she's moved on to her toast will she settle down – and then only by degrees. She won't be fully sat and stationed and at ease until the very end of breakfast, at which point, as if provoked by the first signs and tingles of relaxation, she'll leap to her feet and say something along the lines of 'Right, enough of that, time to crack on with the war.'

Our talk at breakfast this morning is all over the place – religion, Colorado, the importance of putting the butter next to the kettle to soften it in the morning – but it winds up at her mother. 'My mother was a worrier,' says Winnie. 'She did very little else. Hardly surprising when you consider that she lost a son at such a young age. Children are precious things. They're meant to be your future. Not your past.' She says her mother was cremated. Remembers her ashes being delivered in a Mothercare bag. Winnie thought that was fantastic. Laughs her head off at the memory. (Before leaping to her feet and cracking on with the war of course.)

It's kedgeree for dinner. The turmeric and curry powder she's using are fairly mature, I notice, after she's deposited half of each into the pan. But they're positively youthful compared to the cream of tartar. It was made by Mitre, who went out of business in 1959. She says her spice cupboard is prize-winning. Says that one of the grandchildren came home from school saying they had to find the oldest spice in Granny's cupboard. Winnie won by a quarter of a century.

**15 November.** At Winnie's behest, I have the remaining ked-geree for breakfast, while she has her standard diptych of muesli followed by marmalade on toast. She's down to one jar of marmalade – hence her pushing me towards leftovers. Says she can't make another batch until Seville oranges appear in Lidl. 'Why Seville oranges?' 'It's their bitterness. It tempers the sweetness.'

My friend Andy visits. The three of us go out for a walk, and in so doing create the social highlight of my week. Andy and I are both slightly terrified when Winnie crosses a busy road with suicidal boldness. She's unapologetic. 'One has to plough one's own furrow, I'm afraid.' We go to Cannizaro House, a hotel whose extensive garden is open to the public. Andy wants to know what Winnie makes of me. She says that my cooking has been 'rather busy' and that my sense of humour is 'best avoided'. Our lap of the garden finishes at the aviary by the entrance. Andy says the birds should all be released. Winnie knows where Andy's coming from but argues that the birds serve a purpose where they are – they breed a fondness for birds. 'No love without awareness' is how she sums it up.

Winnie's daughter Rebecca calls by. We have a chat on the driveway. She's surprised to learn that Winnie was out for so long. Says it's been years since she walked that much.

Rebecca's also a widow, I've been told. Lost her husband to cancer two years ago. He was in his fifties, a scientist, researching the cancer he knew would kill him. How about that for a game of Poohsticks? There's obvious love between Winnie and Rebecca – a love steeped by or in empathy. That's not to say they don't bump or grate – they most certainly do – a few times already since Rebecca turned up. They're too alike not to, I suppose. Birds of a feather, in my experience, can clash as much as chalk and cheese.

Winnie remarks on a few of the paintings lining the stairs. Points to one and says, 'Henry's father looked at this one and said, "What does it mean?" And I said, "No idea." And he said, "So why on earth did you hang it?" And I said, "Because I like it." Well – you should have seen his face. The notion utterly befuddled him. "There's no value without efficacy!" he said. Or shouted rather. He couldn't handle the slightest hint of ambiguity. A military career will do that, I suppose. Instil a prejudice against things that are nice but don't do anything.'

**16 November.** With each day that passes, common inclinations become apparent. For example, we've similar priorities in the morning. We both like to share various biomechanical complaints before flipping through the paper and having a joke at the expense of the high and mighty. Whoever cautioned not to match May with December didn't reckon on the two bonding over a mutual distrust of July. Speaking of distrust, a white dove has just landed in the holly tree and has started having a go at the berries. Winnie is not amused. 'My brother used to have a rifle for such occasions,' she says. Yikes. Also 'yikes' is the sight of her climbing a stepladder to get at the old clock in the kitchen. She wants to synchronise it. Says it's fallen behind. She's clearly struggling to wind it up but refuses my offer of help. She gets there in the end. 'Back on track,' she says. 'For a few hours at least.'

**17 November.** Nearly two weeks into the lockdown. I don't wear a pedometer but if I did I'm pretty sure it would tell me that over the last fortnight I've walked an average of 36 steps a day, mostly in the direction of the kettle. I'm learning to wake up in the morning with nowhere to go. It's not an entirely unpleasant lesson, I must say, but it's a lesson none-theless, and I never was a good student.

Speaking of the kettle, I make us both a tea. Drinking said, we talk about a neighbour who's been dead seven years. She was the mother of two girls, one of whom had cerebral palsy. Eileen, the youngest, did a lot for her disabled sister growing up. Too much perhaps, for when Eileen was sixteen or seventeen she walked into an oncoming train. Winnie made a point never to ask Rebecca or Stewart to care for Arthur, and she supposes the two things may be related. She feels guilty about Arthur's cerebral palsy and always has. Blames herself. Perhaps she shouldn't but she does. The thing is, she couldn't have a Caesarean because her blood type is rare and she was in the Philippines. If she'd been in London it would have been otherwise. 'Stupid woman,' she says, get-ting to her feet and leaving the table.

Things happen for a reason. A girl walks into a train because she carried too much too soon. A woman doesn't share her burden because a girl walked into a train. A woman feels guilt all her life because she couldn't have a Caesarean. People tend to say that everything happens for a reason when they don't know the reason. People don't tend to say that everything happens for a reason when they do. In any case, Winnie makes me laugh twice in the space of a minute and the reasons are these: first, she opens the fridge and says, 'I've been harbouring this wretched egg for yonks and it's giving me nightmares,' and second, she points to a picture of Matt Lucas in the paper and says, 'He won't survive the pandemic.'

A leaflet lands on the mat advertising a residential aged care facility. 'That can go in the bin,' she says emphatically, going out the back door to scatter some crumbs. As she does so, the house alarm goes off. (Both of us had forgotten to unset it.) A minute later the doorbell goes: it's a police officer who happened to be passing. 'I heard the alarm. Anything wrong?' 'Nothing at all, officer. The alarm goes off when we run out of coffee.' 'Do you live here, sir?'

After lunch (broccoli soup), I sit in the living room and read *H is for Hawk*. Winnie says she'll join me. Says it's been ages since she sat down and read. She's got my book. (I gave her a copy of my latest, chiefly to substantiate my claim that I do have a job of some sort.) She reads maybe half a page and then falls asleep. She wakes up a few minutes later, reads a few lines, asks what a TED Talk is, then falls asleep again.

After a few micro naps of this sort, she ploughs through a couple of pages. It's nice watching her out of the corner of my eye – dark blue gilet, turquoise jumper, colourful scarf, reading glasses perched on the end of her nose. 'Now who told you that an owl can lift up and carry away a lamb?' she says without looking up from the book. In terms of feedback, that's about all I get from her. Got more when I brought a load of coal in from the shed this morning. Ah well.

**19 November.** Morning. I put the kettle on, and as it boils I collect the coal from the coal shed and then attempt to provoke the still faintly orange coals of yesterday back to life. I have an instant coffee and then work on the crossword until Winnie appears, and with her the outside chance of some toast and marmalade. (I daren't help myself. Not yet. Might be years before I take that approach, I fancy.) She enters. I say good morning. She says, 'I must get that tart round to Arthur today, even if it kills me.' Then she heats her teapot, which basically involves filling it with boiling water, letting it stand for a minute, and then emptying it. Then she pops a bag in and fills it again. After giving it at least five minutes, she'll pour herself a mug (milk already in). And then, more often than not, she'll forget to drink the damn thing, having been diverted by a task or a phone call or another dove in the holly tree. So it goes.

Winnie's in charge of dinner. She salts the salmon so thoroughly that I'm led to believe she means to preserve it for years, rather than serve it in minutes. She says (passing me the lemon) that her mother had a nervous breakdown in

America. She didn't take to the diplomacy, says Winnie – too much stress, too many dinners and receptions, too many strangers. Which means that off the back of New York, Winnie's dad got the medal of St Michael and St George and her mum got a psychiatrist. There you go: things happen for a reason.

**20 November.** I'm in the drawing room, testing out the chaise longue, when Winnie returns from the Co-op. She says there was a bit of a scene. The ATM spat out her cash and receipt, but not her card. So she spoke to the young lady on the checkout, who got on the phone to someone to ask them to come down and have a look, at which point Winnie found the card in her purse. 'Damned if I know how it got there,' she says. 'I must have had it in there in a flash. I'm too efficient for my own good.' She looks at me on the chaise longue more curiously, as if only realising now just how unlikely a spectacle it is. She laughs and then says, 'I suppose I better take some marzipan biscuits round to Carlotta. I'm told she's not exactly getting a kick out of the lockdown.'

She does take some marzipan biscuits round to Carlotta (95, Austrian), but not before unloading her shopping. Three blocks of butter to go in the freezer (despite there being roughly a cubic metre of the stuff in there already). Two granary loaves from Mr Spinnici. And some special puddings for Arthur. I'm starting to get an idea of her essentials.

Dinner prep. I'm struggling to get the flesh off some chicken legs. 'Ah,' says Winnie, spotting my struggle. 'Nightmarish, aren't they? You'd better move out the way. I've dealt with turkeys.' Turns out Winnie worked on a turkey farm one summer when she was in her late teens. The previous summer she'd spent in Italy, in a palatial villa owned by the father of a friend. Winnie's mother didn't think much of that sort of vacation, said it was about time Winnie came down to earth a bit – by spending a summer on a turkey farm. 'The local girls who worked on that farm were what you would call indelicate. They taught me everything I needed to know about sex, and much more that I didn't. In any case, I became a dab hand at sorting a turkey out and did it every Christmas thereafter.'

**21 November.** There's been a reduction in the garage. Stewart arranged for some men to come and take away what he'd earmarked as pointless. Winnie oversaw the whole operation, said the removal men were jolly good chaps, though they might have left her the unplayable piano she hasn't sat at since 1984. 'The old bathtub's gone as well, I'm pleased to say. Has a lot to answer for that tub – not least a slipped disc and a broken toe. Not the kind of memories to cling on to. But much of what's been removed is surely *useful* – like the rocking horse without a head.' She points to some things that she rescued from removal: some wood from the Philippines that she's waiting to mature before having it turned into furniture, and a helmet from the First World War.

After lunch, I take some biscuits and his laundered electric razor to Arthur, then go to the common. I sit on my new favourite bench in the light rain and watch what happens. It's all and nothing, really. Dogs pull on leashes. A man yells into his phone that something wasn't enough. A lone crow ambles along the footpath, as if out for an evening stroll, its wings sort of tucked in behind its back, whistling as it goes. The rain briefly stops, and then starts again.

Most of the people she knows have died, which is an odd thought. Over lasagne, she mentions a friend whose first wife dropped dead during a yoga class ('or flopped rather'), and whose second wife dropped dead on the doorstep. She looks at me. I compliment the salad dressing. She says Ron did it.

'As in Ron the former carer of Henry?'

'That's him.'

'And he left when exactly?'

'Oh, about ten years ago.'

Washing up, she points to the back of a house on the far side of the garden. 'I've been in there once,' she says. 'Years ago. I think one of their cats got into the garden and I took it back. Anyway, he became governor of the Bank of England if I remember.' 'The cat did?' 'Wimbledon used to be quite communal, believe it or not. Not like it is now. I was always returning cats or hosting children. And there was the Women of Wimbledon Association. I used to call them the mafia – once you were in, you were safe. They'd even eliminate bothersome local councillors if you gave them an address. They would go up and down the streets, calling on members, making sure they were alright. They can't now of course.

People could be as sick as parrots and nobody would know. Bloody pandemic. The new normal. Hey-ho.'

Drying up, I ask Winnie what she made of the lasagne.
      'Hm? Oh. Well. It was certainly solid. Quite rich.'
      'A mark out of ten?'
      'Well it's hard to measure such things.'
      'Five?'
      'Alright.'

**23 November.** I've been asked four questions in five weeks. I come downstairs and say, 'Hello Winnie,' and she says, 'Scottish Widows are a jolly nuisance.' Or I say, 'Alright Winnie?' and she says, 'This Caitlin Moran winds me up. I could kick her around the block.' I have on more than one occasion felt remarkably like a utensil. Which is neither complaint nor criticism, I hasten to add. Winnie has no reason to give a monkey's about me. As far as she's concerned, I've been installed to deter burglars.

**24 November.** At dinner we talk about what's under our noses. The dining table was bought in a second-hand shop in the Cotswolds, where the family used to rent an old farmer's cottage every summer. They'd take the children, go down to the river, catch dragonflies and hunt for flowers (and occasionally furniture). Winnie and Henry would share with the children what they knew of nature, what they loved, what they admired, what they marvelled at. Of the children, Arthur was the real enthusiast. Less able to swing across a river or charge off into a field, he'd find sanctuary in botanical super-iority. 'Anyway, the table was a bargain,' she says. 'That's the long and the short of it. Excellent wood, mahogany. Its grain is a picture, and it extends to cater for fifteen, useful at Christmas. Not this Christmas, mind you.'

Some things are more than what they are. More than what they stand for. Her table is such a thing. She's protective of it. Fiercely so. She scolds me when I put anything directly on it that is warmer than eleven degrees. When eating she uses two placemats (one on top of the other) as a rule. And if it's sunny she will always have the blind down to prevent fading, even though she adores the light. For Winnie, the table is tantamount to family.

**25 November.** I wake up to two voicemails, the second an escalation of the first, in terms of tone and content. Together they amount to: 'Ben. Winnie. Where the hell are you? Wakey-wakey. You HAVE to start the fire. You CANNOT expect me to do it. Come on. Get up. Make an appearance. NOW.'

I'm angry. For about four minutes. Then I reason that today is a big day for Winnie (she's taking Arthur to the hos-pital) and she probably didn't sleep much. The discovery of an extinguished fire and a missing lodger must have provided a useful outlet for her angst.

I nip downstairs and quickly dispose of the ash and bring in the coal and get the thing going again – all in silence, for I'm not yet ready to be pally with Winnie. I think she knows she blew a gasket in my direction because when I'm adding the final touches to the fire she comes in, puts her hand on my shoulder and says, 'Thank you. Very much. A lot on our plate today, that's all.'

As I'm wondering about her use of the word 'our', she says, 'Right, we better be off.' She senses something in my reaction suggesting surprise, so explains that I'm to drive her to collect Arthur, then drive the pair of them to the hospital, then deposit them outside the appropriate unit, then commence the arduous task of finding somewhere to park. I manage to avoid saying something uncharitable. Instead I offer a Hollywood smile and say, 'Of course, Winnie. Get yourself set and we'll head off.'

Arthur is getting a Botox injection to reduce salivation. When we get to the care home, we both have to be tested for the virus and wait in the carpark for half an hour for the results, giving Winnie half an hour to complain about waiting for half an hour. When the time comes, I put Arthur's 'wheelie' (walking frame on wheels) in the boot and help him with the descent into the passenger seat. I ask him if he fancies the radio on. He answers by saying that so-and-so nicked his paper again this morning, which tells me that Arthur's a chip off the old block alright.

This is the first time Arthur has been out for months. As a result, when I ask him a few questions, he's so intent on studying the world he doesn't even hear them. I drop the pair outside the appropriate unit then try to find a parking space, but it's quickly obvious I don't have a hope in hell and so drive home. Just as I'm sitting down to do a bit of work, Winnie calls. As I'm telling her about the parking situation and that I'm back home and will come and collect them when she gives me the nod, the doorbell goes. It's a middle-aged man in a tracksuit. Bob Mustard, he says, family friend, wondering if Arthur's in. Bob explains that he'd heard on the grapevine (i.e. via his mother) that Arthur was being busted out of jail for a few hours. I explain the situ. He says he might head down to the hospital. Asks if he'd stand more chance of getting admitted if he wore a vicar costume. Sensing my confusion, Bob hastens to add that he's a chaplain at a local prison. As I'm processing this new piece of information, two things happen: the postman turns up with a parcel that needs to be signed for and Winnie calls on the phone. 'Ben,' she says, 'it looks like we're just about—' 'One second, Winnie. What's that, Bob?' Bob's jumped into a taxi, says he's off to the hospital. I sign for the parcel. 'Winnie? Listen up. Bob Mustard's coming down in his vicar costume.' 'Don't worry about that. We need picking up.' 'Already?' 'Yes.' 'OK, I'm on my way. But look out for a vicar.'

I find them all outside the appropriate unit chatting. We offer Bob a lift home but he's adamant it would be sinful, so gets a cab back. Back at Windy Ridge, Arthur comes in against the rules. Winnie does him some eggs – the freshest she has, which goes against every grain in her body. I watch Winnie become overtaken by an entirely different operating system; in the face of her son, she's swift, instructive, insistent, exacting – parental, in short. Over the next hour, Winnie presents Arthur with a series of reheated leftovers – small plates, if you will. Fish pie, half a spud, a tranche of apple crumble, a venison sausage. After eating 4,000 calories,

Arthur goes upstairs (which takes a hell of an effort from the man) to spend some time in his old bedroom, where he promptly falls asleep. Winnie later tells me how she'd put her head around the door and found him snoring with a book over his face.

'Hardly salivating at all, which was good,' she says.

'What book was it?'

'*A Hitchhiker's Guide to the Galaxy.*'

'27.'

'27 what?'

'Just 27. The meaning of life, the universe and everything. That's what the author—'

'I think you'll find it's 47.'[1]

**27 November.** Dinner is a curry. Winnie slices a banana on top of hers, which might be the first sign of dementia. The conversation is typically non-linear. Lard comes up, and then Merton Council, and then the memory of her granddaughters asleep on the floor under the table of a local restaurant she liked to go to with Rebecca and Henry. Doing the dishes, I ask for a half-term report. 'Do you think it's going alright, Winnie? Me living here.' 'I think you've been incredibly tolerant,' she says, passing me what might once have been a plum. 'Now would you do something with this? I fear it's growing a beard.'

---

[1] It's 42.

**28 November.** I wake at 9.15. Whoops. This could spell trouble. The fire's bound to have gone out. I hasten downstairs: the paper's on the mat, which means she hasn't been down yet. There are still some bright embers in the grate, thank the lord, meaning there's something to work with. Ten minutes later and it would have been a goner. I tidy the grate, empty the tray, fetch the coal. The fire needs a fair bit of encouragement – yesterday's headlines, a bit of tinder – but survives, stabilises and then flourishes. Winnie appears as the kettle's boiling. I act like I've been up for hours.

'Morning, Winnie.'

'Stiff as a post this morning frankly. How was the fire?'

'Terrific. Yeah. No problems. Good as new. Yeah, fine. Blazing.'

'Would you kindly shift so I can access the telephone?'

She phones Liz the hairdresser. Says she can't see a thing. Liz explains that it's illegal for her to come round. Winnie says, 'But I can't *see*.'

**29 November.** Because she's getting low on marmalade, I've been using alternative toppings of late. This morning, I ask if I can borrow a banana. She rather likes the idea of someone borrowing a banana; it makes her laugh – until, that is, I start spreading the banana on my toast, at which point she drops *The Times* and says, 'Good God! What are you doing? Have you got scurvy?' She's never seen it done before, never even heard of the notion. She says it's a bit rum, if she's honest, and not exactly aesthetic. I say, 'That's a bit rich seeing as you'll merrily stick banana on a curry.'

The front page of the paper carries a story about *The Crown*. Helena Bonham Carter, who plays Princess Margaret, reckons it should be made absolutely crystal clear that the drama isn't a documentary. Winnie says, 'Is there anyone stupid enough to mistake it for a documentary?' and then goes on to answer her own question: 'Yes, I rather suppose there is …' She says that Henry's father (the art critic we met earlier) was rather fond of Margaret, thought she was rather good fun, rather jolly.

'Ron, on the other hand, reckoned Princess Anne coarse,' she says.

'Ron the Zimbabwean who did the salad dressing ten years ago?'

'That's him. Apparently he was manning a jump at an equestrian event in South Africa.'

'As you do.'

'When Anne approached (on a horse), by all accounts she rather had the feeling that Ron was in the way, and so said in no uncertain terms that he ought to shove off, which seems fair enough to me.'

'I see.'

'Anyway, one thing causing another and so on, Ron rather went off Anne thereafter.'

'Want to try some?' (Banana on toast.)

'Not in a month of Sundays.'

'I thought you said you'd try everything once.'

'Yes but there's everything and then there's that.'

I discover a huge pumpkin in the larder. It's been quarantined, and is covered in Post-it notes. 'Do NOT dispose. Do NOT compost. SEEDS will run amok.'

I go out for a long walk. I told Winnie I'd be back at 7ish, and not to wait for me before eating, but get a call at 7 along the lines of:

'Ben. The fish pie is done – where are you?'

'About a mile away.'

'Why?'

*Why?* 'I'm homeward bound, Winnie.'

'Bound to home might be better going forward.'

'For who?'

'Can you get some peas?'

She doesn't like eating alone. That's the thing. Hates it even. But I can't conceivably have dinner with Winnie every day for the rest of my life. (Can I?) When I get back she's heating a glass of red wine above the fire. She's still a bit off with me. I remind her that I told her I wouldn't be in for dinner. She says, 'Yes, but I did a fish pie and hoped you were lying.' It's nearly nine by the time we sit down to eat.

'You should have eaten, Winnie.'

'You say that, but I'm afraid there's just something about eating dinner alone that I'm not good at. Anyway, cheers, all the best, your good health.'

'And yours.'

'So tell me. What's happening a mile away?'

'You wouldn't believe some of the prices in the village. £2.40 for a yellow courgette.'

'Bayley and Sage?'

'Sage and Bayley.'

'You wouldn't catch me in there. I'm surprised they don't charge an admission fee.'

**30 November.** I go to the common, sit on a cold bench, watch the lamplight on the water of the pond, the leafless trees, a dog being carried around like a loaf of bread. An eavesdropping: 'But one can't understand Sussex without an acquaintance with Kent.' This being Wimbledon, one can't be sure whether they're talking about counties or dukes. But I like the thought nonetheless, its logic, that understanding is relational, that it's comparative. For Sussex and Kent, substitute light and dark, happy and sad.

For dinner she revives some ratatouille labelled 2001. Tucking in, she says she went round to Arthur's today and saw en route a mother pushing a child in a buggy while gazing adoringly at her phone.

'You must *talk* to the child,' she says. 'You must share with them what you know.'

'But what if you don't know anything?'

'Then talk to the child and perhaps you'll learn something.'

'I remember asking my nephew all sorts of questions – about the moon, about taps, about grass – which caused him to ask one of his own.'

'Which was?'

'"You don't know very much, do you?"'

'He was right to ask.'

'Ouch.'

'What was it you asked the other day? "What's a conifer?"'

'There were no trees in my garden, Winnie.'

'There were no Egyptians in mine, but I still know all about them.'

'I'm protective of my innocence.'

'Well don't be. You should know what a bloody conifer is.' (It's the first time I've heard her swear.) 'Now what are we thinking re pudding?'

*At the age of five, and largely against her will, Winnie is living in Oxford. She attends a co-educational school, where she tends to mix more with the boys than the girls. Among her peers, she has gained a reputation for being able to use words to her advantage, including several Latin ones. Winnie is very much a social animal. Although she will occasionally sit alone with a book in the air raid shelter her father erected in the back garden, mostly she prefers to be around others (even if she doesn't like them very much). As things stand, Winnie's best friend is her eldest brother Thomas (presently thirteen and at naval college), closely followed by the dog, Eeyore. If she cannot be the king when she grows up, she'd like to be a chambermaid. She has a way of looking at the camera as if it were a bit of a nuisance, and is fond of marmalade but not honey, which she cannot stand. And that's another thing about Winnie: she has strong opinions.*

# 3

# Never say you know the last word about any human heart

**1 December.** Her thumb is purple. She thinks it might be the blackcurrants she's been handling, but it's not, it's a bruise, a full-blooded bruise. She reckons that if I'm right, that if it is a bruise, then it must have been when she was winding up the clock, trying to get it back on track. I tell her she might want to leave the clock alone going forward.

It's Henry's birthday. He would have been 88. His favourite cake was orange drizzle. I stated my willingness to bake one the other day, but she wasn't sure I was up to it, so found a hefty chunk in the deep freeze last night, baked to commemorate his 76th. Its defrost hasn't gone well: it's gone all soggy overnight; so it turns out I'll be baking one after all, or attempting to. Winnie says I *must* follow a recipe – 'slavishly'. Says there's 'no winging an orange drizzle'.

A card for Henry lands on the mat. I take it through to the kitchen, where Winnie is still trying to treat her bruise with soapy water. She opens the card with a knife. It's from his former secretary. 'You can count on a secretary to send a card,' says Winnie. The card shows a pair of roses. She puts it back in the envelope. Then takes it out again. 'No, I think we'll have that one on display. Jolly the place up a bit.'[1]

---

[1] That evening, the card was put back in the envelope and placed on the chair in the hall with the other bits and pieces she can't decide how to recycle.

From my stool in the kitchen, I notice for the first time a small sculpture dangling from the ceiling at the bottom of the stairs. It consists of two people, figurines, holding onto one another, though not without difficulty. She is doing a somersault, it appears, while he, the lower of the two, is holding on for dear life.

'We've had it as long as I can remember,' she says.

'What's going on? Are they falling?'

'No, they're dancing.'

I stand in a patch of sun, facing south. Winnie's out here, folding a few things into the compost. There appears to be a knack to it. She could be steering a raft down the Ganges, or a gondola in Venice. She stops returning matter to matter and comes to the terrace, where she shows me her recently planted hyacinths. One isn't looking very happy because it wasn't sufficiently embedded. 'The bulbs have to be *properly* embedded, else they don't get the nourishment. If they're not properly encamped it's harder for their roots to wander and thereby source nourishment. If the bulb is neither in nor out then the poor thing's hardly got a chance.' The remark makes me think of childhood, and I wonder if it wasn't the clock that bruised her thumb but the embedding of these bulbs. I ask about an abundant dark green leafy plant taking over most of a flowerbed.

'Acanthus,' she says. 'A hardy evergreen. It was used by the ancient Greeks to decorate porticos.'

'I thought it was lettuce.'

'If you served me a salad of that, it would likely be the end of me.'

'I'll make a note.'

We move on to the mulberry tree, as if moving around a gallery. It used to give decent fruit, Winnie explains, but she can't get to it anymore because the damn thing's got too tall.

'Were they good to eat?'

'Not bad at all. Rather like large raspberries. But boy did they stain. I used to pick them wearing Henry's shirts.'

'How good of you.'

'They were pink by the end.'

'Poor Henry.'

'Yes, poor Henry.'


When I get back from the shop, she's affecting to 'tidy' the driveway. She indicates with her broom the steps that lead up to the front door and bemoans at some length the broken bottom one.

'What caused the damage?'

'Time.'

'Ah. "The reef upon which all our frail mystic ships are wrecked."'

'And too much commotion.'

'Ed Sheeran. If you were wondering.'

'Not to mention a few kicks from Arthur.'

'I don't mind the step like that.'

'Don't be contrary. It makes me shiver.'

'The Japanese have this idea – or some of them have this idea – that something broken is more beautiful for its brokenness, is better for its cracks and so on.'

'Well some of them can keep it.'

Winnie says she'll let me get on with the orange cake as she's a mind to polish the brass, but changes her mind when she sees what me getting on with it looks like. She's suspicious of my recipe for a start, which I found online.

'I just can't believe that simply putting everything in at once and pressing play will work.'

'Why not?'

'I fear it would produce a rather leathery sort of cake.'

'OK …'

'Which Henry never went in for. Let me have a look what I've got up here.'

She pulls down a recipe book from on top of the fridge, first published around the time Benjamin Franklin was mucking about with electricity.

'Now here we are,' she says. 'Now this is what they call a *standard*.'

'Sounds promising.'

'Well it's stood the test of time.'

'Prevailing against mechanisation and enlightenment, etc.'

'Just give the old thing a chance, would you?'

I combine equal parts butter and sugar in a bowl. Then I'm told to *cream* the butter. Then I'm told, as I'm attempting to cream the butter, 'That's it! Keep going! Never mind your arm!' She adds two eggs then asks for a tablespoon – 'That's a dessertspoon, dear' – which she uses to add the flour gradually, all the while telling me to fold, to whisk, to lift, lift, lift! I try to do as I'm told. 'Not just round and round like that! You have to *lift*, to LIFT, in ONE motion!' I try to do as I'm told.

'No, don't lift the bowl, for God's sake! Right, give it here. Now watch. And as you watch, spare a thought for all the women in your life that have done this for you. What do you mean they didn't? What, never? Nonsense. You just can't remember. That's one of the things that used to wind me up about motherhood – you move heaven and earth, and then they don't remember. Now add the orange rind, that's it, and now its juice – slowly!'

We get the mix in the tin (after greasing it with the wrapper of an old block of butter, which explains why she's got about 50 old wrappers filed away in the fridge) and then the tin in the oven. She licks the mixing spoon – a lot. It's difficult to watch. It's by some margin the most improper thing I've seen her do. 'No need to wash it now,' she says, smiling and tapping her nose, as if offering me some great secret that will get me far in life.

I serve up steak and yesterday's veg. To give her food ample time to go cold (and herself cause for complaint), Winnie chooses this very moment to begin carefully arranging some flowers in a vase in honour of Henry's birthday. I ask about the previous one, but she doesn't recall it, not in any detail, says he was bedridden and just three weeks from death. Henry's 80th birthday she *can* remember. It was a large party that spilt out of the sitting room and onto the terrace, and then off the terrace and onto the lawn. They flung open the French windows, despite it being winter. There was music playing, and it wasn't just Beethoven. Indeed, Winnie thinks somebody might have played a Rolling Stones song. Henry was in the *thick* of it. He loved having people in the house. They both did. Winnie can't think of anything worse than an empty house. Yes she can: a house with one person in it. She lights four candles. Says, 'For my dearly beloved.' And then turns to me and wonders if I might have cooked the steak a bit longer.

I wash up. She invigilates.

'Henry would have been 88,' she says.

'You said. Two fat ladies.'

She doesn't get the reference, so I explain it.

'Bingo wasn't in our line of duty,' she says.

'Sorry to hear that.'

'Are you?'

'It's a great sport. Requires precisely no training.'

'We would never have dreamt of going.'

'People grow up in different ways, I suppose.'

'And how.'

'They grow up with different things around them – or not around them, as the case may be.'

'Are you practising stating the obvious? Is that what's going on here?'

'They develop a taste for different amusements.'

'Is this a thought process?'

'I don't think I heard a piece of classical music until I was 24, but I knew all the bingo calls. What do you find amusing, Winnie?'

'Not much these days, I'm afraid.'

'Fair enough.'

'Henry was my amusement. And my security.'

She looks out at the garden. I won't say wistfully. Her look isn't wistful. In fact, I think she's eyeballing a fox.

'And he was passionate. *Very* passionate.'

I'd rather nip this thread in the bud, but mention of Henry's very passionate nature has prompted a memory. The setting: Oxford, early 50s. The context: she and Henry have started seeing each other but aren't yet going steady.

'We were at this party,' she says, 'and there was a girl there, a girl who also wasn't yet going steady with Henry, if you know what I mean. Anyway, she was quite something this girl, had the most *tremendous* bosom. It practically extended to Cambridge. It was the life and soul of the party. Henry clocked it all right. Well, I could have *popped* the damn things.'

'Why?'

'Because I was genuinely terrified they'd come between us.'

'This image is getting confusing now, Winnie.'

'And that's when I realised.'

'Realised what?'

'God – I'm banking on him. I'm *determined*.'

Now she *does* look wistfully out at the garden. 'We just had such *fun*,' she says again, wrapping the remains of the orange cake in foil, and then taking it down to the freezer.

**2 December.** End of lockdown. Whoop. Or rather no whoop, as we're moving seamlessly and as one great big family into a tier system of restrictions. Nonetheless, a tier system sounds like a step in the right direction, so as a treat I have a sugar in my coffee and permit myself a generous splodge of marmalade (when the boss's back is turned).

Winnie's got the paper under her nose. She reads about the so-called vaccine passports that are on the cards (and, let's pray, to be blue and made in the UK). She finds the notion quite amusing. (She finds most ideas amusing, to be honest, apart from skimmed milk and burgers and dementia.) She imagines what a world with vaccine passports might be like. 'They'll all be getting jetlag in Tesco,' she says, somewhat mysteriously. I tell her my nan's not even sure she'll get the vaccine, let alone the passport.

'May I ask why not?'

'She reckons it damages fertility.'

She laughs a fair bit at that one.


An hour later. She's making a sandwich for Kuba, the gardener, and I notice that she butters the bread before slicing the loaf, if you can imagine that. Never seen anything like it. She serves the sandwich with a plate of biscuits and a pot of tea beneath a cosy. She bids me follow with a mug. 'Not that one!'


I do another curry – pork shoulder and squash. Winnie puts about two bananas on hers and most of a yoghurt – anything that will deliver it from its original state or, as she puts it, 'mitigate the damn thing'. We talk about the war mostly. The second one. The second world one. She says her brother kept a weapon by the back door in the event of a German landing in the garden. I suggest the German might have preferred a cup of tea to a wallop around the head. Her dad was at the

Treasury, working out how to fund the war effort. And her mum knitted stuff for the troops: socks and mittens and such things. 'You made your own clothes back then. Everyone did. My mum was doing it well into the 1970s. I remember she made a really smart dress to wear to a garden party at Buck Palace.'

'She went to a garden party at Buckingham Palace?'

'You think she ought to have turned the offer down?'

'No, I mean … Did she speak to the Queen?'

'Briefly.'

'What did she say?'

'Nothing.'

'The Queen said nothing?'

'My mother said nothing.'

'Oh.'

'She wanted to make life easy for the Queen and decided the best way to do that was to say nothing.'

'Right.'

'I said something to her mind you.'

'To the Queen?'

'I was asked – this was on another occasion, years later – what it was like being a governor of Harrow School.'

'Were you a—'

'No. Henry was. So I said to Her Majesty: "He Henry, me Winnie."'

'And what did she say?'

'Nothing.'

'End of chat.'

'End of chat.'

Winnie's neither a monarchist nor a republican, in case you're wondering. Gives the whole thing about as much thought as it deserves, which is to say not very much. I offer to get *The Crown* up on my laptop, to establish a small cinema down here in the sitting room, the laptop propped on some books, themselves propped on a stool, so she might watch the newsworthy drama from her favourite chair. 'I suppose one could have a look.'

**3 December.** I quite like Winnie's habit of beginning conversations with a non-sequitur, if that's even possible. Whereas a lot of conversations will start with a question – 'How are you?' 'What do you think of Chelsea's chances?' – Winnie's tend to start with a statement that presumes a familiarity with the context – 'That's Merton council for you.' Another distinct element of her conversational style is the length of her tail. She keeps going (and going), even after you've left the house and are some distance down the road. Not wanting to be rude, one often strains to keep listening half a mile away. I've lost count of the times I've said goodnight to Winnie, and she's said goodnight, and then I've got halfway up the stairs only to hear that she's resumed the conversation, that she's saying something like: 'Thank you very much for supper. It was jolly good. Are we OK for bread?' I swear some of the nicest and sweetest things Winnie says go unheard, by people that were in a conversation with her about 30 seconds earlier. I might start doing as she does. Keep going when they're gone, or almost gone. I might wait until I've shut the door and she's driven off before saying, 'I love you, Mum.

You're exceptional. I wish I was half as cheerful as you. Can't bear the thought of life without you, etc.'

I take advantage of my freedom to do a pub quiz outside with a friend who lives alone. We lose by a point (note to self, a tennis court is not 45 square feet) but win a bottle of wine for best team name: *One Scotch Egg And Ten Pints of Stella Please.*[2]

**4 December.** 8.15. I silence my alarm. Briefly enjoy that half-conscious state, that slow sleepy 'betweenity' (word coined by Horace Walpole), then rise, don slippers and descend to the tune of 'A Day in the Life' by The Beatles. *Woke up, fell out of bed, dragged a comb across my head ...* Unlock front door, pick up paper, place on kitchen table, consider front page: residents of care homes are to be made accessible, and the Mayor of Liverpool has been cuffed. I stoke the fire, empty the ash pan (into a bucket round the north side of the house, if you're into detail), fill the coal bucket. Make an instant coffee, splash of milk, turn to the charts on page seven that show what new level of disastrousness we've arrived at. Winnie comes down around 9. 'Good morning, Winnie.' 'I've only been up an hour and I'm already knackered.' The news about care home residents being made accessible doesn't please Winnie.

---

[2] This topical reference will mean nothing to readers unfamiliar with the micropolitics of lockdown restrictions in England in 2020. In short, it was enshrined in law that one could only have a pint of beer at the pub if they had a 'substantial meal' with it. When Michael Gove, then cabinet minister, was asked on Sky News what constituted a substantial meal he said, for example, a scotch egg.

'Accessible in the carpark a few degrees above freezing? The man will perish.'

Evening. I go to a pop-up art exhibition in an old branch of Debenhams, where Megan (my girlfriend) has two paintings on display. As I'm considering what appears to be a frog on a skateboard, Winnie calls to ask if she should turn the ragu off now. The question throws me somewhat: before I left the house, I'd taken the ragu downstairs cooked and had told Winnie just to warm it through in the microwave when desired. Ergo, it shouldn't really be *on* anything. 'Yeah I would have thought so, Winnie.' 'Right you are.' We can barely hear each other so I hang up thinking that's the end of the matter. But when I get home an hour later, the house smells on fire. I go through to the kitchen.

'There's been a disaster,' says Winnie happily.

I manage to say without the use of words, 'Oh really? Pray tell me more, Winnie darling.'

'The thing is, I had everything in order.'

'I'm sensing a "but".'

'But then Grayson Perry came on the telly, and I didn't bank on him being so engaging.'

She picks up the pot, looks at the mostly black carboniferous mass therein. 'It's this pot, you see,' she says, passing the buck shamelessly. 'It gets tremendously *hot*.' The ragu is a shade of black hitherto unseen on earth, never mind in a kitchen. Looking at it wondrously, I loosen my tongue sufficiently to suggest to Winnie that it was less the pot and more the Perry episode that did the damage. I manage to rescue the uppermost ragu. The thinnest of edible slivers. I ask if Winnie would like it, perhaps with some fresh pasta or something? 'Oh, no. I'm fine. I had some before all this happened.'

**5 December.** Dinner is sausages. When Winnie's in charge, it's either eggs or fish pie or sausages. The first two on that list are pretty harmless, but the bangers aren't doing me much good. By the end of my time in Wimbledon my arteries will be blocked entirely by sausage, like a sideways oil tanker blocking the Suez Canal.[3] Speaking of blockages, Winnie tells me over dinner about her friend Ellen, and in particular their trip to Florence when they were eighteen: four weeks, sharing a room in a hostel, touring the city's historic galleries. Her most vivid memory from that trip is of Ellen in the bath, and in particular the sight of her bosom floating on the surface like a couple of giant lily pads. The sight had Winnie curled on the floor next to the bath in hysterics. 'I didn't know they could float!' The story jumps forward several years (which is probably a good thing). 'Ellen went on to marry a rather boring man from Oxford. Humphrey. They moved to Paris. I've been out to see her a few times but not for years and years.' I ask why it's been so long. 'To tell you the truth, since Henry went downhill I have felt utterly separate, almost like an alien, completely out of joint. And I'm

---

[3] Oil tanker simile astonishingly prescient. The most prescient thing I've ever said or written or done. In March 2021 a huge sideways oil tanker blocked the Suez Canal for two weeks.

not alone. I've got four friends who have lost husbands in the past year.' I suggest that the four of them get together, pool their complaints, their sorrow, be unhinged together.

'We used to.'

'What?'

'Get together to be unhinged.'

'Oh yeah?'

'At the keep-fit class every Tuesday.'

'When's that coming back?'

'Who knows? Apparently we all pose too big a threat. But I do agree, in a sense, that I could do more to reach out.'

I ask if she feels less unhinged now, a year on from Henry's death.

'Now and again,' she says.

We watch a bit of telly. Bob Ross painting a landscape in less than half an hour on BBC4. Bob's on most nights from what I can tell.

'This guy makes me sick,' says Winnie.

'How on earth?'

'He's so *serene*.'

**6 December.** There's a note on the table when I come down in the morning. Its author wonders if 'someone might be willing to rescue the bird table, which has been beaten up by the godless squirrels.' Winnie is not a lover of squirrels. They pinch the walnuts and hazelnuts and have done so since she can remember. One year, if only to give the squirrels an unpleasant surprise, she went out and picked all the walnuts when they were unripe and pickled them. Seventeen jars of pickled walnuts remain in the basement. And it's not just squirrels Winnie has little time for. She can't tolerate pugs (or any dogs that wobble). She can't tolerate people getting out of bed later than 9am. She can't tolerate people who put damp logs on fires or baked beans on anything. She can't tolerate chicken served with red wine, or anything for breakfast that isn't muesli or marmalade on toast. More than anything else, she simply cannot tolerate *relaxing*. And yet, when it comes to things larger than chicken and baked beans, things like gender, race, religion, sexuality and so on, she's about as tolerant an 85 year old as you will find. Indeed, I'm quite sure she would rather share a prison cell with fifteen pansexual pagans than one pug. I mention all this because she just got back from church and is satirising the vicar again. She's not impressed. Not one bit. Says it was all about shepherds again. She does an impression of the vicar, which involves plenty of arm gestures and warbling.

'Anyway,' she says, 'I better get out the front and sweep the leaves. Only Carlotta and I bother anymore. Carlotta bothers too much. Practically waits outside with her broom for the leaves to fall. I swear she even polishes her plants. They *glisten*. I've never seen anything like it. I dare say she'll polish her own gravestone when the time comes.'

**7 December.** Midday. Upstairs working. Miss a call from Winnie. It's alright: she's left a voicemail. 'Ben. Winnie. You mentioned a Spanish omelette. Are you proposing that for lunch? Or did I get the wrong end of the stick? Not sure where you are exactly. Would be useful if I knew. I struggle when things *disappear*.'

I go downstairs. She's in the kitchen – her default setting. 'Ah, just the man. I'm having an argument with the lid of this soup.' She makes no mention of the omelette: has the soup and some bread for lunch. I have a cup of tea and two biscuits. Winnie asks me to ease off the ginger stem biscuits because she's read about a global shortage of ginger. I flick through the paper. The virus has been relegated to page four – an unprecedented demotion. Might one hope that's the brunt of it dealt with?

We cook separate meals (Winnie doesn't fancy my proposed pasta dish) but convene around 7 to eat together. I ask if the chairs are Chippendales, having just learnt something about Thomas Chippendale and his chairs and their extraordinary value, and she says, 'If they were Chippendales you wouldn't be sat on one, my dear.'

'Fair enough.'

'And nor would I. They would be downstairs.'

'Doing what?'

'Increasing in value, my sweet pea.'

I set up my laptop so the eyeline is right for Winnie in the recliner. I put the subtitles on and the volume up and tell her that she can bow out of *The Crown* at any point. I needn't have worried. She's into it. Her nose is almost touching the screen. That's not to say she's without reservations. She's quite sure King George VI was much thinner in real life, and says that Clarence House didn't look like that one bit. I half expect her to say, when there's a close-up of the cancerous lung the King's just had removed, that they haven't got the likeness right at all. More than anything else, the first episode proves provocative. When Winston and Lady Churchill pop up, Winnie remembers how the latter would wave at her when they crossed paths on the deck of the Queen Mary. When we learn of the King's dodgy lungs, Winnie remembers when her mother-in-law came to stay in the house at the end of her life and had to be hooked up to a tank of oxygen. At the end of the episode, Winnie says, 'A terrific documentary. Now where's my hot-water bottle?'

**8 December.** I almost just killed myself. Winnie was downstairs eating smoked mackerel and soft cheese. I was in Arthur's room, stood on a chair, trying to provide overhead illumination. I'm pleased to say I've never felt anything like the electric shock that sent me flying off the chair. For a while, perhaps a half a second, there was a fair bit of electricity in my body. Fair to say I didn't take to it ever so well. My dismount was neither quiet nor elegant. Death by electrocution would have made a fine ending to this chapter of my life. I went down to the kitchen and said as much to Winnie, who didn't stop eating as I retold the story. She imagined adding a final entry to my diary: 'I only asked him to change the light bulb!' I just stared at her, unamused, desperate for some sympathy or consolation or love. Credit to her, she picked up on how I was feeling and gave consolation and love her best shot by saying that it never occurred to her that I'd be so foolish as to attempt such a thing without checking the light switch was off. Then I said something along the lines of, 'I'll tell you what though, Winnie, I'm feeling pretty lively now.' And she said, 'Good, because we need some milk and something for supper.'

I go to Tesco, still in a state of shock. I grab whatever I like the look of, no thought given to price or fat content. A slap-up dinner to celebrate my reprieve. Gammon shanks in maple syrup, dauphinoise potatoes, chocolate and orange pots, and a small bottle of brandy for my nerves. *For God's sake, Ben, never be as foolish as you were about an hour ago.* Arthur can change his own bulbs in future.[4]

We go for a drive down to Raynes Park to a hardware shop. Winnie wants to summon an electrician and is adamant this is the best way to do it. I could do without the excursion, if I'm honest. I thought I'd had my fair share of shock for the day, but evidently not. It's not that Winnie's incapable behind the wheel. It's more that she seems determined to do as many miles as possible within the immediate area. There's some method in the madness: she likes to give the battery a 'going over' and the brakes a 'chance to shine'. Occasionally she'll neglect to put the handbrake on when parking but only, one

---

[4] The wiring was really dodgy, in my defence. There was a bit of wire just hanging out of the socket, or whatever the bit where the bulb goes is called. I didn't know what it was, this bit of wire. It looked like it shouldn't be there. So I had a feel. As you do. Out of curiosity. And almost killed myself. That's the trouble living in a house that was built and kitted out and electrified in the Dark Ages.

presumes, to give her reflexes a chance to shine as well. She's got the windscreen wipers on full pelt throughout, despite a cloudless sky, so perhaps they're getting a going over like the battery. She's certainly a cordial driver, I'll give her that. She's got something to say to just about every car that passes. ('Now those sunglasses are fun.' 'He's got a face of fuzz like you.' 'Did you see that, Ben? That baby had a face mask on.') And when someone gives way, she will demonstrate her thanks by getting within a whisker of the other car's bumper, flashing her lights half-a-dozen times and giving a regal wave. All this done, it should be added, in a pair of outsize baroque sunglasses, a floral bandana and a polka dot face mask. When we eventually get to the hardware store, they tell Winnie to look on the internet.

I set up the home cinema again. She settles deeper into the chair, inclines the footrest until it's almost horizontal. Then we watch the King die and Elizabeth become Elizabeth Regina, to the disappointment of her husband, who happened to be on safari and could have done without the change in circumstances. As the credits roll, Winnie says, 'No, I must say I'm rather pleased about your machine. I must get the hang of mine, I really must. I haven't a clue what's going on in the world.' Having drunk most of the brandy, and still under the influence of circa 1,600 volts, I say, 'There are many good and beautiful things going on in the world, Winnie.' And then, when she's in the kitchen and out of earshot, I add, 'And you're usually one of them, my friend.'

**9 December.** I like breathing the cold air in the mornings, when I take the ash out the front and get the coal from the back. The cold air is more animating than the two cups of coffee I've got into the habit of drinking first thing, while listlessly surveying bits of the paper. It's a stalling tactic – the coffees and paper – though quite what I'm putting off is a mystery. It's as I'm drinking my first coffee at the kitchen table that Winnie enters wielding a knife. She says it's Japanese and is meant for special occasions, which does nothing to calm me down. The knife, it turns out, is for the Christmas cards that are steadily arriving. She opens one and says, 'The trouble is they don't put their *surnames*, which makes it hard to remember who they *are*.' She opens another and says, 'Ah, well, I know who *that* is, that's June Mendoza. You don't get many Junes, thank God.' As she slices open the envelopes and tries to identify the people who wish her well, I return to the paper, whose front page carries a picture of the first person to get vaccinated. Said person looks beside herself. I show Winnie, who says: 'Let's hope that's not one of the side effects.'

I take myself off to the hospital, to see if I've done any internal damage. Call me a hypochondriac, but some light reading online has led me to believe I might have scuppered my innards beyond recognition. A triage nurse waxes 5 per cent of my body hair while performing an ECG. She's not in two minds about anything, this one. Her verdict is essentially that I'll be absolutely fine, but I might want to pluck up some courage going forward. 'We used to electrocute ourselves for fun as kids,' she says. 'Why?' 'Well there was no Netflix or nothing.' I'm not sure what I expected from my hospital visit, but it wasn't to come out of A&E asking myself whether subscription-based television has stopped an entire generation from self-harming.

She says she'll only have half a profiterole, then devours one and three quarters before the opening sequence is done. (For one so disapproving of richness, she can certainly put a fair bit of it away.) We're watching *The Crown*. When George VI says (in a flashback), 'Love. It's the greatest thing of all,' I turn to her expecting a meaningful expression, but instead she's asleep.

**11 December.** *Desert Island Discs* comes on the radio.

'Who's the presenter nowadays?' she says.

'Lauren Laverne.'

'Don't know her.'

'Who do you know?'

'Roy Plomley.'

'When was this, back in the nineteenth century?'

'I'd put my breakfast on your head if I wasn't so thrifty.'

'What would be your luxury item?'

'A secure house, so the bugs can't get in.'

'Even on a hypothetical desert island your first concern is security?'

'Yes. And yours?'

'My luxury item?'

'Yes.'

'It's a hard question. Gets to the heart of one's character, doesn't it?'

'Oh come on – it would be a bottle opener, wouldn't it?'

**14 December.** Breakfast talk: I mention a news item about the BBC having too many left-wing comedians and Winnie says, 'I didn't realise the BBC had *any* comedians.' Post-breakfast talk: she says she just had a row with Rebecca about a favourite jumper of Arthur's, a lovely sentimental royal blue jumper that Winnie won't allow to go to the care home because the staff boil the clothes until they're unrecognisable. Rebecca borrowed the jumper about a fortnight ago, Winnie tells me, to keep warm on her walk home. Winnie agreed to the loan but now wishes she hadn't – regretted it instantly in fact. First thing this morning, Winnie phoned Rebecca telling her to bring the jumper back. Rebecca said she'd bring it back at the weekend. Winnie said she shouldn't have taken it in the first place and ought to bring it back at once. Rebecca said she took the jumper with Winnie's blessing. Winnie said that a blessing isn't permanent. Then Rebecca hung up. And then Winnie looked at the phone like it was the quintessence of malice. 'Hey-ho?' I suggest. She shakes her head. 'Not this time, I fear.'

I'm going out the door in a bit of a rush.

'Right, see you after lunchtime, Winnie.'

'Ah, bring back something for lunch, would you?'

'But I won't be back until—'

'Just a hunk of cheese and some ham. You know, stuff for a ploughman's.'

'What did your last slave die of? Was it exhaustion?'

'Cholera actually.'

10 o'clock news. It seems that London hasn't behaved at all well since the end of the national lockdown a couple of weeks ago and will be relegated to tier 3 of the national coronavirus championship as of Wednesday, meaning everything's shut again and everyone should stay at home if they can. Whoop.

**17 December.** She slides the marmalade across the table then indicates the front page, which says that the elderly should avoid family at Christmas.

'No skin off my nose,' she says.

'Hm.'

'But you do wonder what they'll come up with next.'

'I know, I know.' (I'm trying to read a supplement.)

'I hardly know what century it is. Haven't got a clue where my friends are. It's driving me mad.'

'It's a shocker, Winnie.'

'And those squirrels, they're not doing much to mollify me. They've had the bird table down again. American they are.'

'Who are?'

'The squirrels. American imports. Alien animals.'

'I met a bloke once who said that a lot of Brits would be scared of themselves if they knew what they were made of.'

'Henry counted himself a Norseman.'

'Did he often go berserk?'

'I don't follow.'

'A subgroup of Vikings called the Berserkers, so ferocious and lustful of violence they would have to chew on trees to control their aggression.'

'Oh I like that.'

'Thought you might.'

'I nearly went berserk in M&S yesterday. I went to buy some clothes for Arthur but it was hopeless. The larger the waist the shorter leg. They're aiming for a world of tiny porkers.'

She makes a note in her diary. About the tragedy that is M&S and the squirrels being American. Wrong side of the bed, methinks. That or the headline about not being able to see family has put her nose out of joint. I expect it's just one of those days though. Some days she has the jolliest attitude and perspective, and some days everything is wrong. It's not deliberate. It's not something she's in control of. There are just some things in life – grief, pain, upset, injustice – that quietly and fundamentally chip away at one's capacity for jolliness. Winnie was wired jolly but has suffered setbacks. That's my tuppence worth. 'Shall we go out and find some Christmas lights?' I say. 'If you drive and don't mind going to Lidl after then you're on,' she says.

We pass Carlotta on our way into town. 'Is this your young man?' she asks Winnie, after covering her face at the sight of me. (A man did something similar yesterday – he covered his face with the letter he was on his way to post. I don't blame the guy. Not given the volume of terror that's been drilled into him. I do worry about intergenerational relations going forward, about the long-term accidental consequences of all this, if the received wisdom holds that anyone under 40 is a biological threat.) Anyway. Back to Carlotta. Let's not keep her waiting. She's saying she's been reading about clouds. 'I spend hours and hours learning about it all, the names and the subspecies, and then I just wonder, "Isn't it enough just to look and say it's lovely?"' She points to the heavens. 'That one is a stratus – stratus cumulus. It will be out of the way soon. There'll be sunshine shortly.' I say to Carlotta that if she ever needs a hand with anything then she's to let me know and I'll send Winnie over, which gets a laugh from Winnie but not from Carlotta.

'It's opening things that's a problem,' says Carlotta.

'Tell me about it,' says Winnie.

'Wine bottles especially. It became a real issue. But I've got an instrument to help me now.'

'What's his name?' I say.

Carlotta doesn't answer. Instead she nods serenely and judgmentally while looking at me curiously (not easy to do). And then she says, 'Remember to enjoy the clouds. But do watch out for lampposts.' The remark reminds me of the front page of every newspaper published since March 2020. Don't know why exactly, just does.[5]

Back from the shops, we sit down for a mince pie and a cup of tea. Or rather, I sit down. She won't. It's one of those

---

[5] Being asked to do something that will benefit you but also potentially harm you. Stay at home. See nobody. Etc.

days. The lady is not for settling. Couldn't if she tried. She has cards to deliver, and some washing to do, and papers to go through, and she *must* get Arthur's copy of *The Spectator* round to him. I don't need to ask why the magazine isn't delivered directly to Arthur. It would be another feather plucked from motherhood's cap. I ask how Arthur is, how he's been lately. 'He's fed up,' says Winnie. 'He just wants to get out, to nose around, to see what the people are up to. It's not a lot to ask.'

There is a prevailing sadness in the house at the moment, and the current is getting stronger. It's coming up to the anniversary of Henry's death, a sad fact made more complicated and poignant by Christmas, to say nothing of the virus and its various setbacks and curtailments. Two weeks ago she might have found the sight of me attempting to bake biscuits a jolly one, but now she's worried about the mess I'm making, says it's too late for me to learn how to bake. She goes out to post some cards and deliver something to Arthur, says I ought to have it all cleaned up by the time she gets back.

We swap steaks halfway through dinner, in defiance of government guidelines. Hers was a bit tough, and mine wasn't. She describes the gesture as noble on my part. I say that when it comes to ethics and such things, I always try to behave as if my grandmother were watching, which can make it difficult when Megan is over. She pours herself a second glass of wine and knocks it back more or less in one. 'That'll put me to sleep,' she says.

**18 December.** She's already at her post when I go down in the morning.

'Sleep well, Winnie?'

'I was up at 4.'

'Why for heaven's sake?'

'Thinking about all the things that need doing.'

'You need to learn how to relax.'

'Nobody can relax the week before Christmas.'

'They can, Winnie. I promise you. Just watch me.'

'But you don't have to *provide* for anyone.'

'Aren't you going to Rebecca's?'

'Well who knows. Could all change. Better to be prepared *in case.*'

'In case of what?'

She looks at me. Crossly. Then walks out of the room.


The Christmas cards keep coming. Keep landing on the mat. The number is rising exponentially, statisticians are warning. She got a nice one from a friend called Wilma, in the Netherlands, who hasn't seen her daughter or grandchildren for eighteen months. Wilma's heard that Winnie's got a 'young man' living with her, suggests that she wouldn't mind one herself, but for the sake of propriety has to content herself with the dog, Rubens. There's also a card from Henry's younger sister, who lives alone and lost her daughter this year.

'Is she lonely?'

'What do you think?'

'Could you visit her?'

'You can't just start visiting again after fifteen years.'

'Why did you stop?'

'Because Henry had a stroke. That's why. And then another. And then another. Good enough reason?'

'Give her a call.'

Winnie answers by picking up the stack of cards and saying there's nowhere for them to go so they'll just have to go in a drawer.

Megan comes over for a sort of pre-Christmas dinner. I put the chicken in the oven when Winnie's out in the garden, to avoid having a conversation about it. Some minutes later, Winnie materialises and asks after the chicken.

'Did you wrap it in bacon?'

'What, to keep it warm?'

She looks at me. The look says: *Are you stupid or taking the piss, because I'm genuinely not sure.* 'To keep it *moist*, you cretin.'

'Ah.'

'Nobody likes a pair of dry breasts.'

I add the bacon.

'Not like that! Rashers should go *with* the grain.'

'Why?'

'Because.'

'Because what?'

'Because …,' she takes the bacon from me, pulls the chicken her way, '… that's how it's always been done.'

'Which is a terrific reason for persisting with age-old customs. Like decapitation as a way of knocking sense into someone.'

She lifts up the bacon-clad chicken, turns to me, smiles

sarcastically and says, 'Open the door would you?' In fairness to her, she does laugh when I open the back door.

There is peace on the western front until it comes to carving the chicken. Winnie watches with her hand over her mouth. And to be fair she's right to – I'm not a dab hand at it. According to Winnie – who now has both hands over her mouth (a pose that suits her as it happens) – I'm less carving and more unleashing. Winnie takes over and shows me – over the next half an hour, as everything else gets cold or dry – precisely how one does it, which is to say by first ascertaining who likes what; then removing the appendages by cutting through the 'ligaments, dear, the ligaments, *never* the bone for crying out loud'; and then meticulously carving the breast from *the outside in* as if one were playing a violin very slowly; and then finally transferring each piece or slice to an awaiting plate (which must be heated) with the care and caution of a brain surgeon. I swear to God by the time she's carved three portions of chicken my patience is more cooked than the bird. We sit down, pull crackers. Winnie's arm nearly comes out of its socket.

'What does a frog do when it breaks down?' she says.

'Dunno,' I say.

'Dunno,' says Megan.

And nor does Winnie know by the look of it: she just stares intently at the answer for about a minute, at which point she abruptly and silently puts the joke down, gets up from the table, goes through to the kitchen, comes back with an A–Z of amphibians or similar, parses it, then says, 'As I thought. A toad is not a frog.' One hell of a way to deliver a punchline. To lift the mood and artificially inject some festive bonhomie, I ask about yuletides hitherto. My plan doesn't work. First she says, 'We used to have 25 people around this table and this year we'll be lucky to have one.' And then she says, 'For a fair few years when I was young I got a sock each Christmas. We'd get the other the next year. It was meant to teach us restraint.'

Megan has a sad moment on the sofa. Her grandad has advanced cancer. There's not much that can be done for him, and therefore not much that can be done to banish Megan's upset. Some things are just strongly and stubbornly sad. Winnie calls up from the basement. Says a bulb's gone. Calls me down to investigate the fuse box.

**19 December.** I attempt to illuminate the front of the house with the fairy lights purchased a few days ago. Winnie has me on a ladder threading the lights through the barren wisteria above the garage. When the job's done, I stand back to admire my handy work. 'It's better than nothing,' I say. 'Not sure if I agree,' says Winnie.

**20 December.** Days after saying it would be inhuman to cancel Christmas, Boris cancels Christmas. A 'stay at home' order has been issued, or reissued, on account of a new variant of the virus first discovered in Kent (by a man walking his dog). So no family gathering in Portsmouth for me then. Winnie doesn't plan to stay at home. She plans to go round to Rebecca's, which is fair enough. Maybe I'll get a curry.

Or a pizza. Or I'll source a really small turkey and eat the whole thing unaccompanied by vegetables, like a Tudor. The world's my oyster.

I do a curry from the leftover chicken, adding a chunk of butter and a dollop of cream and a deal of salt, to suit Winnie's tongue.[6] We eat watching Michael Palin, who is remembering his journey in the Himalayas.

'The chap who used to live behind us wrote a terrific book about that part of the world. *A Short Walk in the Hindu Kush* or similar.' 'Eric Newby?' 'That's it. Nice chap. He had us over one night, served very large glasses of whisky. Henry and I rolled home!' Then Joanna Lumley turns up (on telly, not in the sitting room), and Winnie says, 'Now *she* was something else. Lived across the road of course. Rebecca once saw her in the buff at the piano.' And then the Dalai Lama pops up, and I say, 'I suppose he lived next-door-but-one did he?'

**21 December.** I'm watching *Bargain Hunt*. She brings over a picture from the paper. A painting by Joseph Wright of Derby. It shows a group of people marvelling at a scientific experiment. Its theme is enlightenment and its unsteady progress, its tension, its blind spots, etc. She likes the use of light and shade, likes how the one enhances the other. She asks me to keep it for Megan to look at when she next

---

[6] A deal is an obsolete unit of volume for stacked firewood. A UK deal equalled 7ft × 6ft × 2½ inches, which gives you an idea of how much Winnie likes salt.

comes and then returns to the kitchen to the call the plumber. She's thoughtful like that. Sees something, thinks someone else might like it, puts it to one side. She won't always show interest or concern or gratitude when you might expect her to (like when Megan gave her the drawing she did of Ellen in the bath which Winnie gave a cursory appraisal of before passing on to me to deal with), but she will carefully keep back an article or picture that she thinks might be of interest to someone. Her warmness comes out in odd ways, at odd angles, at unlikely times. And, frankly, you'd be tempted to forgive her if it didn't come out at all – not at any angle, not at any time. I can't even imagine what it's like to lose someone you've loved (and lived with) for 60 years. The effect must be giant; it must feel unbearable, impossible. There's no two ways about it, she's got a lot on her plate, and when you've got a lot on your plate, emotionally speaking, then it's bound to be hard sometimes to recognise what's on others'.

And on top of Henry – or on top of the lack of Henry – there's Arthur. In practical terms, she's lost him as well. Not to death but the pandemic. She can't visit. He can't visit. She can't be the mother she is. *She can't be something she is.* She nonetheless thinks tirelessly of Arthur – of his wellbeing, his needs. She frets and fusses with him in mind, hours every day. Arthur is a seismic drain on her emotional resources. So when you weigh up Henry and Arthur, you start to understand how Winnie's stock of care and compassion and curiosity gets spent each day on these two people, one living, one not.

She has a big heart, but there seems to be only two ways out of it. One way leads to Henry, the other to Arthur. Of course there are other minor roads that lead to other major people – to Rebecca, to Stewart, to Carlotta, to the grandchildren – but for the most part these pathways are used by incoming vehicles, by Stewart when he phones, by Rebecca when she comes over, by Abigail when she drops in after school. A telling episode: when Stewart and his wife and their children moved in after Henry died, when the pandemic started, Winnie couldn't accept any changes to Arthur's old bedroom. She couldn't allow her grandson to make Arthur's old room his own. She couldn't accept old things being moved, being cleared. It can't have been long before the situation became untenable. The character of Winnie's devotion (to the past, to Arthur, to how things *were*) made change impossible. Stewart and his gang moved out six months into the familial experiment.

It bears repeating: she's in the wake of a trauma, in the midst of one even. The absolute loss of Henry and the practical loss of Arthur have turned her world upside down. She is essentially reeling. And yet, here I am, feeling she could ask me more questions, feeling undervalued. Mad! Ludicrous! I recall saying to Megan, 'She doesn't have a curious bone in her body! She doesn't like me and doesn't want to! She's unkind!' It's unfair to judge someone, to form an opinion on their character, to reach a verdict on who they are, when they are in a state of quiet, daily, incalculable grief. That's what I'm getting at, getting to. She doesn't know who I am. Fine. Whatever. But she hardly knows *herself* these days. Here's a harsh formulation: she couldn't care less for me, because she couldn't care more for others.

Over dinner we talk about Oxford. Winnie moved there from London when she was a toddler because her father, quite reasonably, wanted the family out of the firing line. Winnie went to a school called The Dragon, whose graduates (or old dragons as they're known, not inappropriately in a lot of cases I would have thought) include John Betjeman, Alain de Botton, Lady Antonia Fraser, Hugh Gaitskell, Hugh Laurie, Emma Watson, Jack Whitehall and the 3rd Baron Tweedsmuir, which means we can safely assume that not many old dragons required free school meals. She says she was decent at school but not decent enough to get into the local university, so she went to the Ruskin School of Art instead. Henry, a few years her senior, was at the same time commencing a degree at Queen's College, Oxford, while her brother, Jacob, a pal of Henry's since the pair met on national service in Germany after the war, was doing classics at Magdalen. Henry started off doing physics before switching to PPE. When I say, 'PPE? What, gloves and masks and that?' Winnie just stares at me for some time before changing the topic of conversation entirely by pointing to the drawing Megan did of Ellen in the bath (which I put on a dresser behind a photo of Winnie's parents) and saying, as if considering the drawing for the first time, 'I must say it was very sweet of Megan to do that. Though she's got the shape wrong entirely.' As far as compliments from Winnie go, it's a fairly typical one, it being three weeks late and qualified.

We watch an episode of *The Crown*. In the episode, an artist called Sutherland goes to Winston Churchill's house to paint his portrait. Churchill wants the painting to flatter him, but Sutherland sticks to the truth. Churchill burns the portrait. Doing so, Winnie nods along in approval.

**22 December.** She's got marmalade on her chops and is reading a piece in the paper about fronds. It's reported that the type Winnie's got an abundance of in the garden (pampas) are worth £28 a head. Winnie works out, with an alacrity I've not seen before, that she's sitting on about 1,500 quid's worth. She sends me out with clippers to fetch an armful, which she means to store in the larder. Cutting the fronds, I please myself thinking: *Heavenly Father, never allow Winnie to learn the value of her spare kidney, else she'll have the thing in storage in the back kitchen.* By the way, the reason she wants a batch indoors is because she's wary of entrepreneurs hurdling the fence and helping themselves, having read the article in *The Times*.

Her breakfast is brought up short when she gets a phone call from Arthur. He had a fall in the night. No damage done, just a courtesy call. Winnie's defence mechanisms flare up. She wants to see him. Demands an appointment. Insists on talking to the manager – who concedes to Winnie's wish and suggests midday in the garden. Arthur reiterates that he's fine, really he is, then asks if Winnie wouldn't mind bringing a pudding along, and perhaps G.K. Chesterton's *What's Wrong With the World*?

I walk to Waterloo to meet a friend – Camilla. Across the common and Putney Heath, with Helen Macdonald's *H is for Hawk* in my ears.[7] The book is a memoir about grief and falconry in the main. The author has lost her dad and is bereaved. She tells us the word 'bereaved' comes from Old English, meaning deprived, robbed, emptied. She tells us how things lose their sense: how you'll see a letter on the doormat but fail – if only for a second – to know what it means, what it is, what it signifies. Ditto a ladder. Ditto a knife. Ditto when the telephone rings. Comprehension is delayed as all things fall into meaningful gaps. The author says, 'I try to cling on to a world already gone.'

I dodge the wettest mud, hurdle fallen trees, pass people together and people alone, including a young girl attempting to scooter through what is effectively a swamp. I sit on a bench. Check my phone. New voicemail. 'Ben. Winnie. Are you here? Arthur will survive. What are we thinking for supper? Keen to hear from you.' I reach Putney, then the river, follow its bank north, then east, then south, then north. It's dark, and quiet. London is staying at home, penned in by the shapeshifting virus. I watch people in their riverside flats. People working out in their kitchens, doing squats in the lounge, lunges in the study. Helen's words keep coming. They're useful. They provide an insight. My dad's parents died before I could care; my mum's are ongoing. I need the grief of others to give me a clue. I'm pretty sure about one thing though: grief has been a part of Winnie since her first

---

[7] The hawk-eyed among you might wish to know why I'm now listening to a book I was previously reading. The truth is that I can sometimes behave in an exceptionally decadent way: I got both out from the library.

son was born. She has said more than once that it was her fault. I get where I was going, sit with Camilla by the river. When I get home around ten the fire's gone out.

**23 December.** My sister arrives. She has a meeting in Mayfair, is parking on the drive. (Winnie's happy with the arrangement as vehicles suggest occupancy and deter burglars.) She hands me a bag containing a gift from her, plus some cheese, biscuits and red wine from my mum, to be enjoyed on Christmas Day.

'Nice of your mum,' says Winnie.

'It is. I told her not to get me anything, but she couldn't help it. Bit like you running a yoghurt round to Arthur.'

'I dare say Arthur would prefer a bottle of red wine.'

'But it's a mother's instinct, isn't it?'

'Not all mothers. I've known a fair few that wouldn't dream of sending cheese up to Wimbledon.'

Her toast pops up. She holds it in mid-air for a few seconds, inspecting it. For a second I think she's forgotten what it's for. She must decide it's a bit on the burnt side, because she puts it in front of me and says, 'Here. Eat. I'll put another one in.'

While eating the other one she put in, she phones Stewart re a winter fuel payment she's not sure she's received. He can't talk, he says, is off to hospital, this second practically, severe abdominal pain, doubled over as he speaks. 'Of course, darling. You go. Right now. The fuel allowance doesn't matter; I'll chase it, you get yourself sorted. You must. Now. Off you go, darling. Will you drive? If you drive

remember the Hammersmith Bridge is closed. It can't support traffic anymore apparently. Which is a shame really as
it's a lovely looking bridge, especially when lit up at night.
No, you go. Absolutely. Your grandfather had awful gas-
tric issues. Blamed it on pollution. How are the children?
Stewart? Are you there? No, quite right. Make haste. Get
yourself seen to. Call when you can.'

Stewart calls. It's just an infection. He's got some antibiotics.
But best to cancel tomorrow's lunch, OK? On the phone
Winnie says it's a shame. Off the phone she says she doesn't
mind one bit because she wasn't exactly looking forward
to it – to facing up to her nemesis, Jane, whose maternal
instincts clashed with her own the summer just gone. I dare
to ask if Winnie's ever thought about perhaps getting over
what happened in the summer. She says nothing, just looks
out the window, then decides to take Arthur some mince pies.

She leaves the house to deliver the pies, only to return twenty
minutes later having forgotten to take them with her. I tell
her there are worse things to forget than a pair of mince pies,
but she can't see the funny side. In fact, she's furious with
herself, disproportionately so. 'Stupid stupid stupid stupid
stupid stupid woman,' is her verdict. Then, before she's left
the house and is back on the road, Carlotta phones to ask
what day it is, which makes Winnie feel a lot better.
    'I told you there are worse things to forget, Winnie.'
    'One-nil to you.'
    'Was Carlotta alright otherwise?'

'Not really. She was meant to be going to Austria for Christmas, but now she can't because Brits are banned from all nations of the world because of Kent.'

'Fed up was she?'

'Fuming. She's even talking about voting Green. I've never heard her rant so much. In other news, she's taken up yoga.'

'Crikey.'

'Apparently she does it on the toilet.'

**24 December.** The fire went out overnight. I spend an hour sat on the floor in front of it, watching it take, watching it give. I make kindling of *The Times*, feed the timid coals news of rising infections, rising admissions, rising deaths. My dad sends a message: would Winnie like a blue tit box? I ask her and she would. I ask why the box is for blue tits only. She says they need the security.

Henry died a year ago. She puts on his hat, his coat. She's so wrapped up she can hardly move. She says she's going to post a final Christmas card, then doesn't come back for an hour. When she gets back I'm watching Fanny Cradock doing a Christmas cake in fifteen minutes. She's brilliant. As accomplished and adroit as any contemporary telly chef, but thrice as dry, as funny, as ferocious. Things don't always improve. Sometimes things were better before.

I get dinner on the go. We open the wine and cheese gifted by my mum. I'm a fan of the cheese but Winnie thinks it tastes like 'something about to go wrong', which is a bit rich coming from a woman who will eat eighteen-year-old eggs. Over dinner, we mostly talk about Henry being gone a year. I tell her what someone told me in Italy: that grief is fruitful because it gives perspective and a sense of scale. Winnie says that's bollocks. Says that loss begets fear of loss. Says she likes the spare ribs though.

She goes to bed. I don't. I sit in the recliner and finish the red wine. The wine doesn't make me happy or sad. It just makes me unsure what I am (which, depending on where you started, isn't always a bad place to end up). I go outside. The night is quiet. A fox sees me and dashes. A light goes off, another comes on. I sit on the old swing and swing absentmindedly, childlike. The symbolism strikes. Like all genuine symbols, it's accidental. And like all good symbols, it's unclear. Am I the child here? I get a message at midnight. From my mum. It brings a tear.

**25 December.** I open my bedroom window and can only hear birdsong, no hint of car or train. I clear the ash, fetch the coal, feed the fire. Then a coffee outside, facing the sun. I phone my dad. He's finished the bird box. We both forget to say Merry Christmas. Winnie comes down, eats her muesli, her toast, says it's just occurred to her that my hair resembles the hazel tree. She phones Arthur. He says it's quiet, very few staff, has been chatting with the accountant mostly. Winnie switches to Radio 3 (I didn't know she knew how) for the carols. She says there's been a few drops of snow in Yorkshire so the BBC are calling it a White Christmas. I say that's like calling me a vegetarian because I eat peas twice a week. I open presents from my mum and sister, a coat and a shirt. Both are very nice, but my family underestimate me – I can no longer squeeze into a 'slim-fitting' medium. When I break the news to my mum she takes it personally, as though it were my fault. Winnie reckons Arthur would get into both no problem.

Our taxi is due at 12.15. (Winnie didn't like the idea of getting a taxi alone so I've agreed to break the law and go with her to Rebecca's for dinner.) At 12, or just after, Winnie says that we need to make some brandy butter. 'Some what?' '*Brandy* butter. The mince pies are *ruined* without it.' Rarely have I seen somebody transition from relative calm to relative mania in less time and for less reason. She throws what's required into a mixing bowl and then shouts – in my direction – 'Now beat it, beat it, beat it!' I get the butter and sugar nicely entwined, losing all sensation in my wrist so doing.

'Can you finish it off, Winnie? I need to have a shower.'

'A shower?'

'Yeah.'

'You can't have a shower. It's out of the question. The taxi is due and we've got to *finish* the brandy *butter*.'

But I'm off, halfway up the stairs. I spend two and a half minutes under hot water, mostly saying, 'Now beat it, beat it, beat it!'

She's worked up. That's the thing. She's stressed. About going to her daughter's, about Arthur being alone, about Henry not being here. There's a little ball of ferocious anxiety inside her, and it's ordering her thoughts. 'No!' she cries at the taxi driver when he sets off down the hill. 'No, no, no! UP the hill! Turn around this instant!' I explain to Winnie that the driver's following instructions, that the driver's phone will have worked out the quickest route. 'Don't talk to me about his phone! I've lived here for 50 years! There's all the *traffic* down there. Turn around!'

There's no traffic down there, and within seconds we're out of Wimbledon and heading towards Wandsworth – smooth sailing. The driver looks at Winnie in the rear-view mirror. He allows himself a smile (you can tell, despite the mask), and says, 'Next year I will go uphill, OK?' When we arrive, she can't remember what house it is. The driver knew of course, but Winnie insisted he was wrong, but now she's not so sure. She says it's been years since she was here. We're admitted by Abigail, eighteen, then offered sparkling red wine by Victoria, 21. Rebecca, 59, is checking on the turkey, eighteen months, deceased.

I'd like to say the next five hours are jolly. I really would. But they aren't. It's like a Harold Pinter play, in that it's tense and full to bursting with underlying sadness. Normally when a strange guest is present, something is done to puncture the awkwardness – but not on this occasion. I feel like I've been cast as a judge, invited to watch and listen and then measure degrees of upset and anger. I feel sorry for Winnie, who barely says a thing, save to offer unwanted guidance regarding the carving of the turkey. She might as well not be here. It's hard to get my head around because I *know* that Rebecca cares, and I *know* that Abigail does. But around this table the emotional temperature is freezing. Winnie is handed a present. She opens it. It's from Rebecca. She looks at the present – a scarf – and her first thought is to ask Rebecca if she'd like the wrapping paper back. (Rebecca would, as it happens.) There are no more presents. Winnie arrived empty handed, save for the brandy butter. We pull crackers. I put on my paper crown. I tell my joke. It's awful. Everybody tuts.

As I'm making a dent in the washing up, Rebecca thanks me – sweetly, meaningfully – for coming along and perking things up a bit. If I've perked things up then I dread to think how it would have been without me here. I wanted to leave after my mince pie on arrival. I know it may sound exceptionally ungrateful but I actually did. I wanted to stand, offer a toast to the absent, and then join their ranks.

At 5, Winnie is asked if she'd like to go. I'm at once happy and sad when she says yes. Rebecca orders a taxi. Winnie waits outside on the pavement. I give Rebecca a hug, careful to keep my mouth a metre from hers. When we get home, something hits me. 'Winnie this bag smells unmistakably of turkey.' She taps the side of her nose. 'It's a leg,' she says. 'And a whopper. We'll get two meals out of that.'

I go to the common, walk laps of the pond in the dark. Partly to digest turkey and bread sauce, partly to make phone calls – to my mum, my grandparents, my siblings, my friends. It's so calm, so still, so peaceful. The uneven light on the dark surface – that's what gets me. There were a hundred people here this morning, and now not a soul but me. What an odd relationship with darkness we have.

It's about seven when I get back. Winnie's watching a

spoof of *The Red Shoes*, says it's the most amusing thing, absolutely brilliant, about a girl that just could not stop dancing. I'm oddly shocked that she can be so much more pleased – superficially at least – by something on BBC 2 than by her own family.

I help her put fresh sheets on her bed. Her bedroom is full of photographs: of her brothers, her husband, her children, her grandchildren. Her room is in no small way a shrine to her family, to those she cares about most. I point to younger versions of Abigail, Victoria, Rebecca – and she offers long sweet descriptions of each. I think of something Henry James said: 'Never say you know the last word about any human heart.' Or any human family, he might have added.

**26 December.** Breakfast. She has toast and marmalade. I have turkey and eggs. (She can hardly bear to look.) I ask if she had a Boxing Day routine, with the family, with the kids. 'Well first I'd gather up and put away whatever wrapping paper wasn't torn to shreds, and then we'd walk up to the common, or I'd walk with the children and Henry would run. He'd do laps and wave at us on his way round. There was *always* snow. And we'd skate on the pond usually. It was lovely to skate on the pond. One really lost oneself.'[8]

---

[8] Not long after, I had a dream in which Winnie was skating on the frozen pond – forever. She just kept going, and going, and going, somehow outside of time and space. Then she stopped abruptly and peered down between her legs, and saw my face beneath the ice. The dream was curtailed by a phone call from Winnie, asking if the bins were out.

**27 December.** A beautiful storm was playing several instruments all night long. The coal shed is flooded, and the fire is out. If you'd like an omen, there's a couple. She does me a bit of toast. Doesn't ask, just does it. I know what she's thinking: solidarity in adversity. She even opens a new pot of marmalade – a gift from Stewart, who makes his own. I break the news that she might have to rely on the central heating for a couple of days. She looks at me as if I've just asked her to handwash her knickers in Champagne. If she could somehow remove the slice of toast from within me, she would. 'Then in which case you'd better see if there's any dry wood in the basement.'

I clean my bathroom. Do some washing. Make a quiche. Tidy my inbox. *I'm keeping busy.* That's what I'm doing. Because if I sit down and there's nothing, just room to think, then it hits me – what are you doing here? What are you *doing*? What is *anyone* doing? I can't call it depression, but, at moments, it's the edges of a very stubborn sadness. Or weariness. Or apathy. Or bits of each. Perhaps we are all, at heart, at root, somewhat depressed. Perhaps the least depressed people are just those that successfully avoid the idea, that keep it at bay – that keep busy. No, that's rot. Christmas does this. As Friday nights do this. They are psychologically tricky. One thinks the grass is greener – out there, over there, anywhere. I wouldn't feel like this if it were October, or March. I would take life for what it was – coldish, darkish, dullish – and then get on with things that provide distraction, amusement, fulfilment. But at Christmas the idea of home seems to glow. But this is my home. And so I go back to the common and do laps of the pond at sunset, listening to the book about the hawk. I only notice the moon once the sun has gone down.

**28 December.** She always puts the telly on in the kitchen when she's just pottering around – dipping forks, transferring loaves, trying to get through to the council. She'll occasionally stop what she's doing to point at the screen and say something like: 'Henry's dad was like Captain Mainwaring in *Dad's Army*. Absolutely determined to impose discipline. He had five children – all beginning with H. One of the girls married the most boring man in Christendom. She used to defend her decision by saying he was very well endowed in the financial department.' And then she'll return to making a pudding for Arthur, or writing in her diary, or pretending to be a scarecrow, until the next opportunity arises to point at the telly and say something like: 'Henry's great aunt had a face like that. You could tell the weather by it. She visited us in the Philippines. Got a boat to Malaya, then another onto Manila – aged 86. She locked herself in the cabin for the whole passage. Didn't care for the goats. Fair play to her in any case. I know some people who are barely willing to go to toilet on their own, let alone sail to the Philippines.' And then she'll leave the kitchen and go upstairs or into the garage and keep talking as she goes, a remark about the great aunt, or a thought on the goats, or a non-sequitur concerning Arthur. Winnie Carter: must be seen to be believed.

**29 December.** Margaret Keenan, 91, is the first person in the universe (available to speak to the media) to have had their second jab. I enjoy the fact that her surname suggests impatience and enthusiasm. When I share this thought with Winnie, she answers by presenting what she claims is a butternut squash. I've never seen anything like it. It's barely identifiable. It's caving in, eating itself, turning into foul, viscous gunk – the sort of transformation a gremlin goes through when introduced to water, as imagined by Steven Spielberg. A mutant variant of squash. She hands it to me. 'Salvageable?' she says.

She's got the picture I gave her for Christmas leaning against the vase on the centre of the table. She likes the child jumping in the puddle, and the adult cowering beneath the umbrella. She reads aloud what I wrote on the back: 'If violets are red, and roses are blue, then I'm half mad, and so are you.' I ask (not sure why) if Henry's side of the family were nice to her when they first got together. She says they were, very much so. Says if there was a frosty element then it was her own mother. Says her mother was always very doubtful – and didn't become any less so after the death of her eighteen-year-old son. That loss was character building – it made Winnie's mother relentlessly fearful that her surviving children would come to harm. 'She just didn't want to lose me, to lose another child. It could have been Pythagoras wooing me, she still would have found grounds for suspicion.' Fear as an expression of love.

She goes up to bed at about 9.30. I stay in the lounge with a cup of herbal tea to watch the news and the football highlights. About an hour later, she calls from above. 'Ben? I do think you should go to bed now. We've a very important appointment tomorrow morning. I don't want you drinking the rest of that wine. Ben?' I have to laugh. The alternative is to cry. She's worried about the coal. The coal that's being delivered at 7 tomorrow morning. Because coal means fire means heat means security means *home*. I turn off the television, finish the last of the tea. 'Good idea, Winnie,' I shout. 'You're quite right.' Besides, there is only one more game left to be shown – an old champion versus a misfiring newcomer – and I already know the result: a point apiece.

**30 December.** I barely sleep. I'm worried, both consciously and subconsciously, about not waking up for the coal delivery. I have two dreams that I can remember. In the first I'm involved in some kind of accident, and a civilian first-aider has to pull all the skin off my face. In the second I wake up in the afternoon and have to incur the uncensored wrath of Winnie. I prefer the first one to be honest. My alarm goes at 6.45, but I'm already awake. It's cold – colder than ever. I layer up, descend, enter the back kitchen, where she said the key to the side gate would be. (The side gate needs to be opened so the person delivering the coal can access the coal shed.) There's about a hundred unmarked keys. I feel like Indiana Jones trying to choose the cup of Christ. I choose wisely (fifth time round), open the gate, clear all sorts of wood and foliage that was upset and displaced during Storm Bella, then retreat inside to boil the kettle and read the paper, which says the Oxford jab can be stored in a normal fridge, which is good but does present certain risks – namely, that Winnie will start hoarding the stuff. I watch the start of dawn from the dining table, looking south. Faint upward (or downward, I suppose) lines of pink augur the coming of sun.

And the coming of coal. For here's our man. The doorbell is alien at this hour, a scream in a museum.

'Alright?'

'Got your coal here, mate.'

'Need a hand?'

'Nah. Just stick it on the drive shall I?'

'Hm?'

'Stick it on the drive?'

'Ah. Well. The thing is. The lady of the house was expecting the coal to be loaded into the shed round the side.'

He laughs knowingly. 'I bet she was. She knows very well you're meant to specify that you want "split and tip". It's 50 quid extra. This happens every time.'

'Does it?'

'Yup.'

'Right. And what is the outcome every time?'

'I end up splitting and tipping for nothing.'

I offer him a hand, a torch, a coffee, some toast. He refuses everything, refuses all. It takes him half an hour to split and tip – time he probably won't get paid for, seeing as he's officially self-employed and gets paid by the job. A stoic man, good natured, despite the cold, the setbacks, the unforgiving minutes spent alone, at the wheel, on the road. Halfway through the splitting and tipping, I offer some moral support by going outside and watching him do it.

'Sure I can't get you a tea?'

'Nah, you're alright.'

'Sure?'

'I've got a flask in the cab.'

'Rolo yoghurt?'

'That's ten bags. Ten more to come. Done in a jiffy.'

I feel a bit angry with Winnie. She's fundamentally a sweet, decent woman – I hope that's coming across – but I wouldn't mind splitting and tipping her right now. Fancy pulling a fast one like that twice a year for the last God knows how long? Here she is now, poking her head out the front door as Patrick is climbing into his cab, job done. She's in her dressing gown, has the carefree look of a politics student who's been up all night smoking weed and listening to Woody Guthrie.

'Is it twenty bags?' she says.

'Good afternoon, m'lady.'

'Is it twenty bags?'

'It is. Five-hundred kilos, all split and tipped and ready to burn.'

'Excellent.'

'But you owe them 50 quid.'

'Hm?'

'For the splitting and tipping. It's 50 quid extra.'

'Over my dead body.'

'Is that right?'

'A man called Tony set a precedent in 1983. I asked about the surcharge and he tapped the side of his nose and said that if he was made a cup of tea and lent a hand all would be well. So I'm afraid they've rather made their bed when it comes to that.'

'Speaking of beds …'

'You're not going anywhere until there's a fire going.'

It doesn't prove easy. Needs a lot of encouragement. To generate more kindling, she takes some old picture frames out to the garden and starts smashing them up with a hammer. It makes for quite a sight. Winnie smashing away in Henry's cascading anorak, pausing to breathe, to smile, to grimace. I offer a hand but she turns it down, says it can be rather satisfying if one mentally substitutes the wood for other things.

'I hope you're not imagining me, Winnie.'

'Oh I wouldn't use this hammer on you. It's our best one.'

I'm leaving. For the night. She says thank you, for being around at Christmas. I say it's been a different Christmas, but a nice one. She says that's good news. As I'm feeling like giving her a hug, she asks if I'd retrieve a loaf from the basement freezer before I disappear.

# 1945

*Winnie is stood next to her mother in the kitchen, watching her cook a vast pot of marmalade. This is no ordinary domestic moment: the sugar ration was carefully saved up for the purpose. Unbidden, a cricket ball comes through the kitchen window and lands straight in the marmalade. Winnie's mother swears three times, and these three times will prove to be the only three times Winnie will hear her mother swear. For the life of her, Winnie cannot believe her brother's cheek when, in response to his mother's swearing and steely glare and accusing finger, he simply says (albeit without confidence), 'How's that?'*

# 4

## Beyond the pale of her curiosity

**1 January 2021.** 'Morning, Winnie. Happy new year.'

'Same to you.'

'I've made a resolution.'

'To have a shave?'

'To learn Esperanto.'

'You have two cups every morning as it is.'

'Huh?'

'Joke.'

'And you? Any aspirations?'

'Survival.'

'No chance.'

'Actually, scrap that. I want to be *jabbed*. That's what I want. As much as possible. Then I might be able to get into Arthur's flat and give it a proper sorting out.'

**2 January.** Not a blistering start to the year. Yesterday literally nothing happened, and today I got out of bed around ten and had chocolate for breakfast. On top of learning Esperanto, I'm meant to be learning Polish and Spanish and French, cooking and exercising more, writing letters to loved ones, and reading for at least three hours a day. As it is, I'm stood in my pants watching the news and drinking instant coffee. Come on, Aitken, pull your socks up. Indeed, put the damn things on. That'd be a start.

Up to the common to meditate and learn the present perfect in French. On my way back, attempting to be a different sort of person, I buy reduced smoked mackerel fillets, wild rice, and a high-fibre portion of soup. Winnie's not in when I get back. She comes in an hour later. She's been with Arthur at the hospital. 'He cut his head open this morning,' she explains. 'He got up to make a cup of tea, started making the tea, did something peculiar, smashed the back of his head, got to his feet, finished making the tea, then took it to bed with blood pouring out of his head. I dread to think what the pillowcase looks like. He was discovered an hour later fast asleep, which was when I got the call to get him down to St George's. Sixteen stitches. He didn't seem to mind a bit. When you've fallen as many times as Arthur, one doesn't tend to moan about it. But he did miss his lunch, the poor dear. Speaking of which …'

3 January. When I come down in the morning, the fire is on its last legs. Most of yesterday's 'Review of the Year' is sacrificed in its revival. I sit in front, willing it on, urging the brief flames of the paper to get the small log going. If you get a log going, then its slow steady burn gives the coals half a chance. It's not half as much fun to watch – the slow burn of a log – but it's a damn sight more useful in the long run. I notice a large wooden fish under the old square piano. It's a curious thing – like a rocking horse, but instead of a horse it's a fish, so a rocking fish if you will. I hadn't seen it before. But then I've never sat down here for so long before. New angles, new sightlines. The fire afoot, I move to my preferred spot by the French windows, whose blind is being kept neither up nor

down by a pair of wooden pegs. Something about the sight of the two evergreen conifers in the garden makes me think: *A long few months ahead. Low temperature, little sun, heavy restrictions.* I sigh. Could be worse. Could be a full-on lockdown.

Winnie enters. She always comes down in the morning fully dressed (I'm pleased to say) and ready for the day – thermal waistcoat, scarf, handbag, trainers. She sees me. There's mischief in her eyes. She's going to ask if I've made a start on the midlife workout regime she hooked out of the paper. 'Look at your hair!' she says happily. 'It's nearly touching the ceiling.' In an effort to illustrate her opinion, she goes on to pretend to be something monstrous (i.e. me) emerging from a bush or similar on Wimbledon common. It's a bittersweet spectacle. I try to look amused, but she can tell that I'm torn. 'Oh, just a bit of fun,' she says, throwing the whole thing away with a hand, on her way to the kitchen. I stop her before she goes. 'Winnie – what's that fish? Under there.'

'You know, I haven't a bloody clue.'

'I might have a go later.'

'Would you mind doing it on the driveway? I could invite Carlotta.'

I head up to the village, come back with a piece of beef – silverside, apparently. The beef's packaging says to roast uncovered on high for ten minutes, then low for 30 … 'Ah,' says Winnie, 'best to ignore that. Silverside is a *slow* cook. It's a pot roast. It will want at least four hours.'

'But the packaging says 40 minutes, Winnie, and so did the recipe I looked at online. I'd say that was a consensus.'

'Consensus is a poor substitute for leadership.'

'Meaning?'

'Meaning neither the internet nor a piece of packaging has what you might call *lived* experience.'

'I can't argue with that.'

'So we'll give it four hours and then take a look.'

Is it a generational thing? That I want to follow instruction and she wants to follow intuition? Are we getting worse at doing what we *feel* and getting better at doing what we're told? Do I slavishly and mindlessly obey guidelines, headlines, instructions, inducements, diktats and directions when I could be thoughtfully and reflectively and independently deciding what's right for *me*? Put simply, do I act according to feeling or prescription? I fancy it's the latter, and I fancy that it shouldn't be; I fancy I should be more like Winnie. Viz: trusting my gut, drawing on hard-earned ken, believing in my hunch and my inkling, rather than just submitting to the packet. We each have our own truth. That's what I'm getting at. Just as we each have a distinct sense of humour, and a distinct sense of purpose, so we each have a distinct sense of what is right, what is queer, what is good, what's best when it comes to cooking a piece of silverside beef. We need – urgently – to listen to our senses.[1]

Afternoon. I run on the common. I try to get lost. Set confusion as a target. The experience is relaxing. I seek out odd

---

[1] We gave the beef four hours then took a look and immediately wished we hadn't. It was but a fraction of a shadow of its former self. We ended up getting a takeaway – Korean – which she described as *sturdy*.

ways, narrow paths, hidden tracks, and the stream of novelty they afford puts me in a state of pleasant suspense, refreshing ignorance, quiet excitement. The novelty also limits awareness of pain. I don't think about my legs or my panting or the lactic acid because I'm thinking about what's ahead, what's below. I'm successful – I get lost. Attempting to get unlost is less relaxing, of course.

It's been harder lately. This game of intergenerational Big Brother with only two contestants. The reality is kicking in. That I live with an 85-year-old woman who has asked me three questions in two-and-a-half months. I've said it before and I apologise for repeating myself: I am outside of her empathetic range, beyond the pale of her curiosity, and I know it shouldn't but it gets to me. You're giving a person more than you're giving anyone else in your life (time, attention, support, love), and yet it's plain as day that that person doesn't give the slightest sliver of a monkey nut about you. I'm not whingeing. Just sharing. Imagine, for a second, that Winnie and I had been set up on a weird sort of blind date. I don't think either of us would have been much in the mood for a second, not least because Winnie wouldn't have asked me a single question. See below.

'Hello.'

'Sorry I'm late.'

'It's alright, Winnie.'

'I was in M&S looking for some trousers for Arthur.'

'Can I get you a drink?'

'Couldn't possibly. No joy of course. Poor love is destined to spend the next ten years in his underwear.'

BEYOND THE PALE OF HER CURIOSITY

'Hm.'

'Come to think of it, I'll have a large glass of cheap red wine. Have you seen the barmaid?'

'What about her?'

'She could sink the *Lusitania*.'

'The what?'

'If it wasn't already sunk of course.'

'So what do you do, Winnie?'

'Survive, my dear boy, survive.'

'Hobbies?'

'Fretting.'

'Is that a hobby?'

'And toast and marmalade.' *She takes a glug of her wine. Then another.* 'Tastes like seabass.' *Takes another glug.* 'I'm sending it back.'

And sometimes, when I'm really bored, which is always these days, I imagine what it would be like if we were married. If I'd been born in 1936, say, and we'd been matched cynically because I was a duke or we were both Protestants or something. I'm pretty sure we would have divorced before we were out of the church. I don't think I would have been able to put up with her passion for storage, her off-the-scale pedantry in the kitchen, her stubbornness. While, on the flip side, I don't think she would have been able to put up with my unthinkable lack of knowhow and my resemblance to a Neanderthal. The bond of matrimony could not have coped with such a mismatch.

And yet here we are. To all intents and purposes married. Looking back, the first month was sufficiently bizarre and novel and amusing to pass quickly and be quite pleasant, but the subsequent months are starting to limp somewhat. I know that the context is important. I know that this is cohabitation on steroids and that she's bereaved and all at sea. I know it's wrong and daft for me to expect this living arrangement to be a laugh a minute, and I know it's right and good for me to play the role of anchor, of ballast, of fall guy and scapegoat, if by playing such a role Winnie is aided, is helped, is settled. I know all that. But I also know that I'm not perfect and nor is she, that on the spectrum of nobleness and magnanimity I'm in the middle and Winnie isn't far away, that we're just two lost souls swimming in a fishbowl (to quote Pink Floyd) and there's no one around to change the water.

I put David Attenborough on, *Perfect Planet*, fancying she might like it, then go into the kitchen to wash up. I've not washed a single plate before she's calling me in to the sitting room. 'Ben! Do come! Otters in the snow!' I appreciate the otters and then return to the washing up. I've not washed a single plate before she's out of her chair and in the kitchen and dialling a number. 'I simply must tell Arthur to tune in …' Arthur doesn't answer, but she leaves a sweet message, an affectionate one even, which is something of a rarity. 'I do hope you get this and can tune in. Hope you're feeling better today. Rotten luck yesterday. But they patched you up, that's the main thing. Also rotten that you have to isolate for ten days now. Damn nuisance, the whole thing. But do look at the beavers if you can, darling, they're really quite wonderful in the snow. Thought of you often today. I do miss you. I do hope to see you soon. God bless. Thinking of you. Bye.'

The dishes done, I catch the second half of the show. I like the land iguanas. We're shown a female entering a volcano to lay her eggs. This is not without danger, but the temperature of the volcanic ash is *ideal* for incubation. Winnie reckons they've got the right idea, reckons it's much more practical to just plant the eggs somewhere toasty and then let them incubate *outside* of the body, thereby sparing the mother the terrific hassle of getting something rather large out of something rather small.

And the baby flamingos are adorable. They can't fly at first (quite understandable) so have to wade through lots of viscous caustic soda mud stuff in order to reconvene with their mothers, who are waiting by the water's edge. This business of wading makes them easy pickings for marabou storks, who look more like pessimistic solicitors than merciless predators. Their faintly ridiculous appearance doesn't make life any easier for the flamingo chicks who get stuck in the mud, mind you. Watching the slightest and slimmest of the chicks getting picked off by the storks is hard. There's a lot said – and rightly so – about how humans treat animals, less said about how animals treat each other. That marabou stork needs to take a look at itself. I'm quite confident it wouldn't be happy with its image.

And finally there's the wildebeest. We're shown a mother giving birth to a pretty sizable infant with remarkable insouciance, as if she did such things most afternoons. Having offloaded her young, the mother actually turns around and looks at the bundle as though she hasn't the slightest idea where it came from – a bewildered beast indeed. At first she refuses to feed her young. First she must teach it to stand, and then walk, and then trot, and then run. Only once it has learned how to run does she permit it to feed. It's tough love: she knows that if it can't run, it won't survive – the hyenas would have it for brunch. Winnie's seen enough. She gets to her feet. Says, 'I must get on with taking Arthur's new trousers up four inches.'

**4 January.** The paper carries an interesting headline regarding a surge in clandestine breast reduction during the pandemic. Winnie suggests two things: 1) that she quite understands the trend, given that large breasts please nobody but men who like cartoons; 2) that 'clandestine breast reduction' sounds like a fancy French dish that's been translated poorly.

She's gathered up the Christmas cards. They're in a pile on the dining table. I flick through them. (Winnie said I could.) Some are just going through the motions. 'Dear Winnie and family. Season's Greetings (and all best wishes). Laura and Alan.' Some mention me. 'Very pleased to hear of your new arrangement. Well done you. Would you leave him to Peter and I in your will?' Some mention Henry, and offer supportive words and so on. But the large majority read something like this: 'Dear Winnie. I do hope you manage to experience a semblance of joy this Christmas, despite everything. It's been an utterly horrid year. I genuinely don't recognise the world. Haven't seen Liz or the grandchildren since last year. Don't think I've been into town since the summer, and only then to buy a thermometer. Here's praying next year is different. I don't think I can cope with the isolation much longer.' And there's one very moving card from a lady who has lost her sight and so apologises for the handwriting. She writes: 'Being stuck inside for the best part of a year might have been sufferable had I the capacity to read.'

It's a lazy afternoon. I decide at 3 to sit down and watch a film – *Mary Queen of Scots*, starring Vanessa Redgrave as Mary and Glenda Jackson as Elizabeth. Because of the adverts, it goes on for about four days, which is nothing to what Mary suffered, in fairness. Winnie's here, working on Arthur's trousers. As is commonly known, she wants them up by four inches, and at this rate they'll be done just as the weather's changing and he'll be wanting shorts, in which case she'll just have to keep going, keep bringing them up, until they're short enough to be useful in the warm weather, by which time it will be winter and the whole process will start again. Which will probably suit Winnie just fine.

About half an hour later, the fire burning strongly and warmly, Winnie all of a sudden gets a bee in her bonnet. She starts telling herself off for not achieving anything today.

'Winnie,' I say, really quite seriously, 'you are permitted sometimes to simply relax. So stop telling yourself off and keep sewing.'

'Yes, sir.'

'*Pointless* is on now anyway.'

'What's that?'

'A gameshow.'

'Oh heavens.'

'Fancy it?'

'Never seen one in my life.'

'Try everything once?'

'OK.'

But then the phone goes and she's granted a reprieve. It's Arthur. He's in tears. He says he's hungry. Says they're not feeding him enough. Says they're used to feeding people in their eighties and nineties, not someone in their sixties with cerebral palsy. (Because of his cerebral palsy Arthur burns off calories practically non-stop.) 'I thought they knew the drill?' says Winnie. 'Would you like me to bring you over some butter stollen, and maybe have a word with the kitchen while I'm at it?' And before Arthur has finished saying 'Yes please' she's started putting her shoes on.

I watch a programme about fake news on BBC2. Afterwards I watch the news and I hope – really hope – that it's fake, because Huw Edwards is saying a new national lockdown will start tomorrow morning, in response to a new mutant surge. Exercise is to be limited to one walk a day in a southerly direction no longer than 75 metres within a furlong of your house, assuming you've got one. It's past midnight. Which means it's 5th January. Which means it's Epiphany. Here's an epiphany for you: I'll be seeing a lot more of Winnie going forward.

**5 January.** I'm in the sitting room. She's in the kitchen on the phone to Stewart. 'Stew. There you are. Glad I tracked you down. I need you to come and have a look at the tumble drier. It's on the blink. I know it's unlawful but I thought you could wear a balaclava or something. Think about it. In the meantime – have you seen they've opened a new John Lewis in Putney? You haven't? No you're quite right to avoid the shops – I've been doing much the same. Of course there are lots of things I *could* pop out and get, but one just *can't* anymore. Hey-ho. Lots of love. Must go. I'm just nipping down to— just nipping across to deliver Arthur's trousers. Yes again, that's right. Lots of love, darling, take care, must go.' She hangs up and then heads upstairs, convinced I'm up there. 'Ben! Ben! I'm just nipping down to Morrisons. I want to see if they have any meringue.'

**7 January.** 'I've been summoned,' says Winnie.

'Oh?'

'For the jab. Four o'clock at the Nelson Centre.'

'When?'

'Today.'

'Today?'

'That's what I said.'

'That's great!'

'Yes and about bloody time.'

'Wouldn't mind seeing how long it took you to engineer, trial and then distribute a new vaccine, Winnie.'

'Wouldn't you?'

'Not in the least.'

'I'm a bit worried about parking. So I'm going to walk. It's only a mile. But I can't say I like the prospect of coming back in the dark.'

'I'll come with you, if you'd like?'

'Would you mind?'

'Not at all.'

'OK then. Thank you.'

There's a gathering outside the entrance when we arrive. A volunteer gives Winnie a number – 363 – as though she were in a queue at the butcher's. We're invited through to a waiting room. Winnie takes a chair; I stand nearby. One man in line for the jab is reading the paper. He's the only one seemingly at ease. Everyone else is alert, watchful, eager or anxious. I wouldn't mind reading a transcript of their thoughts. The gentleman opposite drops his number. 340 is on the floor and up for grabs. I tell the man what's happened, joke that I was tempted not to tell him, tempted to swoop on his number and get the jab myself. 'You can have it for a fiver,' he says. His wife – long suffering, no doubt – tuts and hits him on the shoulder. 'You wally,' she says, 'that's worth at least a tenner.'

Winnie is called. A nurse called Trudy invites her to remove some layers, and I don't stick around to see which ones she goes for. I wait in the corridor, where I can hear Winnie telling the nurse all about Arthur, how he was breached, how he's struggled, that his razor is playing up – which is hardly a surprise, given that it started off as Henry's father's razor. She emerges.

'How was it?'

'A jolly good prick,' she says.

'Is that right?'

'Barely felt a thing. Just what you want.'

We're moved to another waiting room. We're to stay here for fifteen minutes before we leave.

'Why's that again?' says Winnie.

'To see if you die,' I say.

We walk home wearing our masks – more for warmth than protection. Back up Merton Hall Road, and then across the railway bridge. I pause halfway across the bridge to watch a train coming out of Wimbledon station. It rushes under us. I turn to watch it shooting southwest. It's dark. The only lights to speak of are the red tail lights of the train and a green light further down the line, signalling for the train to advance. It's cold; water vapour is visible around the street-lamps. I hear Winnie making steady progress behind me. There's a heaviness to the moment, to the crossing. The dark contributes to that heaviness, and so does the cold, and so do the red, green and amber lights. And so does the sound of Winnie passing, crossing, descending, the sound of Winnie going home.

**10 January.** I can't find my shoes. I left them by the front door. Winnie can't be sure she didn't move them somewhere. I check everywhere. I go down to the basement to check the pile of Henry's boots and brogues and flip-flops. I've never really explored the basement. It's huge. There's about six rooms. One contains old wine. One contains old tools. One contains old magazines and suitcases and speakers and egg boxes. And one – the largest – contains a ping-pong table. I'm excited. Delighted even. Then I'm less of these things by an order of magnitude because the only person I can play is Winnie. I shouldn't assume her inability. That's the essence of ageism. I'll ask her for a game. I find my shoes – they're on my feet. Is senility contagious?

**11 January.** Breakfast. Kitchen. The front page of the paper carries a picture of two toddlers enjoying a walk in the woods. The caption has to do with protecting the NHS by not travelling outside of your local area for exercise. I show Winnie the picture and then pretend to read a different caption. 'Toddlers issued £200 fines for being happy in public.' She cottons on, has a stab herself. 'Tiny drug lords on the run in Cumbria.' Elsewhere in the paper, there's news of a 'Hip Fracture Death Risk'. I suggest that Winnie might well get a call from government demanding she gives up her hips in order to safeguard her future. It's that kind of morning. A mixture of fear and dismay and madness. Which is to say normal.

She goes to Arthur's and comes back in a flap. It's his razor. It's broken. Kaput. It needs to be fixed or replaced – urgently. I nip down to Boots and see what they've got. It's a particular model she's after – a Remington – but they don't have one, so when I get home I order one online. I tell Winnie it'll be here tomorrow.

BEYOND THE PALE OF HER CURIOSITY

**13 January.** I come down wearing my running stuff. This has happened many times before.

'Going to play football?' she says.

'No, I'm going for a run.'

'Never seen you do that before,' she says.

'Have you not?'

I like to think that the combination of stress and grief and her busy mind allows certain things to slip through the net. That's what I like to think.

We watch an episode of *The Crown*, which ends with a lingering shot of Prince Philip's empty bed, implying his absence, in more sense than one. The implication isn't lost on Winnie. 'He ought to be mindful of where he isn't,' she says. She gets to her feet. Looks at the spine of *The Wine Buyer's Guide 1993* upon which my laptop is perched, says that Henry's brother-in-law got into importing wine and Henry was very keen to keep up with the Joneses. 'Never read a page of course. Far too busy. We've got some bloody valuable stuff down in the cellar, you know. I used to give Kuba a bottle every Wednesday, when he came to do the garden. Then I realised they were worth about 300 quid a pop. So I give him a can of lager now, as you know. After a month or two of getting lager each week, he said to me, "Mrs Carter. Can I just say thank you for changing to lager – I prefer it immensely."'

**14 January.** I wake up at 10.30. Whoops. Completely slept through the alarm. My first thought on waking is: have I enough credit in the bank to get through this with minor bruising? Probably not. I go downstairs, enter the kitchen, try to be as jolly as possible, rather than sheepish and sorry.

'Slept right through my alarm!'

'I hoped you were dead.'

'Oh calm down.'

'At least then you'd have a decent excuse.'

She gives me a look. It's a novel one. She's somehow looking down on me even though she's five foot and sat, while I'm six foot and not. I check on the fire. It's blazing.

'Fire's looking good.'

'Almost broke my neck bringing the coal in.'

'I'm sorry to hear that.'

'I took the ash out to the bucket – trusting there'd be room for it.'

*Bollocks.* 'And?'

'Lucky for you, there was plenty.'

'You would have cursed me if there wasn't.'

'I would have gone upstairs and bashed you over the head.'

'Sorry, Winnie.'

'The hoover's fully charged if you'd like to atone.'

I do my penance while she has another bit of toast and goes through the paper. I hoover the kitchen first. When I turn off the machine she says, 'Are you Japanese, by any chance?' I give her a look inviting her to explain herself. She reads from the paper: 'A Japanese man has earned an enormous online following and a modest living by renting himself out to the bored, lonely or needy as a companion who does nothing. Under the name "Rental Person Who

110                                  BEYOND THE PALE OF HER CURIOSITY

Does Nothing," Shoji Morimoto, 35, has received thousands of requests for his services despite a lack of any particular personal or professional skills. In less than three years he has published books, inspired a television drama and acquired 269,000 Twitter followers. "Rent a person who does nothing," his online profile says. "I am always available, I won't do anything except eat, drink and give a simple response."'

She looks at me. I look at her: *Your point is?*

'Your cover's been blown, Ben,' she says.

'Nightmare.'

'Or shall I say Shoji?'

'You may as well.'

'What do you have to say for yourself?'

I offer a simple response in a sort of robotic voice and then ask for 10,000 yen. We both laugh. She returns to the paper. 'This is a fun headline. "Circus in trouble over Nazi goats".'

The phone goes. It's Keith Lime. He's talking for about five minutes before Winnie twigs who it is. 'Ex-soldier,' she explains after hanging up. 'Friend of Henry's. Married a contemporary of Rebecca if you'll credit that, some 30 years his junior. She was an upstart, I can tell you. She came down to Devon once, to the cottage, brought a great big mobile phone to show how important she was. It was the size of a toaster.' I think: *It's telling what people compare things to.*

**15 January.** She hands me some old photos. There's a nice one of Arthur and Winnie on the former's sixth birthday (judging by the candles). They're in the garden. Friends are gathered around. Most are wearing pirate hats. Washing is on the line. The old swing – new then – is in the background. Rebecca looks unsure. Deeply unsure. Stewart, who clearly wishes it was *his* birthday, is being restrained by Mrs Wilson, the housemaid. Henry is in a vest and sandals. Winnie is behind Arthur, her arms around him, her hand on his, helping him cut the cake. Arthur is looking at the camera. Winnie is out of focus and her fringe has fallen across her face, partially obscuring her smile. My favourite photo in the bunch though is of the children by a stream. Arthur is stood and central, showing off a bottle of murky water that presumably contains tadpoles or something. Rebecca is sat on the rocks at the edge of the stream. She's looking up at Arthur and in the middle of saying something along the lines of, 'They're not yours, Arthur, they're *ours*.' Stewart is on his haunches, to the other side of Arthur, to the left of the image, looking away from the pair, wearing an expression that unmistakably says, *What am I surrounded by? What must I put up with?*

Struggle is not straightforward. Grief does not proceed in a straight line. Like the weather, sometimes Winnie is good, and sometimes she is bad. Like the clouds, sometimes she is low and heavy, sometimes higher and lighter. She's always suffering – that's plain as day – it's just that sometimes she gets distracted. I've started laying traps for her – attention traps. I'll scan the TV listings and put David Attenborough on, or start making something in the kitchen, which always gets her full attention, and so doing gives her brain some time off worrying about Arthur, or the bill that needs to be paid to the tree surgeon, or the relative absence of bread and loved ones.

She will smile and she will laugh – but her smiles and laughs are bits of punctuation in a world of words, words, words. The majority of those words are Arthur and Henry and her lifelong feelings of guilt and insecurity. The other two children – Rebecca and Stewart – are not a cause for concern. They are not a feature of her struggle; indeed, they are a feature of her support, her surviving.

I get angry with her. Sometimes. Once a week, for maybe ten minutes, occasionally longer. After she's snapped at me unreasonably, or got me to do some faintly ludicrous task (buff the bannisters) and then moaned about my technique throughout. But then there are times when she'll shuffle into the sitting room, where I'm drinking tea and reading the obituaries, and tell me she bought some baked beans at the supermarket because she knows I'm a fan and that I'm to help myself but preferably when she's out of the house, and I'm touched, and feel cared for, feel thought about, and am forced to let go of anything I think I know about her. We never know about other people. Not really. Not least because we never know about ourselves. Not really. We only think. And guess. The world is made up of people thinking and guessing, thinking and guessing.

I'm watching snooker and she's leaving a message for Arthur. He attempted to have a wet shave and cut himself quite badly. She's giving him some advice. 'I'm afraid you *must* accept the fuzz, darling. You have to let it come on. It's not something to be embarrassed about. Not this once. A parcel came yesterday and what we hoped was your new razor turned out be a book for Ben. Such a shame. We'll just have to wait. Don't you worry about a bit of fuzz. Look at Ben. He's got fuzz all over him and doesn't appear to give a farthing about it. He's not even *trying* to shave. May he be an example. But only for the time being. You're *not* to cut yourself like that. It *won't* do.' There's a pause. She breathes, fills the kettle, resumes. 'And I'm very glad you've had the jab. But you *must* get onto them about the second one.'

She comes into the sitting room carrying a bunch of daffodils.

'You didn't have to do that, Winnie,' I say.

'I didn't do that. Believe me. They're for the table.'

'Lucky table.'

'90p a bunch. Couldn't resist. I think they might be from Chile, like everything else at Lidl. They'll be coming out here soon enough – February usually.'

'In the winter?'

'Oh yes. Daffodils don't mind a bit. Very eager. Tough as old boots. I remember walking through a field in Oxford – I can't have been very old – and the field was covered in thick snow, with just the heads of daffodils poking out through the top. I remember finding the scene both hilarious and utterly beautiful.'

'Would you let me know when the different flowers come out?'

'You've got eyes, haven't you?'

'Yes, but sometimes things only become visible after they've been pointed out.'

'Nonsense.'

'I promise you it's true.'

'It's one of the joys of spring. My mother taught me flowers sooner than the alphabet.'

'We didn't have a garden.'

'Well that was an oversight.'

'I'll let my mother know.'

'I'll be happy to point them out to you on one condition.'

'What's that?'

'You stop leaving mugs everywhere.'

**16 January.** She calls through from the kitchen. 'There's a completely daft programme on. It's Nazi propaganda no less. I don't know how they get away with it. They're burning books, for heaven's sake. Not in the slightest bit woke.' It's *Indiana Jones and the Last Crusade.*

Winnie has spent the bulk of the day trying to crack the razor case. The one I ordered still hasn't shown, so she's unearthed an earlier one of Henry's, only it doesn't have a charger – or a 'flex' as she calls it – so she's been over to Arthur's to collect his flex, to see if it works with the new (old) razor. For my part, I spent the morning watching golf tutorials on YouTube and then came downstairs to read. Why come downstairs to read? Why not just stay in my room? Because it's undeniably nicer – at a subconscious level – to do solitary things with someone nearby, with someone around. I say someone but I mean Winnie. I mean Winnie in particular. For all the times I've wanted to hit her on the head with a carrot (don't worry, the carrots we have around here are *very* soft), I do like the old girl. Increasingly.

**17 January.** I can hear Andrew Marr in the kitchen saying that the next 100 hours will be the crescendo of Covid, so strap in, everybody. Winnie pops her head in and tells me to cover my ears because there's about to be a crescendo. She jokes, but I know it's getting to her. I've noticed a shift, in line with the nature of the bulletins, in sync with the news. If it's not increasing case rates it's unprecedented deaths. If it's not vaccine worries it's a new variant of the virus. The government has launched a new 'awareness' campaign, which is a hell of a euphemism. It includes a poster that says: 'Don't Let a Coffee Cost Lives'. The poster shows a few people queueing outside a café. It won't be long, I think cynically, before they're saying: 'Save Lives: Stop Breathing'.

**18 January.** A message from Amazon. Arthur's razor has been lost and won't be delivered.

'Winnie.'

'Yup?'

'I got a message from Amazon.'

'Oh is it here?'

'No. It's been lost.'

'I *knew* it.'

It's Blue Monday. Most depressing day of the year. Winnie puts some fresh daffodils on the dining table – tight little buds like bullets – and then a shoe. Arthur's shoe. The sole is clinging on by a thread. His shoes are specially made to suit his style of ambulation; they're like wedges, or platforms. He's currently coping with slippers. She's pulling her hair out. I search for cobblers nearby, go to the nearest, down by the station. The cobbler applies some industrial strength glue and some magic spray and then squeezes the shoe in a magic vice. Then he doesn't charge me. I say, 'Nah go on, how much?' And he says, 'No honestly, it's on the house. Have a good day.' Hero. Winnie is delighted. She's on the phone immediately to Arthur. She passes me the phone to confirm that it was industrial strength glue and that the cobbler didn't charge. She opens a half bottle of dusty champagne.

Message from Jane (Stewart's wife) re Winnie sounding more confused on the phone recently. They want reassurance she isn't going downhill. I send back an honest assessment of Winnie's behaviour the past few months. Phew, they say, everything as it was then.

BBC News. Huw Edwards. Footage of a mortuary – a body being stowed. Footage of a gravedigger – filmed from above by drone, toiling with soil, making room for one more. I think of Carlotta watching this. I think of my grandparents watching this. Is this the *only* way to encourage caution? Ceaseless exhibition of worst-case scenario? Then a report about cracking down on public misbehaviour. Footage of police officers serving £200 fines to four people using the outdoor gymnasium in the courtyard of their housing estate. To criminalise exercise during a health crisis does seem an original approach. Then we see a café being forced to close for permitting a queue to form outside. The tone of the reporting is: *look at our bobbies, aren't they good, catching out the criminals, those brainless citizens with blood on their hands.* Am I cynical because I don't want to believe how bad the situation is? It's probable.

**20 January.** Storm Christoph is in town. I say to Winnie that it was initially Storm Christopher but the 'er' got blown off. She exhales, raises her eyebrows, leaves the house to deliver Arthur's rejuvenated shoe. Then returns ten seconds later. There was a parcel outside, getting soggy. It's the razor at long last. She puts the box on the side, makes to leave.

'Why don't you take it round to Arthur now?'

She looks at the box, at me, at the box.

'It's not going to do any good here,' I say.

She purses her lips, exhales, a silent whistle. 'I do prefer to try these things out first …'

I pick up the box and put it in her bag. 'It's the right one. It will do the job. Give it to Arthur so he doesn't look like me.'

'OK,' she says, 'I see your point.'

She leaves. Then returns ten seconds later. 'Phone Arthur, would you? Tell him to come down to reception for a chance encounter with his mother.'

The daffodils on the dining table, just buds the day before last, are now bright trumpets, taut and optimal – at their very best. I think: *What is actually happening here? What's going on? How is this thing changing its nature?* She's bought some other flowers for the hallway. Poinsettias. She has to say it four times before I can pronounce it properly.

I do a Nigel Slater recipe. She likes it apart from the cabbage, which she says is galling. She puts the telly on. *The Repair Shop*. All of the 'hands' in the shop – metalsmiths, carpenters – look happy and expert and astonishingly practical. I tell Winnie I wouldn't last ten minutes in the repair shop. 'Ten minutes?' she says. 'You'd be lucky to even get in the place.' A bird box is brought in for repair. She says, 'Did I tell you a blue tit got into our one outside? It was quite dubious. Had a look, went away, had another look, went away. Really couldn't decide. It was quite fun to watch. Might have been worried about getting stuck in the doorway, forced to spend the rest of its days with its backside on display – dreadfully embarrassing. In the event it got in and out no problem at all. Went off to tell its friends. Though we *must* move the box. It's too *low*. The cats will have it.'

**21 January.** We used to have quite a big conversation at breakfast each morning. Well, I say conversation, but it was more like an interview, with Winnie in the hot seat. I was trying to learn about Winnie in a hurry, hoping that what I learned would help me understand who she is now. And it did. Partly. There are fewer interviews now. I ask less about when she was seven, fourteen, twenty-one; about rationing, about Harold Wilson, about her mother's character, about her experience of private school. I guess that kind of questioning, that line of enquiry, couldn't be sustained. I guess that degree of interest on my part couldn't be kept up. When I moved to Windy Ridge, I knew I wanted to learn about Winnie's life, about her take on things, and so I set about it. I wasn't prepared to be patient, to let it come naturally – which is to say slowly, in bits, organically and accidentally.

But now I am. Prepared to be patient. And, besides, nobody wants to be asked to consult their deep emotional archives every breakfast time, to be asked about love or regrets or the change to decimalisation. I guess I've settled down now. I know she has a past, of course she does, big deal. She ran around, fell over, went to school, learned to behave, learned French, met a boy, fell in love, developed a distaste for liver and mushrooms, moved away, had a child, moved back, cared for her young, cared for her old, cooked, talked, shopped, built, planted, cried and so on – of course she did. All that is no less interesting to me, but all that has fallen down the pecking order. Without thinking, I have switched course, have changed tack: now I attend to Winnie in the present, Winnie as she is, Winnie ad hoc. And to be honest – and this is not to disparage her form coming into the present – I prefer dealing with her contemporary self.

We talk throughout the day, in patches, in bursts, about the decency of lettuce, or the state of the milk, or the length of Arthur's beard, or the insecurity of the bird box. Such ordinary starting points aren't decided upon; they simply arise, simply present themselves, and so the dialogue, the relationship, is less effortful, less orchestrated. But such ordinary starting points – a lettuce, for example – can lead, via here and there, to something larger, like the time she got assaulted in Oxford aged eleven. We increasingly behave as friends might. Our relationship is more *thoughtless* these days. Our interactions are at once less deep but somehow more meaningful for being so.

A clear morning: sun fills the house. It comes as a shock. I fill the coal bucket in my slippers, make a coffee, read the foremost pages of the paper. Jo Biden's on the front, looking newly elected.

'It's quite a job to take on at 78,' I say.

'Churchill did it at 80. Toast?'

'Did it from the bath. Yes please.'

'Though perhaps he oughtn't have done,' she says. 'His health wasn't the best. He didn't look after himself. He indulged.'

'Hence why he burnt that portrait Graham Sutherland did of him. Couldn't stand the sight of himself.'

'People can't stomach their own image. We're too soft. We close our eyes.'

'Truth is beauty and beauty truth. Shelley.'

'Keats.'

'Shelley.'

'Keats.'

'It's Shelley, Winnie.'

'If you insist.'[2]

---

[2] It was Keats.

I look at the painting above the fire (an abstract inferno), and the painting above the dresser (an abstract cock fight), and the porcelain men on horses on the mantlepiece, and the toucan, and the sea shells, and the chair from Manila, and the photographs of Dartmoor and India – all gathered here today, all in assembly, the spoils of a life. I quite like the idea of a retirement spent softy and quietly in a recliner watching the news surrounded by the souvenirs of my life. But there's a time for such a chair, such stillness, such cushioned reflection, and that time is after the time spent moving, searching, embracing, foraging. For years and years one gathers the stuff for a feast, and only then can one sit down in good faith to eat. I'm not ready to eat. Not yet. And to be frank I'm not sure Winnie is either. Which is why she's out hunting for tulip bulbs.

**23 January.** She comes downstairs with a wad of photographs. She hands the pictures to me, as though they were nothing. Of the bunch, there are several I especially like:

1) Winnie with Arthur and Rebecca in her arms on a building site. The three subjects amount to 5 per cent of the image – meaning Henry, who took the picture, must have been stood ten or so metres away from them, up on a scaffold. It is their house that is being built – the one across the street that they never got round to moving into.[3] Winnie and the children are in the rightmost quarter of the image, half-

---

[3] Windy Ridge was meant to be a stopgap while the new house was built across the street. But Winnie fell in love in a big way and refused to budge.

way up. Behind them is Carlotta's house and front garden. The majority of the photo – the remaining three quarters – is the house under construction. It's an interesting composition: the significance of home is unmissable. It's also an interesting family portrait, at once lacking and harsh and tender and complete. Because Henry *is* in the picture, isn't he? We might not be able to see him, but without him there would be no portrait. It's his perspective. It would be easy to conclude that his perspective belittles the family, favours the building work, etc. But the house was *for* them. He wanted to record and catalogue the creation of their home.

2) Winnie is sat on a sofa looking at Arthur, who is dressed as a consultant and is inspecting Winnie's skirt with a stethoscope. In the background, Rebecca is picking her nose sat on the lap of her uncle.

3) A camping holiday. Early 1960s. The canvas tent (ex-army via Henry's father) has been erected, and Winnie and Arthur are celebrating the fact by posing on its threshold and waving at the camera. There are other things around – a paraffin stove, two potties, the bonnet of a car – but what's first and foremost is mother and child on the edge of their temporary home.

**24 January.** Snow. I spot the first flake. Or nearly first. Difficult to tell exactly when it starts. Winnie's instinctive delight quickly U-turns into acute worry. 'We need salt! *Coarse* salt. Three bags. Big ones. Cheap ones. Sainsbury's will be open. And get a hunk of ham – they go a long way. And maybe a piece of beef for comfort. But you'll have to go *now*.'

I drop what I'm doing (an egg sandwich) and head out. It's not straightforward going downhill. Need to take small steps and lean forward. No big bags of salt in Sainsbury's, so I have to buy four boxes of expensive organic responsibly sourced stuff. I get the beef and ham, plus some daffodils in a pot to go in my room (the first flowers I've ever bought for myself: I must be growing). Upon my return, she hands me a shovel and tells me to clear a path from the front steps to the pavement, then season liberally. I do so. She says my path's not exactly A to B but it will have to do. I sprinkle the salt. 'Not so much!' she barks. I give her a look. She reads it well. 'No you're doing a fine job, a very fine job, and I'm hugely grateful.'

She moves out onto the street to confront three young children. They've rolled a huge snowball and mean to send it down the hill for a laugh. Winnie nips this in the bud. Tells the children to consider what they're doing. Tells them that the snowball is actually an *ice* ball and can do terrific damage. Tells them her friend Carlotta got bowled over by such a ball once and fractured both hips, which isn't easy to do. She pleads with the children to put a lid on their dangerous instincts and *go home*. The children seem to be standing their ground. Winnie seems reluctant to admit defeat. An impasse. I take a photograph. They reach a compromise: the children agree to roll their snowball down a different hill.

I walk to the common. The snow is thick, an inch or two deep, and it squeaks underfoot. The common is busy – uncommonly so. Pleased to see that the snowmen are socially distanced. Several are wearing face masks. The mood – measured how?

BEYOND THE PALE OF HER CURIOSITY

– is good. The snow has been welcomed, the novelty well received, thoughts of the virus have momentarily withdrawn. Yellow wellingtons. A dog wearing earmuffs. Misdirected snowballs strike unsuspecting heads. It's a warming scene, in spite of the cold. I walk home. The bulk of the snow on the streets and pavements has already gone. The path I made and salted, from the pavement to the front steps, is no longer evident. The path was a brief and obvious absence. Its character relied on something being missing.

**25 January.** My miniature daffodils are showing signs of life – a single bud has broken through, if that's the right way of putting it. I have to rotate the pot occasionally to ensure even growth, and I'm not to give it too much to drink – quite sound life advice. When I go downstairs I'm shocked to find the daffodils that were on the dining table in the compost bin outside. Surely a premature execution? I remonstrate with Winnie in the kitchen, who's putting a new batch of daffs in a vase. She's unrepentant. She says you cannot and must not mix the old with the new.

'Why?'

'Because in a few days the new ones will make the old ones look pathetic.'

'According to you.'

'No. According to science.'

Winnie and I sit down in front of her computer. She wants to check her emails. I turn the machine on and am asked for a password.

'Password, Winnie?'

'Hestia.'

'What?'

'A mythical Greek goddess.'

'How do you spell it?'

I type it in. It's the wrong password.

'Maybe put some numbers on the end,' advises Winnie.

'What numbers?'

'Don't ask me.'

'Right you are.'

I reset the password. It takes some doing. Involves two codes, a text message and a telegram. When I'm in, I navigate to her email login page.

'Password, Winnie?'

'Hestia.'

'The Greek goddess?'

'That's the one.'

It's the wrong password.

Half an hour later and we're finally into her account. She wants to forward an email. Henry has left some dosh for a godson believed to be living in a hut near Galway. 'It's going to come as a nice surprise. I don't think Samuel was even aware Henry was alive let alone dead.' Then she wants to order a bird feeder. I type 'bird feeder' into the search engine. I show her some candidates, making sure to talk through each of my clicks and scrolls, principally so that I don't have to do this again. She makes a decision. Knows the one she wants. Great. Just need to access her popular online retailer account in order to complete the purchase …

'Password, Winnie?'

'Hestia.'

**26 January.** I'm sent down the hill to fetch six pounds of sugar for her marmalade. I get the sugar and three small yoghurts for Arthur and some green beans for the lady outside collecting food for local people in need. Somehow there's more room in my head these days to see what others might like, what others might need. By no means has there been a transformation, but there has, at least, been a change. One advantage of a relatively settled and sober mind – it's more sensitive, more aware of others, of things outside of ourselves. Haven't had a drink for nearly a month. I've been abstemious. And I wouldn't have said that were it not for Winnie. (She taught me the word.) Though we can hardly congratulate Winnie for keeping me off the sauce. Practically every night she 'forgets' I'm behaving abstemiously and pours me a glass of wine that she either drinks herself or funnels back into the bottle. I feel a bit bad. She doesn't like drinking alone for some reason. She thinks it's improper. Or sad. Or both. She might be on to something.

A nice passage in my book – *Any Human Heart* by William Boyd. The novel, put simply, is the diary of one man's life, from cradle to grave. Boyd writes:

> 'That's all your life amounts to in the end: the aggregate of all the good luck and the bad luck you experience. Everything is explained by that simple

formula. Tot it up – look at the respective piles. There's nothing you can do about it: nobody shares it out, allocates it to this one or that, it just happens. We must quietly suffer the laws of man's condition, as Montaigne says.'

I show the passage to Winnie. She stands and reads. And reads. And reads. I have to ask for the book back. She asks if she can have a look when I'm done. I ask if I can have a look when *she's* done. Moments later, she spots a tiny moth. She squashes it, looks at me. 'Bad luck,' she says. 'Tot it up, little moth.'

The bird feeder arrives, and so does a set of scales – the former to encourage and attract finches and warblers, the latter to measure time and justice and levels of sadness and sugar. I think she's doing OK. I think she's doing better. That's not to say she's great or delighted or flying high – it is to say she's OK, that she's better than before. How does one measure? She's just asked again if she can have my book when I'm done with it. That's one thing. And she took half a minute or so out of her day to show me, via the medium of mime, how her egg went to pieces when she dropped it into boiling water this morning. That's another. She wants to get on top of the computer. She wants to get her passport renewed. She's buying flowers and a bird feeder and three kilos of mixed seed. She's laughing more. She can sometimes be found reclining in Henry's chair, with a cup of tea and a book, or a biscuit and the remote. (She wouldn't go near that chair when I first moved in.) And the nature of her complaints is becoming more down to earth. It's the price of pasta. It's the colour of Paul Hollywood. It's not – or it's not as far as I can tell – that the world feels upside down, that it feels like she lives in a house at the bottom of the sea.

Having said all that, she's just entered the sitting room wearing a face like thunder. She's got the biscuit tin with her. 'Did I not tell you to go easy on the ginger ones? You let yourself down, Ben. You really do.'

I offer her a hand with the marmalade. 'No. Thank. You,' she says, quite happily. 'This is not a job for a novice. You've got to be quite pedantic, for if it doesn't set properly then you've got some very unattractive marmalade on your hands – literally so. You put it on your toast and before you know it it's not there anymore.'

I like how she puts things. It's arguably the thing I like most about Winnie – how she puts things. I ask myself: *To what extent is how we put things telling of who we are?* She once said, of a woman passing by, 'She's got more chance of travelling through time than remaining upright in those heels.' I liked that the key detail came at the end. I tried to come up with something similar: 'At the party, over several hours and in the company of various people, Alan behaved with uncanny grace and humility for a murderous psychopath.'

Anyway. Back to the marmalade. Her oranges thoroughly poached, she starts scooping the flesh, slicing the rind, fishing out pips and pith. Having scooped and sliced, she's now got the goods going in a giant pot of cartoonish dimensions. Her apron is flecked with flesh and pith. She's stirring the cauldron with a long wooden spoon. She asks me to have a sniff. I get too close and a spit of molten marmalade hits my eyebrow. Winnie says my reaction is a bit on the dramatic side. She adds a touch more water, and then the sugar, about three pounds. Once the sugar crystals have dissolved she cranks up the heat until she's got a rolling boil.

'A what?'

'That's what it's called. A rolling boil.'

'And what does that mean?'

'It means it's bloody hot. So stand back or you might suffer another life-changing injury.'

By the end of the process she bears an uncanny resemblance to Donald Trump.

**27 January.** I take a cup of tea outside, sit beneath the walnut tree, spot some emerging daffodils, and think: *The more familiar you are with something, the more you notice it elsewhere.* As reflections go, it's hardly an original or insightful one, but it's nonetheless the case. It stands to reason, therefore, that the more things we are familiar with, the more things we notice – flowers being an example, and grief being another. Although the sun is behind the ash tree, because it's winter the light is still coming through. It's a seasonal advantage I hadn't considered before. Perhaps that's why sunny winter days have such a different quality to them. There's less getting in the way. Winnie appears on the terrace, spots me. 'Is that Ben or a piece of furniture?'

She said dinner would be ready at 6.30 and she'd give me a shout. At 6.45, I go down to the kitchen to see what the score is. The oven's on – good sign – but it's full of glass jars – bad sign.

'Is this what we're having for dinner?'

'What? Oh. Yes. I'd better think about the dinner, hadn't I?'

'Why are you cooking the jars?'

'I'm sterilising them.'

'Won't they blow up?'

'They won't blow up.'

One blows up. Well and truly. Thank goodness the door was shut, else it would've been a scene from *Oedipus Rex* in here. I take the jars out and put the sausages in (the oven, not the jars), do the spuds and carrots, lay the table, heat the plates, and so on. When dinner's ready, she opts to have hers in the kitchen, picks at it while jarring the marmalade. She says she's not happy how it's turned out, but you wouldn't know it because she seems jubilant. I tell her she should cook marmalade every day, if it lifts her spirits so. 'I'd be dead by Tuesday,' she says, licking a teaspoon. 'Why?' 'Because passion and stress are birds of a feather.'

She sees that I'm stretching my back – arms in the air and so on. 'That's it,' she says. 'Good idea. Stretch it out. We used to do all sorts of stuff like that, down at the YMCA, for the keep-fit.' Then she does a few star jumps, quite rapidly, while staring straight at me, her expression saying: *This sort of thing – reckon you could handle it?* Then she reaches for the ceiling and then for her toes, and then she does some torso rotations, all the while wearing her orange-smeared apron and holding, in her right hand, a long wooden spoon coated in marmalade. I've never seen such a flurry of energy. She stops mucking around, looks at her spoon, inspects it.

'Nothing came off. That's good.'

'Pity the same can't be said for you, Winnie. Is that your left arm under the table?'

She smiles at me – long and hard – then says, 'What?'

She needs to get some hearing aids. She's missing out.

**28 January.** I mention the travel writers festival kicking off today, of which I am a part. We talk a bit about the genre. 'They used to be quite modest. By foot with a backpack. Not anymore. One must travel gymnastically – *Tumbling to Tokyo* and what have you. Or the author has to be a llama, or a pop star, or both. Eric Newby lived behind us. Did I tell you? He wasn't a pop star. He just went somewhere and wrote about it. *Very well*. But like most things now it's all about the wrapping paper.' I ask for a travel book idea. She says I should either go somewhere few people go – Croydon, for example – or somewhere many people go but write about it in a way few people are able to. 'Croydon it is then,' I say. 'Toast?' she says.

I turn down the toast. Take a second coffee through to the sitting room, close my eyes and listen. A Book of the Week on the radio. The drip of a tap that's becoming too hard to turn. The tick and tock of a clock. The turning of pages. And then, 'Now that's more like it. A robin. Welcome my friend.' What do I like about this house? About living here? I quite like this for a start. Sitting by the window, near the fire, watching the garden, able to hear the action of the kitchen. She calls me through. Insists I try her marmalade. It's on the bitter end of the bittersweet spectrum, but I don't mind that.

She's off to the bakery, and then the supermarket. 'I've not been for a while,' she says. 'I've been obeying the Führer.' (Not sure if this is politically correct but hey-ho.) I offer to go for her, but she says my generation aren't canny enough. Before she goes, she says there's one more thing. (There's always one more thing. She's like the fictional detective Columbo in this way.) Could I find it in my heart to fish through the contents of that drawer and hook out some Sellotape?

I could, and I do, and doing so I come across some old birthday cards and the like. One from Henry to Winnie on their anniversary (I assume) in 2002. Feel a little jolt of something on seeing Henry's handwriting. The sight of it makes him somehow more alive, more real. Not that I doubted the man, but you know what I mean. He has the hand of someone brilliant but in a hurry. 'Winnie Darling. With all my love and all my thanks for so many lovely years together! Henry.' And then at the bottom of the page it says, 'xxxx → ∞', which must be code for something saucy. The card, for the record, was bought (though I suppose it might have been stolen) from the V&A Museum in London. It shows a swallow happily plummeting against a pattern of golden leaves.

The next card, found inside the first, is dated 9th June 2001 – Winnie's 65th birthday. 'Winnie Darling. With all my love on this Great Day! Many happy returns! And thanks! Henry.' And again the secret code at the bottom. The card, incidentally, is the same – plummeting swallow sourced (in bulk by the look of it) from the V&A. Within the birthday card is a Valentine's card (2008) from Winnie to Henry, which carries an image of Punch and Judy, looking quite at peace and rather pleased with themselves. The handwriting is more eloquent and legible but still gives the impression that the card was written while riding a bicycle. She probably had a pot of marmalade on a rolling boil and Arthur on her shoulders. It reads: 'Dearest Henry. All my love – It's never changed & we are just as young as ever! Winnie.' And then at the bottom, answering Henry's code, 'xx () () etc.'

We sit and eat. A bit of soup and ciabatta, some cheese, a few cherry tomatoes. She says she ought to call her friend who lives on Spencer Hill. Mary. Hasn't spoken to her for yonks. Says she probably knows a bricklayer who might deal with the crack in the front step. I say she ought to call Mary, crack or no crack. She says, 'That's very true, but it's been a strange time, hasn't it? Busy somehow. Busy being not busy. Somehow no time and nothing but time. Would it offend you if I had another chunk of cheese?'

She calls Mary, leaves a message, gets straight to the point – 'Winnie Carter here. Do you know a bricklayer?' – as though Mary were merely an operator, a public service. It's not that Winnie isn't a warm person, it's just that she's rather rubbish at getting the warmth across. It gets trapped beneath several thick blankets of etiquette and propriety and politesse and so on. Mary's blankets aren't so thick. She calls back and, after dutifully giving Winnie the details of a man who's very good but usually two months late, she asks after Arthur, after her. She sympathises with Winnie, or claims to anyway, says it must be hard not seeing him, agrees that a brief encounter outside beneath a tarpaulin is hardly ideal in winter, says she knows how much Winnie has cared for Arthur, says that it must break her heart. This last gives Winnie pause; its honesty, its relative depth, stills her in her conversational stride, brings her up short.

'Well,' she says eventually, 'one looks after their own.'

'Of course,' says Mary.

'I'd be brought back as a ferret if I didn't pull my weight.'

'Oh, Winnie.'

'Besides, children are an investment, and I could do with the dividends, Mary!'

'I've given up expecting anything from my children. One's in Hong Kong and the other's in Sutton Hoo. And, do you know what, I see the former more than the latter. When they get a pang of guilt or concern I get an email saying they've subscribed me to Netflix or Amazon or something.'

'Ben and I had a go at Amazon the other night, with regards to bird seed, and it turned up, so that's something.'

'Do I know Ben?'

'The nightwatchman.'

'With you.'

She says she's going up to the village to hunt for 'some cellophane to seal in the marmalade', which doesn't mean a great deal to me. She returns about an hour later, upset at the prices in the village. I ask about the cellophane and she looks at me like she hasn't got a clue what I'm on about. Eventually she comes clean.

'You know what, I got up there and forgot all about it. I'm going mad.'

'You'd be going mad if you got up there, bought the cellophane, and then forgot how to get home.'

'Well that's something to think about.'

'By the way, Mary called and left a message. A bricklayer named Terry's going to pop round next Tuesday. So that's something to look forward to.'

'Terry, eh?'

'Yeah.'

'What do you reckon?'

'How do you mean?'

'Well you must admit, it's a bit of an alarming name.'


**29 January.** *Desert Island Discs.* The show has become something of a weekly fixture – by dint of it being on every week, and by dint of Winnie spending 97 per cent of her time in the kitchen, and by dint of Winnie having the radio on for 100 per cent of that 97 per cent – by dint of that lot. I forget the castaway. But I remember they were of an anxious nature, selecting as their luxury desert island item a series of creams and weapons to deal with the creepy crawlies. One of the songs selected to soundtrack the inevitable siege of mosquitoes was 'A House Is Not a Home' or similar. The lyrics caught my attention. I paraphrase: a room is still a room when nobody's in it, as a chair is still a chair when nobody's sat on it, but a house is not a home when *you're* not in it, implying that some things rely on people in order to *be* those things. I mention this to Winnie, who nods and says, 'I've started paying the BBC licence fee in monthly instalments.' 'Oh?' 'To avoid the unpleasant scenario of dying a few weeks after renewing the licence.' Then she looks out at the blue tits nosing around the feeder and remembers the young American who stayed for a few months. 'Chuck his name was. Or Skip. In any case, he just couldn't handle us calling them tits. He would get painfully embarrassed every time I invited him to take a look.'

# 1948

*Winnie is walking home from school. She's in a good mood because that afternoon one of her teachers described her as 'obstinate', which Winnie presumes is a good thing. She stops outside the bookshop on Broad Street to look at the window display – she's got her eye on a new story about a boy who can't grow up. (Perhaps he's obstinate too, she thinks.) Because Winnie was taught to be polite to adults, when a man takes her by the arm and asks her to follow him because he needs some assistance (something to do with his car), she does so. When he leads her down an alley and his mal-intent is clear, she kicks and thumps and screams, and manages to scare the man off. Winnie is left frightened. She is left less polite. She is left less inclined to browse bookshop windows. Hey-ho.*

# 5

## You'll always be late for the previous train

**1 February.** My daffodils are coming along. Six are out now, standing fairly tall and straight. They smell, to my nose, very faintly of lemon sherbet. The stems of the oldest flowers are starting to harden and discolour around the neck and shoulders. I used to try and tidy them up by picking off the ruined flesh, then decided to leave them alone, decided there's no disgrace in gentle maturation, in shifting away from green towards a later hue.

A parcel is on the doorstep. It's a pair of binoculars, which I ordered to get a better look at the foxes and the woodpeckers. I look through the binoculars towards Winnie (who is on the other side of the kitchen table) and pretend to fall off my stool, but she's not amused. She's a bit tetchy because she's been on the phone to someone from the council regarding Arthur. Winnie thinks the council aren't doing enough. The council think Winnie submitted some forms incorrectly. She's admonishing herself for being so damn inefficient, so damn useless, for not being on top of the situation like she used to be. 'I've been useless from the word go,' she says, standing and leaving the kitchen. 'I couldn't even deliver him properly. Useless woman. Useless.'

Arthur moved out of the family home and into an assisted living flat about ten years ago, after he had a fall walking up to the village. The fall precipitated his move – if that way of putting it isn't too full of motion. Prior to his fall, Arthur could get by unassisted. After his fall, he couldn't, and so he moved into a flat which is part of a care home. 'Assisted Living' is how it's advertised in the brochure, though according to Winnie, Arthur is neither assisted nor living much, and so she's constantly pressing for reform.

I tell her that sardines used to go by another name, to which she says, 'No, I quite agree, they used to be much larger.' Winnie's comment prompts me to tell a lie. I tell her I spoke to my nan yesterday and she was full of praise for her new hearing aids, which have made her see (or hear) just how poor her hearing had got.

'Is that a hint?' she says.

'I guess it is, yes.'

'Fair enough.'

'I'm not being judgmental. I don't mind you being deaf as a post.'

'Doornail.'

'Post.'

'Doornail.'

'Anyway. I don't mind you struggling, you can do what you want, but it must be bothersome and tiring having to strain and infer and guess what people are on about. Or getting people to repeat themselves. It can't be much fun listening to me once, let alone twice.'

'Now that is a very valid point.'

'For what it's worth, I just think you'd be happier if you gave your ears a bit of a helping hand.'

'Hm?'

'I think you'd be—'

'I heard you. Little joke. I suppose there's no reason why I shouldn't be going deaf. Both my parents went deaf in their sixties. I shall certainly look into it.'

'Good.'

'If I can find my glasses.'

The shape and colour and texture of the chunk of cheese on her plate reminds her of Portland Bill, which in turn reminds her of the brother who died aged eighteen. He'd just graduated from naval college, was ordered out in a storm in an open vessel to pick up some sailors ashore at Weymouth. Thomas lost control on the way back on account of the conditions. Thirty drowned and the blame was pinned exclusively on Thomas, which really killed Winnie's parents, who couldn't believe the Navy would do such a thing, use their son as a scapegoat like that, would heap ignominy and shame on top of loss like that. Winnie says she buried it. The whole thing. Buried it as far down as she could. Sent it straight down to a filing cabinet out of sight and out of reach. She remembers being asked on the bus about her brother. Just a day or two after it happened. Remembers saying, 'He died yesterday. Drowned. And how is your shop, Mr Townsend?' She says it affected the rest of her parents' lives – of course it did, how could it not? You can't lose a child like that, you just can't. The hurt never went away. It altered, perhaps, but never left. Not for an hour, not for a second. (OK, maybe a second.) On Winnie's 50th birthday, she went to a reunion of the survivors. She met the man that pulled her brother out of the water. She met men who, instead of blaming her brother as she feared they would, told her it wasn't his fault, told her that the whole thing was a damn cover-up. 'I was very proud of my brother,' she says, her eyes becoming wet as she moves along that sentence.

Not long after the tragedy, Winnie's father was made the British Treasury representative in New York. He was more than happy to go, to escape. Winnie's mother reckons Churchill had a hand in it, reckons Churchill knew about the Navy's cover-up and felt such a posting was the least that could be done for Winnie's father. Winnie has a photo of her dad on the boat, the Queen Mary, crossing the Atlantic, looking happy, truly happy, so happy that she almost doubts it's really him. Winnie was gifted some French perfume on that voyage by a certain Madame Dreyfus, whose father had been involved in some sort of scandal, the details of which presently escape her.[1]

She's spoken to Arthur. About his needs and wants going forward. Long and short of it is: he's not keen to move into a room in the care home itself, will stay put in his flat, come what may. He likes his space, that's the thing. Likes his

---

[1] It was the daughter of Alfred Dreyfus, of the Dreyfus affair. Frenchman of Jewish ancestry, wrongly imprisoned for treason in 1894. Sentenced to life imprisonment on Devil's Island in French Guiana, later exonerated. Turns out the powers that be (or the powers that were) knew that the real traitor was a fellow named Ferdinand Esterhazy, but they opted to keep this intelligence to themselves because, well, Esterhazy wasn't Jewish and Dreyfus was. Roman Polanski made a film on the subject, *An Officer and a Spy*, which came out in 2019, based on an earlier novel of the same name by Robert Harris.

independence. So what if he lands on his face sometimes? What's a face for?

**2 February.** Go to St Ann's Hospital in north London, received by Juliet, jabbed by Mary. Get home. 'I'm glad that's done,' I say. Winnie looks at me, smiles, can't remember where I've been. To be fair, she's had a busy day – building up the courage to chuck out an avocado. At about 10pm I start to feel a bit funny – nauseous, achey. I celebrate this development by burning a hole in the carpet. I was loading up the fire when a hot coal (*very* hot coal, let's be fair) some- how liberated itself from the fire and landed on the carpet. With admirable swiftness and presence of mind, I swore several times, kicked the coal forward onto the floorboards (where it was less of a threat to Winnie's future), scooped it up with the little shovel provided for the purpose, returned the offending flaming hot briquette to the fire, and then inspected (and smelt) the considerable damage.

I call to Winnie in the kitchen. Tell her to come and have a look at something. She enters the sitting room, happily curi- ous. Faced with the still smouldering burn in her carpet, it's fair to say the curiosity survives the happiness. She goes to the kitchen and returns with a cloth and soapy water, which is a bit like trying to dam the Thames with a head of broc- coli. She's on her knees, scrubbing away. She looks up at me periodically to check I'm watching.

'I'm sorry, Winnie.'

'Well, you've certainly left your mark.'

'I'll get you a nice rug. Cover up the evidence.'

'Will you fit under it as well?'

'Sorry, Winnie.'

She stops scrubbing, shakes her head, says, 'It's alright. These things happen.'

Very little sleep. Feverish, headache, at once hot and cold, a touch delirious. Strange dreams and visions as I wriggle and fret on the cusp of sleep and wakefulness, sweating and shivering. In one dream the house is on fire and I descend a drainpipe with Winnie on my back. Then I hear Winnie cry out, 'Rod!'. I shoot up. *Rod?* She must mean Ron. In any case: OMG she's on fire. No. Hang on. That's unlikely. Would she be calling me (or Rod) if she were on fire? Probably not. More likely she's tripped over the ironing board on her way back from the loo. Something like that. I creep downstairs, shivering as I go, despite being covered with sweat. Silence. Nothing is doing. No sign of disaster. I put my ear to her bedroom door. Silence. She's either dead or asleep. I can't very well go in and ask. I listen harder: a short snore. I return upstairs, drink a pint of water, take a shower, swallow pain killers, eat a banana, then toss and turn until dawn, hostage to certain weird circles of thought, certain stubborn/loopy misapprehensions – namely, that instead of trying to fall asleep what I am actually doing is trying to cut slices of Spanish omelette. Weird. Get up at 5 to bin the ash, do the fire, take on more water. And then I sleep until midday.

**5 February.** *Gardeners' World.* The best time to prune is late winter. Remove the old, the rotten, the unhelpful. Let in the new, the fresh, the fruitful. That's the thinking. That's the idea. That's what Monty Don is keen to stress. And another thing worth knowing, says Monty, is that adverse weather can cause plants to *self-prune*. (A process called abscission, in case it crops up in a pub quiz.) Which means that sometimes a storm is doing you a favour. Note to self: next time it's blowing a gale, put Winnie outside to see if her dodgy ears get knocked off.

**7 February.** I'm out walking. Snow starts to fall. A phone call. 'Ben. Winnie. I am somewhat marooned. It's the car – looks like it's going to get iced up. And we need more salt of course, to keep us from being fenced in. And the back door won't open. I do see trouble ahead, frankly. I know you only left an hour ago, but I'm not in a position to keep the snow clear. Go to your bosom. Knock there. Ask your heart what it doth know. About old women in jeopardy. It's only going to get worse. It's settling. Consider this a tip-off. Be grateful if you'd come back. Before you get trapped somewhere else. Hey-ho. On with the war.'

She's hoovering when I get back. She shows me the door that won't open. I open it. She looks at the door disdainfully, as if it's let her down. I salt the driveway, etc. and then do pie and potatoes and peas. Afterwards we watch a film – *The Dig*. I suggested it because I fancied its themes might float her boat. She remembers the excavation in question – the Sutton Hoo dig of 1939. An Anglo-Saxon burial ship, full of treasure. I wouldn't be surprised if she was there in person, aged three, helping catalogue the relics. She watches intently, not nodding off once, saying nothing acerbic or irrelevant until: 'I don't think lemon drizzle cake had been invented at that point, to tell the truth.'[2] I bring her through some sticky toffee pudding. She says she would never dare buy such a thing. I tell her we clearly have different ideas of danger.

It's recycling night. She comes into the sitting room with about ten plastic soup containers, asks how many I think we need to keep.

'I wouldn't keep any, Winnie.'

'Five?'

'I wouldn't keep any, Winnie.'

'Six would be ample.'

'I wouldn't keep any, Winnie.'

'Four?'

I laugh.

'Three?'

'Winnie.'

'Two?'

'You know my feeling.'

'Two it is.'

'Fine.'

'Two's company.'

'It is.'

---

[2] And she wasn't wrong. Or, rather, she may well have been right. A website run by film nerds with a fondness for anachronisms has the following to say: 'In the garden party scene near the end, Ralph Fiennes' character mentions lemon drizzle cake. According to the Oxford English Dictionary this term was first recorded in 1969.'

'Got that cleared up.'

'We did.'

'Which is a relief, I can tell you.'

*8 February.* I go to the common on foot, up to the windmill. It's the surface of the earth that pleases me most. The dark wet mud has been frozen and the result is excellent for walking. Like stiff Christmas pudding dusted with icing sugar. Nature in dessert form. When shallow puddles snap underfoot, I think of crème brûlée. I enjoy the stark contrast of buttercups on gorse: the delicate yellow and the off-putting spikes. The snowfall is light but steady – small feathers, as if from a pillow, easy to dodge. I leave the common, continue north, cross the main road, enter the town of Roehampton, which is like nothing else. No: it is like something else. It puts me in mind of Poland. Sixteen high-rise blocks, some on concrete stilts, arranged sweetly on sloping land. I look up at the balconies – socks on the line, tiny bikes, hardy plants – and then enter Richmond Park at Roehampton Gate.[3] Still the odd crunch underfoot, more sponge and burnt cream. I phone my mum. She's in the car, at a petrol station, wants to know what I want for my birthday. A backpack, I say. I leave the park through Richmond Gate, descend Richmond Hill. I pause to take in a famous view of the Thames (Turner got it down on paper), but more than the river I am drawn to a kite that's snagged in the middle branches of a tree.

---

[3] For 40 years Richmond Park was inaccessible from the Roehampton estate. The locals were kept out. A gate was introduced in 2010. Odd to think of an absence being introduced, but there you are.

When I return, she's polishing her forks, her trinkets, her tankards. I watch her apply the pink lotion to a rag, and then massage the silver with an index finger. She shows me a tankard gifted to Arthur on the occasion of his christening. Arthur was christened twice, she says, once in Wimbledon and then again in Exeter, where he got in with the God squad at university, who dunked him in the River Exe. She looks at Arthur's silver arranged on the kitchen table, and as she does so I can see, actually see, her mood alter, her mood dip. She says life's not been fair on Arthur, and it was she who pushed him out towards it all, towards all the unfairness. 'Anyway,' she says, 'how was your walk?' I tell her about the sponge, the river, the balconies. She latches onto the river, gains a foothold there, says that Rebecca and Mark (her late husband) and Bilbo travelled down the Thames from Oxford in a punt once, years ago, to raise money for charity. It was a disaster. Bilbo hated it. Henry and Winnie had been dubious as soon as they got wind of the idea. But when Rebecca wants something, she often gets it – even Winnie's dog in her punt. I ask Winnie if she'd like to walk in Richmond Park one day. We could drive to Roehampton, I say, and then proceed from there, just an amble. 'Nice idea, but the traffic wardens would have you in a flash.'

I'm watching *University Challenge*. She enters, comes towards me holding an open biscuit tin, stops, turns to face the TV, stands in front of it with the biscuit tin, as if offering one to the set. 'I don't know why you bother,' she says. 'It's simply measuring the extent of your ignorance. Gosh, look at

Daunt, Warwick.' 'What about him?' 'I'm surprised he can see beyond his nose. It's like the Rock of Gibraltar.'

I watch the first episode of a Danish series called *Legacy*. At first, it appears the legacy of a wealthy artist who is terminally ill will be fought over by three children – two sons and a daughter. But then a fourth child, illegitimate and unknown, enters the fray. When the wealthy artist dies, the eldest son pops open a bottle of champagne, starts celebrating with his mother's big house in mind. One suspects that by the end of episode 2 he might well have stopped. You don't put a gun on stage if it isn't going to go off.

**9 February.** More snow. It's got Winnie's back up. The kitchen has become the centre of operations. She'd like the car uncoated. She'd like it ready to go. 'Go where?' 'Never mind where. It needs to be able to go.' And she'd like the drive cleared as well, a path at least, the width of a car, a car that's ready to go. I do as I'm told. Because I can see that she doesn't want to *feel* trapped. Because I broke the shovel the other day (don't ask), I use a dustpan. I start with the car, with its windows, its windscreen. I shave off the snow in wide sweeps – like shearing wool. Then I get on my haunches and scrape until there's a catwalk from the front door to the pavement. Of course, as soon as I clear the way, the way is freshly covered. But she's satisfied – for now at least. Next she'd like the bird bath defrosted. And then she'd like to know what I think about going to the shop to stock up on meat.

'Would you really like to know what I think, Winnie?'

'Probably not.'

'I think there'll be no shortage of meat in Wimbledon.'

She's not convinced. Not one bit. I flip a coin in my mind. It lands on heads.

'I'll go to the shop and have a look,' I say. 'To be on the safe side.'

'That would be very much appreciated. Just some mince perhaps. And two blocks of butter while you're at it.'

'Butter is a red line, Winnie.'

'What do you mean?'

'I can't buy butter in good conscience. Knowing how much you've got.'

'But it's the price, Ben. It will go up. It *is* going up. You do know we're leaving the common market, don't you?'

'Fine. But if anyone asks about your hoard, from the Home Office or wherever, I had *nothing* to do with it.'

'Deal.'

We watch *Portrait Artist of the Year*. She reckons a good portrait captures the sitter's character, as well as their physical likeness. She did a self-portrait once. When she was nineteen. She didn't like what she saw, so painted a landscape over it. Hasn't bothered since.

**10 February.** I read a poem from the anthology I took out from the library. Piet Hein. That's the poet. Piet liked writing a type of poem called a grook ('gruk' in Danish), which tend to be short and aphoristic and rhyming. He wrote 7,000 of them. 'The Road to Wisdom' is one.

*The road to wisdom?*
*Well, it's plain*
*And simple to express:*
*Err*
*And err*
*And err again*
*But less*
*And less*
*And less.*

I recite the poem to Winnie. She eats her toast as I read, chewing in sync with the metre, biting down on less and less and less. And then I read another of Piet Hein's grooks. One about waiting on a station platform.

*It ought to be plain*
*how little you gain*
*by getting excited*
*and vexed.*

*You'll always be late*
*for the previous train,*
*and always on time*
*for the next.*

Of this second poem, Winnie says, 'And what if the next train doesn't turn up at all?'[4]

---

[4] Some say that the name 'gruk' is a coming together in Danish of the words for laugh and sigh, which appeals to me as an idea.

An observation. She will start saying something – 'Television these days is just advert after advert' – and then segue into what's really on her mind – 'The doctor does agree that Arthur has lost weight' – so that the complete utterance reads: 'Television these days is just advert after advert, and the doctor does agree that Arthur has lost weight.' Why is this important? Because the second clause is Winnie's subconscious popping its periscope above the surface. Or not *quite* subconscious. (Pre-conscious? Pan-conscious?) Either way, you get the picture. Her sense of self is dominated by Arthur. He is the start and end of her day, the start and end of her sentence. And there is something both admirable and tragic about the fact.

**11 February**. It is a morning of things, a breakfast of *minutes*. Some mornings have many, some have none at all. This morning's things, in no meaningful order:

1) Winnie enters the kitchen saying, 'He's always been a reliable plumber, and I just think that now is the time to strike.' *Strike the plumber? Strike him for being reliable?*

2) An adult goldfinch (red face, yellow stripe on wings) drinks from the bird bath that I'd recently defrosted with a kettle full of boiling water. Winnie looks the bird up in the directory she keeps by the phone. 'Notably sweet dancing flight,' she reads. What a job to watch birds and describe their ways. I think of an entry for Winnie. 'Won't stray far in fussy manner.'

3) Winnie reads the news. A couple in Wales, Mr and Mrs Tweedy, bought a zoo in 2017. Neither of the pair had any experience managing animals. A lynx escaped and

had to be shot by a 'council marksman' on Bangor high street. Another lynx was accidentally strangled, which doesn't seem the easiest feat to pull off, especially by accident. After running up huge debts, and several more escapes, the zoo has been 'wound up'. Winnie looks at me. Is aghast. Can't believe it. 'Surely they mean wound *down*?'

4) I say I was cold last night. She says she was cold last night. I suggest we economise and share a bed. She says she'd rather perish. Then she says, 'Henry and I used to curl round each other all night.' 'That's romantic.' 'Well it was less about that and more about not putting the heating on.'

I tend to my daffodils. The full contingent are out. Ten heads, alike in dignity, unequal in extent. The green leaves are long now, shooting out and up at sharp angles. Necks of stems are turning brown and crisp, like deep-fried onion. Some petals (perianth segments) are inverting, while others remain straight and proud like the blades of a propeller. I would argue the plant is at its most beautiful.

**12 February.** Marvel at Winnie's discipline and restraint. Despite knowing she's got twelve jars in her locker, she applies so little marmalade to her toast. If I were she, I would splurge for three months then suffer for nine. Is moderation the key to longevity? I ask the question of Winnie, but she must mishear me because she says, 'You can blame Tony Blair for that.'

Speaking of political leaders, Boris is on the front page. His dog has caused a stir. Until recently, Dilyn was homeless and malnourished, but by getting on his bike and knuck-ling down and dreaming big he now resides towards the top of the social ladder, in 10 Downing Street. When a couple of enterprising journos discovered that a trio of taxpayer-funded photographers were being employed to document Dilyn's activities, there were loud calls for a taxpayer-funded public inquiry. A Number 10 spokesperson (and former schoolmate of Dilyn) had this to say: 'Anyone who thinks this is a big deal is barking.' She turns the page. And then again. 'Butcher throws philosophy student into Humber,' she says. 'To what end?' I say. 'Somewhere near the mouth,' she says.

**13 February.** My birthday. I open some cards in bed and some gifts. An Allen key set from my nan and some sturdy boots from Megan. Winnie reckons they're trying to tell me something. 'What's that then?' 'That they'd prefer a more practical version of what's currently available.'

She's not really one for music, from what I've heard. It's never playing. It's always Radio 4, and she doesn't go near the CD player. And yet this evening I find her ironing while dancing (or vice versa) in her bedroom to Curtis Mayfield's 'Move On Up'.

**15 February.** We've gained ten degrees overnight. The bird bath doesn't need defrosting. I watch a blackbird bathe enthusiastically. Watch it dunk its head and shake its wings underwater. It keeps this up for a minute or so and then a great tit jumps in after, does similar. I had no idea they behaved in such a fashion. Frantic ablutions. Rather stupidly, I thought a bird bath was simply for drinking from. It's quite lovely – and amusing – to watch the birds clean themselves up, give themselves a wash. In other news, the crocuses appeared about a week ago, and are already full of themselves and practically long in the tooth. And the garlic flower, which has a wild mind of its own, now has the house surrounded. The bird box is busy. Getting more traffic than the port of Dover.

Stewart calls. They talk about the new and unexpected warmth, and mention in unison that the forecasters are saying it might be seventeen by Saturday. She says she went to the common yesterday and saw lots of families, which was cheering.

'Righto,' she says.
'Righto,' he says.
'God bless then.'
'God bless.'
'Many thanks.'
'Off you go.'
'Hey-ho.'
'As you were.'
'On with the war.'
'Night-night.'
'Love to all.'
'Righto.'
'Alright then.'
'All the best.'

'See you soon.'

'Bye, darling.'

If they were in the same room I'd be tempted to bash their heads together. For what good is love on the tip of a tongue?

**16 February.** Shrove Tuesday. The trouble is, I've nothing left to give up. My days are lean enough as it is. I've given up vices, and I've given up virtues – freedom, chiefly. I suppose it will have to be coffee. Or my sense of humour. That wouldn't be missed a great deal. Giving it up might increase Winnie's life expectancy. Might increase *my* life expectancy. I doff my sense of humour. For lent. For a laugh. Because there's bog all else to do.

The other day, when Winnie had a beige beanie hat on, she said she looked like a peanut. Well she must have forgotten she said that, because when she came downstairs a minute ago and I said, 'Here comes the peanut', she treated me to a look that could kill a fox from twenty paces. I brush it off and go outside to top up the bird bath. 'Not the filtered water!' she cries. 'They're not discerning you know.' When I return to the kitchen she's wringing her hands about ordering some coal. She wants to order some because we're running lowish, but her instinct to run a healthy surplus is jostling with the fact that the price per kilo drops in April. A genuine dilemma that has her stumped.

I'm off to Dulwich, a small village to the east, simply to have a butcher's. Winnie used to volunteer at the gallery there. I ask if she wants to join me. She says she does but she also wants to get down to Boots (make-up), and then across to Arthur's (yoghurt and *The Spectator*), and old wants pull rank over new ones. I take the train to Tulse Hill, start walking. It feels indulgent. Transgressive. To head out with no larger ambition than to look at a new place. I guess the value of anything – indeed the character of anything – is contingent and unstable. I'm only valuable in certain situations, for example, which I can count on the fingers of one hand. Recent events have altered the character of things. That's what I'm getting at. Things like taking a train to Tulse Hill and then walking to Dulwich, pausing to watch pigeons, stopping at a bakery, reading a plaque that remembers six people killed by a V2 rocket in 1945. Confinement reframes existence. Its reduction is fecund – new desires, new affections, are grown.

**17 February.** She can't remember the name of a tree in the garden (the one behind the two conifers), and she's *furious* with herself, absolutely livid. She goes out to deliver Arthur a panna cotta, slams the door behind her. When she gets back she launches unbidden into a detailed overview of everything in the garden (copper beech, New Zealand flax, acer, mayflower, honeysuckle, silver birch), as if to prove she's still got it, that she still can. Buoyed by her performance, she declares enthusiastically that she'll do a cauliflower cheese this evening, so long as I've no objections? This won't be the first time she's done a cauliflower cheese for dinner. She just doesn't seem to understand that it's a side dish.

**18 February.** After dinner, a film, *Edie*. The opening scenes are somewhat close to home. A man in a stairlift. A woman caring. His death. Her isolation. Some hoarding. A stubborn streak. A difficult daughter. Winnie watches, a wry smile, closed mouth. 'Wouldn't catch me hoarding baked beans,' she says. 'Not if they were the last thing on earth.' The story unfolds. Edie is fed up with life, feels contained, stifled. Determines to scale a mountain. Packs a bag, takes a train, is knocked over on the platform by a young person in a hurry – typical. To make amends, the young person gives the old person a lift to where she's meant to be staying, but there's no room in the inn, so Jonny takes Edie back to his, at which point Winnie's had enough and changes channel.

'Not a fan, Winnie?'

'Insipid.'

'I thought it was quite sweet.'

'Not for me. Better things to do.'

'Like what?'

'Wipe down surfaces.'

**20 February.** To Portsmouth via Basingstoke. I want to check my father's alright. To do so is illegal, but I've had a test and a jab, and he's had a jab, and Winnie's had a jab, and he hasn't been anywhere, so I think, I decide – I'm going to see my dad. We play Scrabble. Watch the football. He shows me what he's been practising on the keyboard – 'Ballad for Adeline', by someone French. The song's quite lovely – and lovelier still for being played by my dad, whose battered-sausage-like fingers cruise along the keyboard like impostors.

A private recital. I'd pay to be on his shoulder. I thank him, on Winnie's behalf, for the bird box. 'I've started on what I'm calling a bird temple. Do you think she'd like it?'

I go out the next morning to break the law some more. I drive up to my nan's. She prepares a whopping fried breakfast, while Granddad listens to the West Ham match. She lost her friend Polly of late, tells me that when Polly's daughter was sorting out the house she discovered one thing in particular – that Polly was an incomparable hoarder. She found more margarine tubs than she thought possible to manufacture, but nothing of value – no jewellery. Eventually the missing jewels were found in a cool box in the porch, individually wrapped in tinfoil – under the burglar's nose, exactly where they wouldn't look. Sort of thing Winnie might do. Wads of cash in knickers in the microwave. I make a note to tell her. I'm often making notes to tell Winnie things these days.

After Nan's, on to Granddad and Grannie Annie's. Chat on the doorstep – they're not admitting anybody, negative or not. They look alright. Not top notch, I wouldn't go that far, but alright. She shows me a picture on her phone of Granddad aged fifteen, up the park, with his football mates, Christmas Day 1950. It's a group shot, two rows of half-a-dozen. Granddad's in the back row and has got his left boot resting on the shoulder of the lad in front. At fifteen, he was well on his way to being who he is now. I love them but find it difficult to say so when I'm leaving.

Winnie shows me the mimosa tree – which bloomed when I was away. A riot of yellow. Didn't see that coming. That's quite a thing to have up your sleeve. Apparently Stewart got up on a ladder and cut some off for her, and it's presently in a vase in the back kitchen. (There are thirteen ladders in this house, by the way, which is telling. Not sure what it tells, but it tells something.) Later on, Winnie joins me in watching a documentary about Margot Fonteyn, the prima ballerina assoluta. Winnie says she used to pretend to be a ballerina, would dance from one room to another, until her mother nipped the habit in the bud, citing the risk of injury.

**22 February.** She's on the phone. She's telling someone that she ordered the coal weeks ago and is about to succumb to the cold. The lady at the coal company says that, in point of fact, Mrs Carter ordered last Tuesday and was told it would be at least seven days. Mrs Carter, ever reasonable, says, 'Well I suppose that is one way of looking at it,' and then hangs up. She looks at me, unperturbed, unrattled, quite happy. 'Never hurts to drop them a line,' she says.

Apparently she's never done a stew before – quite incredible. She's done a chop, roasted a joint, baked a cake, fashioned a soup, assembled a salad, sorted a pie, but never done a stew. I cut the fat off the meat at her behest. It smells of vinegar. I raise the matter; it's not a problem, she says, stop being a snowflake.

An hour later. The stew's bubbling away. She says she might borrow a carrot from Carlotta, thinks it will help bring the dish together. She phones. 'Could I, by any chance, borrow a carrot?' I don't hear Carlotta's reply but Winnie giggles and giggles and giggles, and then collapses into a fulsome laugh. My feeling is Carlotta just made a joke. The doorbell goes. A delivery of one carrot. Winnie says she'll repay the debt and so on. More laughter.

An hour later. The telly's on in the kitchen. She's in her apron, hand on corresponding hip, watching the government's daily press conference, while keeping an eye on the stew. 'Can they say any more about it? Is it possible do you think? It's overkill. The words lose their sense. So shut up.'

Half an hour later. The telly's still on in the kitchen. 'For the love of God will they ever shut up?' 'That's *EastEnders*, Winnie.'

The government briefing that was going on and on and so exercised Winnie's patience pertained to the government's new 'roadmap'. I'm given to understand that 'roadmap' is a carefully selected euphemism for 'major lockdown extension'. Another five weeks before I can meet a friend in public in any weather not for exercise. Two months before I can dine alone al fresco up a tree. And so on. Some good news for Winnie though – from 8th March, Arthur can receive one nominated visitor, so long as that visitor tests negative and wears a wetsuit throughout.

An hour later. She joins me in the sitting room. Flicks leisurely through a gardening magazine. The sight of Winnie doing this would please me if I didn't know she had a stew on a rolling boil in the room next door.

'How's your stew getting on?' I say.

'Hm?'

'Your stew.'

'Oh that old thing.'

'Yes that old thing.'

'Probably needs checking on.'

'Should I?'

'Would you?'

At 9, with her stew more reduced than any set of freedoms could ever be, she decides she fancies a baked potato with it. We sit down an hour later and something about the lateness of the meal prompts her to bring up the family 'holidays' they used to take down in Devon. (She puts the word in scare quotes because as far as she's concerned a woman's work was never done.) She says there was something magical about those holidays, now that she thinks about it. 'We bought that cottage for fourteen grand. You couldn't get a back door for that money nowadays. But that's what happens. Things change. I mean, look at me. If I found myself at the back of the fridge I wouldn't think twice about throwing myself out.' I ask if she worries about getting old. She snorts. At the question's stupidity. 'The trouble with death,' she says, 'is that it stops you *doing* things.'

**23 February.** My daffodils. You know the ones. Heads bowed across the board now. Stems bent and buckled and bruised, despite my ministrations. Petals furling, curling up, caving in: coming, as Icarus, to the end of their triumph.[5]

---

[5] Icarus image taken from Jack Gilbert's poem 'Failing and Flying'.

There's a carrot on the table. No, that's stretching the truth – it's half a carrot. Half a carrot that's seen better days. Winnie enters wearing gardening gloves and a happy look that suggests she's just scared something away or warded off danger.

'What do you mean to do with that?'

'Return it to Carlotta.'

'Are you joking?'

'No.'

'I'm not sure she'll want it, Winnie.'

'I wouldn't be so sure. Carrots come in handy.'

'Yes, but that one?'

She huffs. Gives me a look. Dares me to persist with my line of questioning. I back off. Raise my hands in surrender. She picks up the carrot, marches out of the house with it, still wearing her gardening gloves. She's back before the kettle's boiled.

'You were quite right,' she says.

'Was I?'

'She laughed at the carrot.'

'Oh well.'

'Didn't stop her accepting it though.'

A thought. Winnie struggles to believe that something can be gifted – even a humble carrot – without expectation of repayment. To Winnie, a gift is a 'You Owe Me', is a debt obligation. Receipt of a gift is a tacit promise to repay. Because she understands gifts as contracts, she's not into them, not one bit. She doesn't want to receive, because she doesn't want the obligation to give. Her attitude to gifting (cold) doesn't do her character (warm) justice. At Christmas, she bought only one gift. A pair of trousers for Arthur. I wouldn't be surprised if she's expecting a pair in return.

**24 February.** I sit on the swing and there enjoy the strange warmth, unfelt since October. The crocuses abound nearby. Two types. Some wild, some well-bred. The flimsy lilac type is wild. The other – deeper, richer, with bright ornamentation – was cultivated elsewhere and bought in a shop. Two flowers, alike in nature and name, different in form and story. Winnie prefers the wild ones. 'They're more reliable,' she says. I swing over them both.

She's at the kitchen table, her lunch spread out before her, the telly on. I say I'm off for a short walk, up to the common, ask if she fancies it. She does. I say I'll read the paper in the sitting room while she gets ready.

Later. I check on her in the kitchen. She's eating a piece of toast, watching a film called *The Bishop's Wife*. Fair enough – finishing off lunch.

Later. I check on her in the kitchen. She's making a pot of tea. Again – fair enough. No great rush.

Later. I check on her in the kitchen. She's mending a peg, or attempting to. 'Did you want to come for a walk, Winnie?' 'No you're quite right, I'm faffing, one second.' I tell her I'll wait outside.

Later. Outside. Waiting. I stare at the face of her home. The blinds are down against the sun. She loves the light but more than loving light she worries about things fading.

Later. We do a lap of the pond, the wind in our faces. 'It's idyllic,' she says.

'So why don't you come up more often?'

'Because idylls should be rationed.'

Later. We get back to the house. Pause on the driveway. She tells me that the wall that separates the garden from the alley was built by Tom and Charlie, two local lads, ex-soldiers. 'Charlie had no fingers,' she says.

'No fingers?'

'Lost them in battle.'

'And he was a bricklayer?'

'Yes, and a very cheap one at that.'

Later. The fire goes out and we've no coal. I ask if she wants me to get one going with logs. She says it doesn't matter. Says there's less need now. Says we'll survive.


**26 February.** She's never had fish and chips. Or if she has, she can't remember having it. I suggest The Vintage Fish on Leopold Road. She's up for it.

'What do you fancy?'

'Oh I don't know.'

'Cod? Haddock? Battered sausage?'

'Battered what?'

'Battered sausage.'

She looks at me. I explain.

'I can't think of anything worse,' she says. 'No – just a small cod and a few chips, I think.'

'Pickled onion?'

'No. Emphatically.'

'Mushy peas?'

'What?'

'Mushy peas.'

'Oh God no.'

'Curry sauce?'

'Now you're just being daft.'

When I get back from the chip shop she's got the plates in the top oven and the bottom oven heated to 220 degrees. Never mind. Easily done. She tries a chip and says it's the best she's had. Absolutely LOVES the bag the food came in. Insists on keeping it. Doesn't mind the mushy peas (as it happens) and considers the tartare sauce a *revelation*. She asks what the damage was. I tell her it's fine, that she can get the next round. She looks at me in a way that suggests she'll be dead before she's spotted in The Vintage Fish on Leopold Road.

*Gardeners' World* comes on. Once again, I find the show oddly compelling. Monty Don and his sidekicks are veritable scholars of the garden. They know *everything*. I'm glad Winnie's got a crap TV. Because the old way of watching telly will do this – throw up a surprise, defy your taste, invite your interest elsewhere, instead of just feeding you more and more and more of the same. I haven't watched telly like this since … well, since twenty years ago. Winnie comes in and asks why I'm smiling like a Cheshire cat. I tell her I'm in love with Monty Don. She tells me to join the queue.

**28 February.** It's not a bad office. One of the old swivel chairs. Feet up on the old brown couch (with Winnie's permission).

A wooden stool nearby to bear a mug of coffee. The French windows affording a view of the garden. A television at hand should I require distraction. The fire close by. The kettle next door in the kitchen, of course, and below it, in the cupboard, several tins of biscuits. The sound of Winnie above, padding around in her bedroom, or below, padding around in the freezer, or in the kitchen, grazing on cheese and granary bread while on the phone to Arthur or the council, or laughing at a subtitled film on the telly on top of the fridge. I spot two magpies. They seem to be having an argument. Winnie enters and puts a glass of red wine above the fire. Bit early, but whatever.

'Celebrating what would have been our 61st wedding anniversary,' she says.

'Isn't it tomorrow?'

'It's today and tomorrow.'

'I don't follow.'

'Use your imagination.'[6]

---

[6] I did use my imagination and I still don't follow.

# 1955

*Winnie is nineteen and at art school in Oxford, sharing a flat with her brother in the attic of a Victorian terrace. The cohabitation, after a smooth start, is faltering. Jacob is starting to get fed up that his friend Henry will now only come over if Winnie's going to be there. He's also starting to get fed up that in terms of her domestic prowess Winnie bears little resemblance to his mother. According to Jacob, living with his sister is rather like living with a male friend, which isn't really what he was after, now that he comes to think about it. He loves his sister, no doubt about it, but would love her all the more if she could bring herself to cook dinner every night and not be attractive to his friends. The landlady isn't delighted with Winnie either. Mrs Peacock is of the opinion that Winnie's habit of hanging wet clothes in the flat is causing damp to get into the walls; whereas Winnie is of the opinion that any damp getting into the walls owes more to the hole in the roof than her washing. Despite the bumps and hiccups, Winnie will look back on the time she shared a flat with her brother with immense fondness. In particular, she will remember the time when she got up on her tiptoes to look at the River Cherwell through the bathroom window and Henry came up behind her and gently flicked the back of her knee – citing a fly as a pretext. In the years to come, Winnie will pinpoint that afternoon as a turning point in her life. Henry won't. He'll pinpoint an afternoon three weeks before, when he saw Winnie for the first time, queuing up to buy a loaf of granary bread.*

# 6

## Every silver lining has a cloud

**1 March.** A voicemail.[1] 'Ben. Winnie. Problem. The kitchen is flooded. It's the bathroom upstairs. It's got down the wall from the shower. I'm in said bathroom now. Inspecting. It seems to have ... got down the wall somehow. It *looks* well sealed around the bath. I certainly couldn't squeeze through. I mean it's a damn good shower, but I might have to change my mind if it's going to carry on like this. It's all around the kettle. In the kitchen. That's where it's concentrated. The kettle has a moat. Scared to use the thing if I'm honest. I'm well overdue a tea. Think you'd better come back from Croydon or wherever you are and see if there's anything you can do. I've phoned the plumber, left a message with his wife. Trouble is, he's about my age and semi-retired. Always at his allotment by all accounts. But jolly cheap. In short, it's a nightmare. And today of all days. It could be a message from Henry. Oh, confound it!'

She's in the kitchen when I get back – of course she is. You could bet your life on her being in the kitchen. She's on the phone to Liz the hairdresser. 'I look ghastly,' she's saying. 'I

---

[1] I get a high ratio of voicemails to calls because my phone is twenty years old and can only vibrate, and it can barely even do that, meaning unless the phone is resting on a sensitive part of my body when someone calls, I'm likely to miss it. That I've been able to persist with this status quo for a number of years tells you how important I am.

look a thousand years old and it just won't do.' Liz says she can't cut hair until 12th April. Winnie repeats, in a slightly different tone, that she looks at least 270. Liz explains what would happen if she were caught – hefty fines, for both Liz and Winnie. This does the job. Winnie doesn't want a fine, no siree.

She's got a chap from the bank on the phone (may God bless him with patience). She's waiting on a text message containing a verification code. She needs the code before she can reset her PIN – which the bank, Winnie feels, have changed without her knowing. The code isn't coming through. I ask the chap from the bank what phone number he has for Winnie. It's off by a digit. Winnie's poking me in the arm and pointing to her phone number, written down in her diary. The chap explains that to reset the phone number in order to change the code in order to change her PIN, Winnie has to visit a branch. Winnie doesn't think much of the prospect. 'What branch? They've closed them all!' she bellows. There's a branch in Croydon or Richmond, says the chap. 'Well which one is it?' says Winnie. 'Croydon or Richmond?'

Of course Winnie could bank online but is dead against such methods, on the grounds that they are deeply and laughably insecure – might as well leave your assets on the driveway. She hangs up. Turns to me. Says she'd better send a message to Stew because she sent him one an hour ago that might have alarmed him. But she can't get into her phone. She's forgotten the PIN. I ask if she can use her fingerprint instead. 'I used to be able to but it's stopped recognising me.

It's my withered fingers. They won't make an impression. I'm slowly disappearing. What's for supper?'

The plumber has been and gone. His expert opinion confirmed Winnie's suspicion – that the water was getting through from the bathroom above the kitchen. Barry's sure no more water will get through.

'Was it expensive?' I ask.

'£15. Flat rate. Hasn't gone up for years.'

'Christ.'

'I think Barry's a touch in the dark regarding inflation.'

'And you're not inclined to enlighten him.'

'Certainly not. Everyone's on their own journey.'

The paper and card 240-litre recycling bin has gone missing. I suggest it's probably being put to good use elsewhere, but Winnie's not in the mood for humour. 'I was going up the road looking in other people's bins,' she confesses, 'in case I found something I recognised.' She's really put out; I get the feeling she's not enjoying her anniversary. I say we'll let the council know and in the meantime I'll dump our paper and card in a neighbour's bin. She quite likes the solution.

Dinner doesn't improve her mood. Complains the pappardelle pasta is too wide and heavy and slippery. It reminds her of a cleaner she once had. 'With other pastas,' she says, 'you get them round your fork and they come with you. But this stuff has a mind of its own. It's *uncontrollable*.' She leaves the table and disappears upstairs without a word. She's not done that before.

She joins me for a sliver of tart in the sitting room. I mention the walk I took across London this morning. I mention Regent's Park, St James's Square, Savile Row. She knows the names. Each one is a file containing memories, associations. She has happy memories of St James's Square. Henry's workplace (or one of them) backed on to it. She'd meet him in the square on his lunch break. They'd sit on a bench, share a newspaper, a sandwich, any gossip they'd collected that morning, and then he'd return to the office and she'd walk along the river towards Putney to collect Rebecca from school. 'I didn't realise at the time. Or didn't fully realise anyway. How close to perfect such occasions were. When nothing is awry or amiss. And you're not late or ill. And nor is anyone you love. You don't, do you? And if you did it might spoil them.' She looks at the television. It's *Gogglebox*. 'Not these clowns again. Why would anyone with a brain cell want to be exposed to other people watching television?'

**2 March.** Up to the common, where I watch two children wrestling. One's got the other pinned down and is explaining the situation. 'You. Are. Never. Going. Anywhere. Again.' This kid could be a member of the government. When I return, Winnie looks in my shopping bag. 'That's a hell of a leek!' I pretend to misunderstand, look at the ceiling – 'Oh not another one,' I say. I ask about the dentist. How it went. (She lost a filling in her muesli.) 'Fine,' she says, 'though it's not going to be cheap. A thousand quid. I reckon he sees me coming. Silly old lady, on her own, decent postcode – sticks another zero on the end. He's so *inquisitive*. Wants to know who lives where, who's moved, who's died, who's fallen over, all the gossip. Always angling for business. He even asked what state Henry's teeth were in. I said it was difficult to say.'

We watch an episode of *Reginald Perrin*, who sometimes reminds her of Henry. She nods in agreement when someone says that 'every silver lining has a cloud'. I watch her succumb to sleep out of the corner of my eye as the sitcom unfolds – slowly lowering like a flower cut off from its bulb, weeks after its peak.

**3 March.** We talk about her tooth while I dig for the dregs of marmalade from jar number two: while I slide and scrape a butter knife up the side of the jar and then spread and repeat until I've a thin covering. She approves. She almost looks proud. I ask if the tooth fairy used to come in the 1930s. Winnie says that neither of her parents believed in the incentivisation of teeth loss.

Winnie needs to pay Kuba but she hasn't got any cash and can't *get* any cash, what with her ongoing PIN crisis. I offer to nip up to the village, have a go myself, with her card, see if my fingers manage any better. After all, she's *sure* of the PIN, sure of it.

'Of course you can supervise me if you want,' I say. 'If you're worried I'll withdraw a few hundred and leg it to Shrewsbury.'

'I don't imagine you'd do that.'

I know what's coming …

'Shrewsbury's a rotten place.'

There it is.

A few times a week she'll set herself up like this, lay the foundation for a joke, take another bite or another sip, and then deliver the punchline. You could put her on the telly. I swear you could. I don't swear she'd stay on the telly, but I swear you could put her on it. You could stick her on one of those ten-a-penny comedic panel shows. Or *Bake Off*, even. That would be something to watch. Or she could even have her own review show. She's so abrupt and concise she'd get through most of the week's culture in about five minutes. It would sound more like a version of *Mastermind* than anything else. See below.

'Winnie Carter. You have 90 seconds to harshly judge the week's television. If you pass or hesitate you'll be propelled into the sky. What did you make of *Gogglebox*?'

'Inexplicable.'

'*EastEnders*?'

'Mistook it for the government's daily press briefing.'

'Casualty?'

'At my age one doesn't want to see on Thursday what could be happening on Monday.'

'Meghan Markle's interview with Oprah?'

'Caused me to micro-sleep seventeen times in an hour.'

'The weather forecasts?'

'Over-optimistic by half.'

'*Reginald Perrin*?'

'Deserves credit for provoking memories of my late husband.'

'Winnie Carter, you scored lots of points. See you next week.'

'If I'm not dead.'

The PIN didn't work, by the way. When I went up to the village. My fingers didn't manage any better. So we'll be going to Croydon.

We set off for Croydon. I suggest we give her bank card one more go at the cashpoint by the station in Wimbledon. She believes her PIN is one of two solid, reliable, historically significant dates. The first – the Battle of Trafalgar – is refused. The second – the death of her first pet, a rabbit called Shaun – is accepted. She gets her 50 quid. Turns out she was never prepared to try the second one, believing a second failure would annul the account and cause her card to be swallowed and obliterated.

'Still want to go to Croydon?'

'What, for no reason?'

'Yeah.'

'Alright.'

We take the tram to Croydon East, have a wander around the shops and the new shopping centre before having a look at the market on Surrey Street. We walk slowly and curiously between the stalls, taken by the fish, the baby aubergines, the kumquats (she used to eat the latter as a child, hasn't seen them since, assumed she'd eaten the lot). At the end of Surrey Street, Winnie encounters a food truck. I explain what it is. She tells me to stop being condescending. I order the goat curry, which comes with rice, peas, cabbage and macaroni cheese. Winnie watches the dish being assembled wearing a look that indicates wonder and disgust. She opts for a chicken patty and we eat our lunch walking to the tram stop on Church Street, in no hurry at all, pausing to stare at lobsters, to point out buildings.

It's proving a pleasant outing until a man on an electric scooter almost knocks Winnie off her feet. I expect Winnie to lose her rag but instead she says, 'That looks rather fun. Can I try your goat?' We're forced to sit apart on the way home. I watch her eat the patty from a distance (which is a sentence I never thought I'd have occasion to write). She's looking out the window intently – at the flats, the towers, the fields, the river, IKEA. At Mitcham Junction it occurs to Winnie that she's not wearing a mask, so she quickly buries her patty in her handbag and falls in line. It starts to rain. At Wimbledon, I ask if she wants to get the bus. She says nothing, just puts her hood up and strides off. She goes through three red lights on the way home.

She's in the kitchen. I'm in the sitting room. She's leaving a message for Rebecca. 'Yes I am glad we went to Croydon – all things considered. It's a different world down there – which is no bad thing – and four sea bass for five quid is not to be sniffed at on any planet. The chicken patty was very good in the end, once it had calmed down. I wouldn't mind knowing what spices the chap puts in the pastry. Croydon certainly has a lot of character. Could probably do with having a bit less if we're honest. Anyway. On with the war. I'll be taking Arthur round his yoghurt in a minute. For your information. Let's hope it doesn't capsize en route. How are you by the way?'

She gets back from delivering the yoghurt. 'That receptionist is *so* miserable. She depresses me, she actually does. I thought you were supposed to be *nice* to little old ladies. I thought that was meant to be one of the few consoling things about getting old and falling to bits. I'll tell you something: by the time I'm living at that place, she had better have cheered up a bit. Is that a hot cross bun?'

I'm watching *Love Island Australia*. Winnie enters, approaches bearing two squares of dark chocolate, stops halfway, snared by what's unfolding on the box. 'Trainers on the bed,' she says. 'Not a good idea.' About half an hour later, she enters with a cup of tea for me. (She's getting good at this landlady business.) A show called *The Terror* gains her full attention. An expedition to the Arctic, circa 1850 – quite scary stuff. She sits on one of the stools, on the edge, and stays there for 90 minutes. I imagine her out of the corner of my mind's eye (if that's somewhere you can imagine out of) doing likewise as a child. The ending is bleak. The credits roll. She rises. 'That was horrifying,' she says cheerfully. 'Night-night.'

**4 March.** A letter lands on the mat. An order to complete the census. Failure to complete carries a fine. I can see she's immediately unnerved by this new chore.

'Where are the damn questions?' she asks sweetly.

'I'm afraid they're online, Winnie. Shall we do it now, on your phone? While the iron's hot? I can type in the answers?'

'Fine. Fine, fine, fine. Fine.'

The following is an approximation of what followed.

'Name?'

'Winsome.'

'Just Winsome?'

'Winsome Delores Lovelock Carter.'

'What type of accommodation?'

'Detached but not nearly enough.'

'Nationality?'

'Am I allowed to say English? Or has that been banned?'

'Sex?'

'Less and less.'

'Are you in paid work?'

'No.'

'Are you likely to take up paid work any time soon?'

'No.'

'Have you ever been in paid work?'

'Well no. But you try running a house and bringing up three children.'

'How would you describe your mental health?'

'I wouldn't.'

'On 21st March, what will your legal marital status be?'

'Same as it is today with any luck.'

'Which is?'

'I'm a widow. That's the brutal truth.'

'Who is your landlord?'

'God Almighty.'

'Have you served in the armed forces?'

'Yes, I was a parachutist.'

'No then.'

'In fact I was a bisexual parachutist living in a bungalow.'

'Religion?'

'Christian. When I can figure out how to log on.'

'Will you have any guests on 21st March?'

'What's all this about 21st March? How should I know? It's unlikely of course. Not to mention illegal.'

'What have you been doing for the last seven days?'

'Trying to fill in this damn form.'

'I see.'

'Plotting a *coup d'état*. Self-combusting. Write what you want.'

'Tea or coffee?'

'It doesn't say that.'

'No, that's me asking you.'

'I suppose I could have a coffee.'

'How do you usually travel to work?'

'Stair lift.'

'Any feedback for the census 2021 support team?'

'Yes: bugger off.'


I stretch on the driveway beneath the mimosa tree. Reach up to stroke its brilliant yellow flowers: soft and cold and lightly wet like a dog's nose. Next to the mimosa is what Winnie calls a *prunus*, which is now showing, after months of nothingness, dozens and dozens of small white flowers. The view from my window each morning is a slowly growing surprise.

The first fifteen minutes of the run are hard going. Then I take an unplanned left and everything is new. I follow thin, meandering tracks – less travelled, less trod – and somehow the novelty diminishes the toil and it's easier to carry on. It's wet and muddy, extremely in places. When I spot a sizable puddle ahead, I've learned to scan the sides of the track for narrow bypasses put down by a long line of runners faced with the same obstacle. Boggy spots aren't random: they occur at low points; and the wayfarers of yesteryear have laid escape routes for today's crop. I used to miss their solutions. I'd plough on through the bog, and slip and curse, and regret the entire run. Now I lean on others, heed their detours, pursue their diversions, the better to proceed. As much as I can, I look up as I go – at trees, at clouds. I turn my ankle considering a magpie.

**6 March.** She hooks out a vintage brick of bolognaise from the freezer, which she perks up with herbs from the garden and some expired bacon. I join her for a glass of red, which she's pleased to see. Her mood has improved. This afternoon she seemed totally frazzled, more like the Winnie I knew in October and November. I think my being out for most of the day might have wobbled her a bit. When you take something away, it's easier to see what it was there for. I'm not blowing my own trumpet, but another person in the house is indisputably useful to Winnie. They serve as a reference point, as a co-ordinate, as ballast. Another person keeps her from spinning.

**8 March.** Passing me the marmalade, she tells me it's Stewart's birthday tomorrow. She says she remembers being 'almost spherical' and going with Henry to Chinatown for a meal a few weeks before he was born (Stewart, not Henry). She says the food came very, very quickly. She says she reckons they didn't want her to pop on site. I suggest that Winnie might have been affecting the restaurant's turnover by taking up too much room. In any case, she enjoys the memory: there's a loving look in her eye as she goes over the evening in her mind. 'The Peking duck was excellent,' she says in conclusion.

I run fourteen holes of the golf course. The greens are being readied for action. Only three weeks now – 29th March, G-Day. I'm going to celebrate by playing golf from dawn to dusk. Should get about 50 holes in. Winnie's going to caddy. I finish my run by the pond, sit on a bench in the sun. A man and his dog arrive at my shoulder. A youngish Labrador, an oldish owner. The latter launches a battered tennis ball for the former. 'Would you like to sit down, sir?' 'I will, but not just yet.' I shuffle along the bench. After a few more throws, the man sits. I ask if he'd prefer to have the bench to himself. 'I don't reckon so,' he says. An American accent. He offers me the launcher. 'Would you care to throw?' 'Sure,' I say. I throw the ball for Colin. And then I throw it again. And again. And again. I ask the man how his lockdown has been.

'Oh I don't mind. It's nice to have Colin.'

'Is he quite young?'

'He's three. Just over. He's quite smart. He seems to know what I'm thinking. Not all the time, but still. You live local?'

'Yeah. Since October. You?'

'Yeah. Since 1950.'

'What brought you here?'

'I wanted to see if you guys were really like you were in the movies.'

'And?'

'And you're not, thank God.'

'And then?'

'And then I fell in love. And then I got a job. And then here I am.'

'Here you are.'

'Colin's not mine.'

'Oh.'

'His owner went to Switzerland for the winter. He'll be back next week.'

'Will you miss him?'

'I don't know yet.'

We sit for a while longer.

'See you around,' I say.

'Sure,' he says.

Walking away from them, I sort of wave at Colin and feel ridiculous for doing so because Colin's not looking and he's a dog. When I get home it occurs to me that that was the first conversation I've had with a stranger for months.

Winnie gets back from the farmers' market with some venison sausages. Absolute whoppers. She pulls out some parsnips from a musty crack in the earth's core to go with them. I look at them with disgust. 'They just need a shave,' she says. 'You'd make an excellent defence lawyer, Winnie,' I say. Stewart calls.

'Stew,' she says. 'Nice to hear from you. Did you have a good weekend?'

'I enjoyed my birthday yesterday.'

She says nothing.

'Spent most of it digging a hole!' he says.

A pause. And then, 'A big one was it?'

'Fairly.'

'Anyone I know?'

Stew laughs, but half-heartedly. He's upset his mum forgot. And she's upset she got the day wrong.

'Hey-ho,' he says. 'Better go. Bye mum. Lots of love.'

'OK. All the best. Love to the—'

But Stew has hung up.

We watch the news. There's a piece on care homes opening up to visitors. Scenes of loved ones being reunited, etc. Winnie watches it all then gets up abruptly and heads to the kitchen. I hear her digging around in the freezer, the small one below the fridge. I go through. She's on her knees, searching for something, behind the peas, the sweetcorn, the ice cream. 'They're in here somewhere …' She finds them. 'Raspberries. Arthur loves them. They'll need a bit of sugar to combat the sourness. The trouble is they've made it so hard to visit. I had all the forms up on my phone – pages and pages. They should thaw quickly enough. He enjoys them mixed with a bit of yoghurt. But I just couldn't make any *sense* of them.' She makes the raspberry yoghurt. Says she's going to run it round to him now.

'Now?'

'Yes, now. Heard of it?'

'Will the reception be open?'

'I'll leave it on the doorstep.'

'It's nearly eleven, Winnie.'

'I'm not scared of the dark.'

'Do you want me to nip round?'

'Would you?'

**9 March.** My second pillow is cold, which means I can't have moved during the night. The fire needs some coaxing. I sit by it, feeding it things I think it needs until it glimmers, drinking a coffee from a mug that carries a motto in Latin: *Arduus ad solem* (striving towards the sun). Winnie comes down saying she's booked in to see Arthur and is running late. I stand in the road as she reverses out of the drive. I encourage her to continue, to keep coming, to turn. I let her know the way's clear.

Winnie returns.

'That was quick.'

'You're telling me.'

'How was it?'

'Hopeless.'

'Why?'

'I turned up at 8.30, as per the appointment. They got me dressed up, shoved it up my nose, then told me to wait in the car for half an hour.'

I enjoy imagining Winnie dressed in PPE waiting in her car for half an hour.

'Then at 9 o'clock someone came out and explained that I was very welcome to visit Arthur's flat but I ought to bear in mind that he wouldn't be in it.'

'Where was he?'

'Of course I thought he'd died or something.'

'Naturally.'

'But apparently he was still having breakfast.'

'Right …'

'Which means they told me to come at 8.30 for 9 knowing full well that Arthur likes to eat until 10.'

'And what now?'

'I've been invited to go back at 11.'

'And will you?'

'Well I've a mind not to.'

'To teach them a lesson.'

'Something like that.'

She shakes her head. Gives it some thought. Shakes her head again. Then says, 'Did you make Kuba a coffee?'

Winnie returns. (Again.)

'That wasn't quick.'

'You're telling me.'

'How was it?'

'I got in trouble.'

'I can believe it.'

'I was supposed to stay for half an hour.'

'And?'

'I spent two hours cleaning his kitchen.'

'Sounds fun.'

'Everything had got muddled up. His biscuit tin had all sorts in it.'

'And how was Arthur?'

'He was wearing his trousers.'

'Well that's a start.'

'The pair I got him for Christmas.'

'Was he pleased to have you over?'

'He didn't say anything to the contrary. Not at any volume. A bit of a hairy moment when he insisted on making the tea. I had to watch through my hands. You never know where things are going to end up. Speaking of which – fancy one?'

**10 March.** We share a slice of toast. And then another. It's her new method – it means one's second half isn't getting cold during one's first. I read a poem from the anthology. It's Larkin. The final line is near immortal: *'What will survive of us is love.'* I look at the stone couple hanging in the hallway, either falling or dancing. She looks at a pigeon making a mess of her bird bath.

**11 March.** Winnie gets back from visiting Arthur. Outstayed her welcome by some margin again, she says. 'Needless to say, he was getting a bit fed up, mum faffing about, trying to organise him. I sat with him for lunch. They make him sit apart because he makes too much mess, which is a bit off. Mashed potato and omelette. Didn't look delectable but there was enough of it at least, and it's hard to choke on either mashed potato or omelette, which is all I ask of anything Arthur puts in his mouth.'

She complains of stiffness getting out of the electric recliner. She turns round and gives the chair one hell of a look, as if it were solely responsible for this unpleasant turn of events. Then she gives me a look, as though I'm in on it as well. I'm reminded of the various times she has blamed her tools when food has burned beyond recognition while she was watching *Gardeners' World*. For all her know-how and savvy, she can't half kid herself. I wouldn't be surprised if she came out of the womb passing the buck to the midwife.

**13 March.** A man from Secom (home security) came yesterday, but nothing's been fixed. Winnie doesn't think the man had a clue what he was up to. She calls the company to share her concern – quite serious – that someone might have stolen one of the company's vans and be going around posing as a technician. I shake my head as I listen to Winnie explain her suspicions, and privately award the chap on the other end of the line a medal for not hanging up. Instead, the chap agrees to send someone else round ASAP.

Highlight of the evening is watching an episode of *Top of the Pops* from 30 years ago. The Christmas number one is the St Winifred's Junior School Choir with a song called 'Grandma, We Love You' or similar. Winnie hears them out and then describes the song as ludicrous.

**14 March.** Mothering Sunday. Winnie says she's never taken the day seriously so she can hardly expect her children to.

**16 March.** She's in the kitchen when I get back from a run. There's evidence of a trip to the supermarket spread on the kitchen table. More biscuits, more cheese and – *drum roll* – a sticky toffee carrot cake pudding. I tell her it looks like my cup of tea. She says that's why she bought the blasted thing. 'Sticky toffee carrot cake pudding,' I read wondrously. 'Who would have thought it? Like combining P.G. Wodehouse with Sofia Loren.'

**17 March.** Megan comes over for dinner dressed as a bubble and freshly tested. Over paella, Megan and Winnie talk about studios and brushes and *trompe l'oeil*, which I think is a kind of dressing. Then Winnie talks about the 'laughable' pasta I served for lunch yesterday (orzo). Megan enjoys the review, which encourages Winnie to extend it. I don't mind ever so much. I suppose it's good for her brain to search for every single synonym of 'wretched' known to man. We have what's left of the carrot cake toffee pudding, then watch a film wherein Robert Redford pretends to be Bill Bryson. At its end, Megan says, 'I like Winnie. There was a moment when I thought I didn't. But now I know that I do. She's sweet.' 'A wolf dressed in sheep's clothing,' I say.

**18 March.** Morning. I find her in the kitchen. On her feet, in a panic. 'It's Arthur,' she says. 'He's had a fall.' She wants to get round there ASAP to assess him, but, sod's law, someone called Dave is coming over to either look at the crack in the wall or the ivy on the silver birch, she can't remember which. I don't like the sight of her in a flap, so issue some unequivocal advice. 'Prioritise Arthur. If this Dave fellow comes round in your absence, so be it. He can come another time. The silver birch isn't going anywhere, and nor is the crack in the wall. Besides, if this Dave is anything like your typical self-employed artisan, he won't be turning up until after lunch.' She likes the cut of my gib. She respects my logic. 'Yes, I've known one or two Daves,' she says. 'You have to pay them to put their trousers on. You'll man the fort, will you?'

Winnie returns. 'He's fine,' she says, coming through the front door. 'Turns out he went to the loo in the night and then fell asleep on it. Which is good news if you think about it. Means he must have been *very* relaxed. Unsurprisingly, he ended up on the bathroom floor, where he decided to call it a night. He was found in the morning, quite happy and uninjured, having what he described as a bog-standard lie in.'

**19 March.** I find Winnie under an occasional table. On her hands and knees, fiddling with something – an ancient extension lead she knew nothing of.

'You find something new every day,' she says, laughing.
'You will in that position, Winnie.'
'True.'
'I recommend you stay down there.'
'I wouldn't give you the pleasure.'

'Change of perspective and all that.'

'I'll change your perspective.'

'Oh yeah?'

'By booting you out of the house.'

I tend to work in Henry's office these days. I was reluctant to use the space, but Winnie doesn't mind, says she quite enjoys coming in and opening the shutters and the window. It's a big desk, whopping in fact, tailor-made for Henry when he joined Transport for London. Perhaps the thinking was that if Henry was delighted with his desk he'd never want to leave it. I'm meant to be getting on with a novella set in Swindon, but the view is proving distracting. I can see the driveway and a part of the street. Lots of people stop walking to appreciate the mimosa tree, which hangs over the pavement. I wouldn't have been one to stop. Not before I moved to Windy Ridge. Not before I knew what it was. But I would be one to stop now, I reckon, because a change of scene – to put it simply – alters what we see, and by extension what we understand, and what we value. That's why it's good to move, to seek, to crane, to stoop. Like Winnie under the table that time, in a novel pose, discovering that extension lead. A change of company can be as good as a change of scene, for different people see different things, and see the same things differently. I've been lucky, I see now, to have had both.

Winnie enters with Arthur's electric razor. She's in the process of cleaning it. She shows me all the stubble that's accrued over the past week. 'I sometimes wonder if he's going round the care home shaving everyone,' she says. I laugh heartily, and Winnie looks at me like I'm daft. I want to say, or feel like saying, 'I love you, Winnie. You're an absolute nutter.' But instead of saying what I want, I say, 'You're one of a kind, Winnie.' To which she says, 'Then count yourself fortunate.'

**22 March.** News of 'vaccine wars' and a third wave on the continent have put a spring back in the step of news outlets and doom-mongers. Histrionic coverage makes for histrionic attitudes among the public – fact. Of course it's necessary to preach caution, but don't wantonly terrify. Elsewhere in *The Times*, the headline 'Rasher of Bacon a Day Linked to 44% Rise in Dementia Risk' catches my eye, which is no doubt what it was meant to do. I bring it to Winnie's attention. 'I'm not fussed,' she says. 'I have two a day and three on Sundays. Besides, reading *The Times* is more likely to give you dementia than bacon.'

I'm up on the common, sat on a bench. I call Winnie to ask if she's coming. 'I just phoned the dentist,' she says. 'He's done me a discount. Promised to use an inferior substance for the next crown. Not the precious metal he hoped to land on me.' I watch a toddler in a dark green overcoat, apparently unaccompanied, and then three whippets in jumpers. An older couple sit down nearby. She's saying that the problem with relationships is that they involve other people. I see Winnie on the edge of the common, scanning the horizon, her hand as a visor. I wave.

Dinner. I do jerk chicken with rice and peas, which we eat while watching an episode of *Fawlty Towers*.

'How's the chicken?'

'I'm sure it was moist once.'

'And the rice?'

'Porridge you mean?'

'You know, Winnie, you might have to start doing a bit of cooking yourself if you're going to moan about everything.'

'You're quite right. I might indeed. Because I'm afraid you're rather in a rut. Would you pass me the salt?'

**24 March.** There's two slices of bread left – a nice, plump, regular slice, and a crust. She looks at them both considerately, then gives me the nice plump slice. I ask her if she's sure. She says she's not if she's honest, so best not talk about it. I notice that the label on the milk has been added to with a fair amount of biro. 'ALERT ARTHUR. COVID. TELL ARTHUR.' I ask if she feels milk is a Covid risk? 'Abigail's got the bug,' she says. 'And I'm worried about Arthur because I took him round a slice – albeit a thin one – of the lemon drizzle cake she made last week.' Not worried about herself, but worried about Arthur. And worried that he'll get Covid via a slice of cake. Winnie in a nutshell.

She shows me a picture in the paper. 'Look at those legs,' she says. 'You could keep a house warm for a month with a pair of those. Arthur's got solid legs. It was always his legs I had in mind when feeding him as a child. As much as I find podge abhorrent, I knew legs like pins wouldn't do him any good at all. I used to give him porridge and scrambled eggs every morning, and then make him promise to tell his teacher he hadn't eaten for a week.' Again, Winnie in a nutshell.

There's also an alarming graph in the paper. It indicates that unless the British people continue to confine themselves there could be a fatal June peak twice the size of the January one. On the surface, bloody terrifying. Beneath the surface (that is, after doing some light digging), less so. The predictive model assumes that there will be a 33% infection rate for the next few months (much higher than any infection rate hitherto recorded), and that the season of winter will be followed not by spring and summer but by a couple more winters. So, in short, what the graph is actually showing is what could happen in an impossible scenario, which is very useful indeed.[2]

**25 March.** I take the ash out and notice blossom on the driveway. Spot a parrot (relative of) in the tree whence the blossom came, looking somewhat guilty. Winnie tells me it was a parakeet, as sure as eggs is eggs. Tells me that it extracts a little sweetness out of the petals somehow, and that she really wishes it wouldn't.

I'm in Henry's office. Winnie comes through the front door.
    'Get the jab?'

---

[2] The peak in June was about 30 times lower than the January peak, rather than double it. I'm not belittling the disease, or its impact on health services and human lives. I'm just saying that some of the reporting – indeed a lot of the reporting – was either wilfully or stupidly terrifying.

'Of course I did. I'm not that forgetful.'

'And how was it?'

'The parking was excellent.'

'You must feel relieved?'

'I'll say. I didn't fancy looking for a spot on Kingston Road. Did you get my note?'

'I did.'

'And?'

'And what?'

'And what are we thinking for dinner?'

**26 March.** Victoria, her eldest granddaughter, arrives from Bristol. She'll be staying with us for a while. She was meant to be staying at home, with Rebecca and Abigail, but because the latter has Covid, Victoria's got no choice but to suffer Granny for a week or so. There's a symbolic tussle between the two regarding where Victoria will sleep. Winnie thinks Rebecca's old bedroom would be best, but Victoria fancies Arthur's, because it gets more sunlight and offers a better view, both of which stand to be a comfort while she's writing her essay (due in a fortnight) on Georgian pornography. At one point during the negotiation (from which Victoria emerges victorious), Winnie says, 'If only we could turn the house *around*.' In any case, I'm not sure Victoria means to spend much time in either bedroom. As soon as she's unpacked and had her dinner she's off to Clapham Common to see friends. Winnie's not completely on board with the idea that Victoria doesn't know exactly when she'll be in.

'But it's the *alarm*, Victoria, the *alarm*.'

'I'll put the alarm on when I get in, Granny.'

'But that provides a window of opportunity, darling.'

'Granny. Listen. It's unlikely you'll be burgled this evening between 10 and midnight.'

'Famous last words, my dear.'

As Victoria says goodbye by slamming the front door, Winnie offers the following words to the contents of the fridge: '*Optima spera, ad pessima praepara.*'[3]

**27 March.** We watch a pair of magpies in the garden. According to Winnie, they're the ones who have built a nest in the ash tree. She says she can't work out their *relationship* – whether they're familial or just friendly or whatever. 'They seem to get on remarkably well,' she muses cheerfully, 'which rather argues against them being family.' Sensing what she's alluding to, I ask what Victoria's grief looked like after her father died two years ago. 'It looked like anger,' she says, 'and I'm afraid it still does, the poor love.'

Anger isn't easy to measure, and nor is happiness. Their explicit tell-tale signs – aggression, laughter – are probably just the tip of the iceberg. Ninety-five per cent of happiness has nothing to do with laughing, as 95 per cent of anger has nothing to do with aggression. Notwithstanding anger and happiness being difficult things to measure, I'd put money on Winnie having felt more happiness than anger over the past month or so. Why would I? For one, time has passed

---

[3] Hope for the best, prepare for the worst.

and continues to pass. For two, it's spring again and the bluebells and primroses are coming through once more. For three, she's now able (albeit with some rigmarole) to get into Arthur's flat once or twice or week. And for four, I've promised not to cook pappardelle or orzo again.

You don't forget loss. You don't heal. You just learn to cope with your injury. That's my hunch.

After dinner, the three of us sit down with cups of tea in front of the telly. Me in the recliner, Victoria in one of the swivels, and Winnie in the armchair she had made in Manila. We watch a film. *American Pie*. When the protagonist starts experimenting romantically with what his mother baked that afternoon, Victoria and I can't bear to watch. Winnie, on the other hand, doesn't blink. Perhaps she's seen it all before. One effect of the film and the awkwardness it engenders is an uptick in the general mood. When Victoria wishes Winnie a good night, she does so in a way that suggests she might actually mean it, which causes Winnie to embark on a hunt for the spare hot-water bottle that she thinks might be in the garage. When Victoria says not to worry because she's adjusted the central heating so it stays on all night, I'm relieved that Winnie doesn't hear.

**28 March.** There's a bit of tension at breakfast. It's 20 degrees in the shade and Winnie is stressed because she's just been out to the coal shed and found nothing there. She's looking at me in a way that implies I'm guilty of both negligence and profligacy.

Later. I find Victoria in the kitchen, looking impatient. She and Winnie were meant to leave an hour ago – to go up to the Sunday market in the village. I ask where she's got to. 'Probably walking around the house on the phone to Arthur while looking for things to worry about,' says Victoria. I tell her I've grown a new skin over the last six months, made entirely of patience. She says she hasn't, and wishes her grandmother wouldn't faff around so much when people were waiting for her. It's selfish, she says. It's self-important, she says. I think about trying to modify Victoria's take on Winnie's behaviour by suggesting that right now Winnie is probably doing something that at some level is designed to improve the welfare of others. Then I decide not to suggest this because it's not for me to tell Victoria about her grandmother. At which point said grandmother enters the kitchen through the back door. She's been in the garden weeding. Victoria privately concludes that the trip up to the village has well and truly fallen off her grandmother's agenda, and gets up and leaves the house unceremoniously. Winnie looks at me and laughs.

'Rather an independent spirit, I'd say!'

'Yes, but not by choice, Winnie.'

'How do you mean?'

'She's been waiting for you so you could go up to the village together.'

'Ah. I've gone and done it again, haven't I? Do you think I could catch up with her?'

'Honestly?'

'Yes.'

'No.'

**31 March.** She's putting the crumbs out for the birds. I'm flicking through the paper. There's a picture of a reed warbler feeding an enormous cuckoo. Quite a mismatch, and not at all what Mother Nature had in mind. Apparently cuckoos are known for it. Interloping. The young cuckoo is deposited by its mother into the nest of a reed warbler (or whatever nest is to hand). The mother warbler discovers a baby cuckoo, thinks, 'Bit weird but whatever,' assumes parental responsibility for it, then ends up feeding the imposter bird at the expense of its own chicks. Some respect for the warbler for dealing with whatever's in front of it, I must say. Some question marks over the conduct of the mother cuckoo dropping her new-born off like that. Can't blame the baby cuckoo at all. You don't have the self-awareness at that age to respond maturely and nobly to an ethically complex situation. I ask Winnie what she would do if she was presented with someone else's baby and expected to parent it. I expect her to say something light-hearted and devious, like 'I'd be tempted to add it to the compost,' but in the event her reply is surprisingly straightforward and sincere – 'I guess I'd just have to raise the poor thing.'

# 1959

*A wedding. St Margaret's in Westminster, London. Winnie and Henry have been going steady for four years. After Henry finished at Oxford, the pair moved to London. Living together wasn't an option, so Henry took a room in a house near Battersea Park, while Winnie took a room in a boarding house near King's Cross, which she described as* fortifying. *When Henry landed a job with Royal Dutch Shell and was offered a posting in the Philippines, he reasoned that he ought to get married so that he could take Winnie with him without offending anybody. Henry headhunted the vicar, liked the chap at St Margaret's, said he spoke sense. Problem was, you had to be resident in the catchment area of the church in order to get married there. But the vicar had a plan (long established, long rehearsed), and that was for Henry and Winnie to deposit their suitcases in a local hotel for the duration of the wedding and then claim the hotel as a residence, which is precisely what they did, with the blessing of the concierge, who got a few bob out of the arrangement. After the service, they went with a scattering of friends and as few relatives as possible to a restaurant on Basil Street. Some food was laid out, a few drinks. At one point, the child of one of Henry's friends went missing. The mother was beside herself, as you might imagine, and angry with the other adults for failing to keep an eye on her daughter. Winnie, not yet a mother herself, was more amused by the situation than worried, and made no effort to conceal the fact. She would later suggest – in defence of her actions regarding the lost child – that something in the cider had mollified her unusually.*

*In any case, the child turned up under the buffet table, where she had been secretly helping herself to strawberries and cream. There was no first dance – an economy that Winnie insisted on – while for their honeymoon the newlyweds threw common sense out of the window by choosing a hotel in Basingstoke, coming together conjugally in a rather handsome four-poster bed. From Basingstoke they proceeded to Cornwall, Henry driving his 1930s MG sports car, occasionally with no hands, which was the sort of thing Henry did. They stayed at The Rising Sun in St Mawes, and spent the next three days exploring gardens, and looking at the sea, and walking up and down hills, hand in hand.*

# 7

## A picture of herself by accident

**1 April.** She's got several other preserves on the table, but she doesn't go anywhere near them. They're to entice me. Traps almost. She's down to seven jars of marmalade and she's having to pull out all the stops. She asks if we can send some of the photos she took yesterday to Kuba and Hannah.[1] She's got some nice shots – of the heather, the tulips, the mimosa. There's a lovely one of the front of the house, taken from across the road. The sky is clear and blue. The red front door is brightly lit. Framing the façade are the mimosa tree, the sour cherry and the japonica. Blossom from the cherry has settled on the driveway and pavement like confetti. Victoria is visible through a first-floor window, walking away in an easterly direction. I'm partially in frame. My right side is visible, but the rest of me is behind the wall put up by the man with no fingers. She likes the picture – or liked taking the picture – because she rarely takes the time to stand back and appreciate the house, not least because she's 'usually up to her eyeballs in the damn thing', and you know what they say about not seeing the wood for the trees. It's a fiddly business sending the photos. She's far from a luddite but certainly struggles to keep her cool in the face of an interface. She taps and slides and squeezes the screen like there's no tomorrow. I

---

[1] Hannah is a friend of Rebecca who lived with the Carters for a couple of years in the 90s.

feel sorry for the phone's software. In the event, both emails bounce back. The addresses are wrong.

Later on, a coincidence: Hannah phones. Before they've been talking more than a minute, Hannah is asking why Winnie's lodger isn't very active in the garden. She says that Donald, her husband, was *very* active in the garden when resident at Windy Ridge. (Well good on fucking Donald, I think.) I'm glad to hear Winnie sticking up for me. 'Well Donald's family were vegetable growers. Ben didn't see a vegetable until he was seventeen. He never had a garden.' Hannah doesn't consider this a reasonable excuse. 'He's got hands, hasn't he?' Winnie is forced to concede that he has. 'Then put them to work, Winnie. Don't let him exploit you.' Christ alive.

**2 April.** Not great at being still, is Winnie. I dread to think what she gets up to in her dreams. How much ground she covers. A couple of weeks ago, I bought her a book of essays on flowers. She received it enthusiastically, liked the look of it, but I could tell, or I could sense, that she didn't believe she'd ever read it. Not really. She took it up to bed that night, then brought it down a few days later and left it in the sitting room for common use. I asked her how she was getting on with it. She said she just didn't seem to ever get a moment. And when she did get a moment, she didn't ever seem able to *focus*. Is there any way I could teach Winnie how to relax? When we walk on the common she never wants to sit. She wants to do a lap, a circuit, and then get back home to the coalface. On one occasion I had a bit of cake and a coffee, and I wanted to sit down on practical grounds, so I asked, 'Winnie, do you mind if we sit down for a bit?' and she answered, without breaking her stride, 'Yes I do actually,' as if sitting would somehow jeopardise her plans or compromise her investments. On that occasion, we kept on walking, but when it happened again, on a lovely warm afternoon, I put my foot down – and my backside to boot. For the first few minutes after sitting, I had the feeling that she was wondering what was going to happen next. I had the same feeling for the next few minutes too. It was only towards the end of our sitting, when I'd just said something like: 'Well I suppose we can't sit around here all day,' that she leant back and visibly relaxed. I'm at a loss, to be frank. I can't see her doing yoga. And she's definitely not one for long baths. Perhaps I should bake some of those space brownies or whatever they're called.[2]

**3 April.** I join Winnie in the garden. She points out the primroses, which she likes very much, especially the maroon and yellow ones, which remind her of her school uniform, and therefore the emotional atmosphere of those years. (Nice that she likes the flower for what it refers to, rather than its

---

[2] It occurs to me now that Winnie's surest route to relaxation is to perform a task that 1) is enjoyable and 2) assuages one or several of her underlying existential anxieties. Gardening is an obvious example. She loves her garden but also has an underlying existential anxiety that it will all go to pot and wreak havoc if left unattended. Trouble is, she can't really garden anymore, not the way she used to, not the way she'd *like* to. So these days one of the surest routes to relaxation for Winnie is to *watch Kuba* gardening, but she can hardly list that as a hobby.

appearance. If she put her hand on her heart, Winnie might have to admit that her fondness for marmalade has less to do with its taste and more to do with the fact that it reminds her of childhood.) A tree at the back of the garden seems to have misjudged the season. It's been bare all winter, but now it's starting to look autumnal. An acer tree apparently. The idea of going backwards from winter into autumn, rather than forwards into spring, makes sense in a way, autumn being a softer sort of winter. The next and final thing Winnie shows me is a hose that needs untangling.

She spends most of the afternoon cooking a huge ham. Big enough to feed a postal district. She does so because an Easter weekend needs 'a hunk of ham in the fridge to be hacked into'. This house contains a phantom family, unlosable, absent, both real and unreal.

**4 April.** Rebecca and the girls come over for lunch. They move the old wooden table down from the terrace onto the lawn, cover it with a tablecloth, bring chairs out, etc. For my part, I bring the tennis rackets down and allow Rebecca to demonstrate joyously and at length how little hand-eye coordination she has. The outside setting, and the warmth, and the element of play, and the imminent arrival of food that somebody else has cooked, have conspired to produce an atmosphere very different to the one that prevailed at Christmas. Winnie is still a touch nervous, mind you, wanting things to go well but not really knowing how to make them do so. The food arrives and the girls set it out in the middle of the table. They want to start, but Winnie's wandered off. 'Granny!' shouts Abigail. 'She'll be an hour,' says Victoria. 'Granny!' shouts Abigail again. And then Victoria joins in and their shared cry of 'Granny!' – loud enough to be heard in Chelsea – has them both giggling, their frustration with Winnie apparently forgotten, or if not forgotten then altered into something else, something fonder. Winnie gets the message. Joins us in the garden and eats stood up until Rebecca says, 'For heaven's sake, Mum – sit down!' which draws accusations of hypocrisy from Rebecca's children, who reckon their mum is worse than their gran when it comes to eating stood up with one eye on what needs to be done in the next room.

One of the dishes on offer contains a single, very large mussel. Winnie doesn't think twice – she swoops for it – and then spends about fifteen minutes trying to prise the mussel from its shell, first with a fork and then with her fingers. She's assisted by her family in the end – all of them. They're yanking on the mussel while Winnie tries to anchor the shell. I'm not sure I've seen anything like it. We have some chocolate eggs after the meal, and talk loosely of things to come. Winnie tries to take a picture of us all – postprandial and in the sun, me with a guitar and the girls with chopsticks in their hair and Rebecca pretending to take a swipe at Victoria with a tennis racket – but ends up taking a picture of herself by accident.

**6 April.** Stewart is over with youngest daughter Mango. I watch them in the garden. He's spotted a rotten branch. On the walnut tree. It's oozing liquid. He's up a ladder sawing it off now. Winnie shares her opinion that Stew's been of more practical use in the last five minutes than I've been in six months. Mango, incidentally, was advertised as head-strong and devilish but proves easy to win round. I just keep deliberately getting her name mixed up with other fruits, and that's it, we're on good terms. She sits on the couch near where I'm working, gets a game going on her laptop, then proceeds to explain every aspect of it for what feels like several hours. To get Mango off the topic I ask her what she thinks the funniest thing about her granny is. She says, 'That she's still alive, duh.'

The branch that's had a chunk lopped off is still leaking, I notice. Crying almost. The red tulips don't look especially pleased either, and just days after reaching their prime. It's the weather. They thought it was their turn in the sun, and then came snow. A reversal of fortunes like that can cause anything to droop, to sigh, to withdraw.

**7 April.** Stewart drops in early to pick something up that Mango forgot. Has a bit of toast while he's here. He doesn't half slap on the marmalade, does our Stewart. He thinks it grows on trees. He's utterly oblivious of Winnie's disap-proving glances. He was born with a slice of marmalade on toast in his mouth, this one. 'Mind if I have another slice, Mum?' he says impudently. *Yeah*, I think, *if you get yourself down to Mr Spinnici and get a large granary in.* No wonder it didn't work out with Stew living here, if this is how he car-ries on. Tch.

A PICTURE OF HERSELF BY ACCIDENT

**8 April.** Towards the end of breakfast, I direct her attention to an article in the paper about a book – *Humankind* – that argues that humans are a remarkably kind species, despite what we're led to believe.

'If the day had 36 hours then there might be time for kindness,' says Winnie.

'Nonsense.'

'Alright – 48 hours.'

'You've been kind to me, Winnie.'

'Hm?'

'I said you've been kind to me.'

The remark has nudged her. She probably wants to say hey-ho and make light of it, or make some overly deflective comment, designed to turbo-suck all the emotion out of the moment. But instead she says, 'Have I?'

She's expecting tree surgeons. To deal with the ivy on the silver birch. I watch her from the sitting room, down at the bottom of the garden, sizing up the job, calculating whether she's been misquoted. I watch her turn and approach the house, steady as she goes, and then I hear her enter the kitchen. She asks me to come and check if we're low on muesli. (She can't access the cupboard where she keeps it, not without a stepladder. Don't ask.) 'We are running a bit low actually,' I say ruefully and on my tiptoes. 'I feared as much,' she says, tonally slapping her thigh in self-satisfaction, pleased with herself for checking. 'Just the five bags left, I'm afraid, Winnie – three nutty and two fruity.'

**11 April.** The 10 o'clock news focuses on the nation's arrival at stage two of the lockdown roadmap tomorrow, meaning hospitality venues can open outdoors. So lots of lovely beer garden action going forward, methinks.

**12 April.** It's snowing.

**14 April.** When I come down in the morning, the kitchen table isn't laid. She's stopped doing that, or stopped always doing that. Sometimes it's set for one, sometimes for two, sometimes not at all. Whether this is an improvement on it being religiously set each evening for her and Henry is hard to say. I get out two bowls, two spoons, two plates, two butter knives, two mugs, two napkins, the breadboard, the breadknife, her marmalade (Seville orange, homemade), my marmalade (grapefruit, shop-bought), salted butter, milk, stewed fruit and yoghurt. I don't bother with the paper. Not this morning. Leave it on the mat. Instead I watch three parakeets in one of the cherry trees, doing their best to dislodge the flowers. Winnie enters. She's evidently seen what I've seen because she walks straight past me and out the back door into the garden, where she gives the parakeets a piece of her mind. 'Go away! Off you go! Clear off!' Two of the birds dash, which satisfies her, but the third is curiously unmoved, which doesn't. She reissues her instructions, but to no effect. Then she starts throwing stones. But still the parakeet won't budge. This could take a while, I think, so close the kitchen door to stop the cold coming in, or the heat going out, or both. Then Hank the robin turns up, and Winnie stops throwing stones.

Carlotta phones. Winnie takes the phone into Henry's office. She reports back: Carlotta had a fall. The hill she lives on tripped her up. She landed on her nose with a thump. Blood pouring down her face. The end of her nose closer to the back of her head than the front. She didn't want to go to the hospital. Didn't want to clog up the health service.

Winnie gets back from Lidl. She's bought a pair of half-price Easter eggs. She decorates the table with them. And then it occurs to her that Carlotta might like one, given what she's been through. I recognise Winnie in this set of events. She goes to the shop, buys a load of stuff for fear of missing out on a bargain or it running out or the price going up, and then, after the event, she'll look at her largesse and think how so-and-so might like such-and-such. Her thoughtfulness is often an afterthought. That isn't meant as a criticism. It's meant to give an idea (my idea) about the way Winnie's mind works. It could actually be quite interesting applying Maslow's hier-archy of needs to Winnie. She exists, for the most part, on the lowest rung of the ladder, worrying and fussing about the basics – shelter, food, heat. She needn't worry and fuss, of course, but she indisputably does, and it's her concern with such things that prohibits her from climbing the ladder and thinking in a more rounded way about her own wellbeing (or 'actualisation' to use Maslow's term). And it's also her concern with such things that makes it likely she'll forget your birthday.

I tell her I'll be away for a night. Cat-sitting for my friend Thea.

'Well that won't involve much,' she says. 'Cats can take care of themselves.'

'Not this cat, Winnie.'

'*Every* cat. If they don't take care of themselves it means they've been spoilt and distorted. They don't need affection. They're independent. I suppose you'll walk it on a lead, will you?'

'No, but I've been told it will sleep with me.'

'How absurd.'

'Otherwise it will cry all night outside the bedroom door.'

'What does it eat? Pizza?'

**15 April.** Morning. She loves me. She must do. Else she wouldn't do the things that she does. Like sleep on my head, or lick my hands, or rub her face against my knuckles. (The fact that Ruby also appears enamoured of every other corner/angle in the house suggests we're not exactly in a monogamous relationship, but hey-ho.) I send Winnie a picture of Ruby resting on my keyboard in the sunlight. It's one of several dozen pictures I've taken of Ruby already.

Evening. Odd and faint feeling of missing Winnie.

**16 April.** Leave Ruby to it. Walk home. Small boy on Barnes Common with his mother (presumably) feeding the ducks sweetcorn. Mother: 'I think we need to go home now, darling.' Boy: 'Then please would you stop thinking that, Mummy?'

Dinner is a quick-fix job from Tesco. Chicken in a Cabernet Sauvignon sauce. It's not ideal, but I'm not sure Winnie's description of it as 'the strangest meal ever' is quite right.

**17 April.** Not feeling so hot this morning. Sit on the back step and drink two cups of coffee. Watch the leaky walnut tree and a pair of small brown birds jumping around the flagstones looking for scraps. The song of various birds, the loud murmur of distant Broadway, the pointed sound of a train passing through, the shadow of the ash tree cutting across the bright lawn. Winnie comes out with the paper. She wants to show me something. It's a picture of a blue tit attacking a wing mirror. Apparently they don't comprehend their own reflections and have a go at the likeness.

I'm in her bad books. Chipped a plate given to her by one of Henry's great aunts. Worse still, it was up in my kitchen when it happened, where it should never have been. She's confirmed in her suspicion that anything of value has its rightful place and there's a jolly good reason why it does. 'I bet you were too enthusiastic when washing it, weren't you?' she says, really quite upset. 'I was careless,' I say, honestly, and leave it at that. Then a parakeet lands in the cherry tree and she's out the back door saying 'Oh no you don't!' and I privately thank the heavens for sending down an unquestionable villain to deflect Winnie's opprobrium.

**20 April.** Megan comes for dinner. It's nice doing the washing up, watching the two of them at the table out of the corner of my eye, carving up a tart, Megan suggesting cream on top, Winnie saying she couldn't possibly and then somehow managing, even going back for another glug. Nothing brilliant, nothing noteworthy, just a slice of life really, and I guess that's what touches me about the scene, that it's just life, that it's just people, at a table, after a meal, with Winnie at the centre of things. I can't help thinking – as I sponge the knives and rinse the bowls – that things are better than they might have been. I think I'm feeling a bit of pride, if I'm honest. And a bit of happiness. I think that's what it is.

**21 April.** Apropos of nothing, she tells me about the time she test drove a double-decker bus to prove to the union of bus drivers that short women could do it. The union members were predominantly male, and they were also predominantly sceptical about the new push to encourage women drivers. To tackle this scepticism, Transport for London (directed by Henry) organised for the press to come down to a racetrack in south west London to be shown that the new buses could be driven safely by a variety of short women. 'I was whizzing around the track quite happily,' says Winnie. 'Even got told off for going too fast.' 'For how long were you whizzing?' 'Oh not long. About an hour and a half. Until the dinosaurs got the message.' The image of a self-satisfied Winnie driving a double-decker bus very fast in ovals while a collection of hacks and bigwigs look on from the side of the track is one that might prove hard to get out of my head.

A PICTURE OF HERSELF BY ACCIDENT

**22 April.** I watch Winnie in the garden, watering the flower-beds, a look on her face that is at once suspicious and smug. She's at the south side of the lawn, beneath the acer tree, which is looking more autumnal with each day of spring. She's had her hair done. Liz came yesterday. She can see again. Decided at the last minute to have a bit of colour put in. (It's always at the last minute by the sound of it.) She's put the hose on the ground, has got her hands on her hips and is looking down at the old tennis court (now covered with hawthorn and brambles), perhaps remembering an old contest, or imagining a new one. She turns and heads back. Pauses between the conifers. Looks up at the house. She's as still as a statue. I'd like to think she's remembering and admiring, but chances are she's checking for open windows and exterior damage. She sees me, smiles, then disappears behind flowers.

**23 April.** She phones Arthur's care home. 'Hello. Winnie Carter speaking. Phoning on St George's Day. Which is also Turner's birthday. Joseph Mallord William. Painter. Very good one. Anyway, can I book to visit Arthur? In his flat, if I may. I know there's a fad these days for sitting outdoors, but count me out. 3.30 sounds fine. After lunch. Yes, I'm aware I'll have to arrive in advance to jump through certain hoops. Shall we say midday? I'm only joking, dear, not to worry. 3 o'clock it is.'

A loud whack-whack on the door. 'Hello there,' says a man, 'I can't help noticing you've got a driveway.' Yes ... 'And I can't help noticing it's been spoiled with lots of white marks and grime and fungal spots.' Yes … 'Well I've got this special machine, you see, and your neighbours will attest to the fact.' Yes … 'Well I wouldn't mind bringing your drive up good as new, like.' I'm prevented from taking the man up on his generous offer by Winnie, who has appeared at my side and is presently treating the man as though he were a parakeet in the cherry tree. She closes the door, gives me a look – *I don't know, the lot of the homeowner, eh?*

But the thing is, she likes that lot. Loves it even. Winnie enjoys – revels in – the day-to-day business of having a home, the bits and pieces of being a guardian. No doubt about it, should Winnie ever relocate, she would dearly miss the demands of running this house. She wouldn't know what to worry about. She'd be at a loss. It's the bittersweet complexity of having a home that gives Winnie purpose, that puts a spring in her step and a sparkle in her eye. I fancy the family across the road, the one that sent a letter begging Winnie to sell up, will have to content themselves with having their eyes on Winnie's pad, rather than their hands, for quite a while longer.

Doing a spot of dusting, find a handmade get well soon card under an occasional table in the sitting room, made by Mango for Winnie, on the occasion of the latter's burst appendix. It's addressed to 'granny lala', and the message inside reads: 'get better soon ok'. The whole card has been lavishly decorated with roughly hewn blue hearts.

*Gardeners' World*. There's a diverting section about a lady who grows chillies in Dorset, including some of the hottest in the world. The lady says there's no better feeling than planting something and then watching it grow and then feeding it to your children. 'Quite right,' says Winnie, 'especially if it burns their tonsils off.'

**27 April.** I sit outside. On the terrace. Face due south and read *The Madness of Grief*. There are some impressive passages. For example, when the author (Richard Coles) writes about how when your partner dies they take your future with them, and that, after their death, when you look forward, you see nothing, you go nowhere. But mostly, instead of reading, I tune in to what's in front of me. A magpie diving from its nest, and then its mate swooping in pursuit or support. A pair of robins playing around, courting perhaps. (Have you ever seen two robins bump into each other by accident? It's quite amusing.) The border of hyacinths and bluebells and heather. Kuba crossing the scene with a wheelbarrow, appearing at once strong and glum and peaceful. I go inside to make him a cup of coffee.

I set the table for dinner. Napkins folded into triangles, coasters for water and wine, two types of placemats (both rubber and straw; a case of belt and braces if ever there was one). As usual, Winnie starts the meal standing up. The habit is lodged soundly in her hippocampus. She waits until she's comfortably seated before she shares her opinion that the stew is the most unusual she's ever had. I don't raise an eyebrow. I eat a few mouthfuls, make a thing of enjoying them, and then look at Winnie and smile and tell her about the book I'm reading – or something about it rather. I tell her the author says that when your partner dies they take your future with them. She can see what he means, but Winnie made a decision not to go around looking miserable. Instead, she tried to remain grateful for what she had been given, which was 60 years of excellent marriage. I mention a line from a poem, about someone's absence being a companion, and she nods. 'Henry's everywhere. Case in point: I've still got all his clothes. Not for sentimental reasons. I would happily invite you to consider his suits, but your work doesn't appear to be office-based. Indeed it hardly appears to be based anywhere at all from what I can tell.' She gives me a warm smile, as if she'd just said the nicest thing in the world to me, then says that another partner is totally out of the question. She says she wouldn't want the responsibility (which strikes me as an interesting point of objection), and that nobody would put up with her idiosyncrasies anyhow. I ask her what idiosyncrasies she has in mind. She says her habit of boiling the dishcloths once a week. I don't share my feeling that when it comes to her idiosyncrasies, boiling the dishcloths wouldn't even make the top ten. She looks out at the garden, says it's been the sunniest and frostiest start to spring she can remember.[3]

**28 April.** When Henry died, she saw it coming. She didn't make a ceremony of it. There wasn't a vigil. She didn't invite

---

[3] And she was right. April 2021 was one of the sunniest and frostiest on record. Not a coincidence. The clear skies that allowed the sunshine also allowed the frost. So it goes.

the children. She just let him go. I'm not sure what made her tell me this. Perhaps it was nothing. Perhaps she was just thinking about Henry dying and decided to let the thought come out. Then she lets something else come out, and I rather wish she hadn't, because it's the following question: 'Can I borrow you this morning? I'd like to go to Lidl for some compost.'

On our way to Lidl, it occurs to me that Winnie is very much an observant driver. She just doesn't observe the things you'd prefer her to be observing, like the road. Instead, she keeps an eye out for things she knows (the poet Robert Graves' former house), things she's fond of (a haberdashery called Elastic Stitch), things she doesn't have much time for (Pizza Gogo), and things that remind her of other things (like the Nelson Health Centre, which reminds her of the time she got a nosebleed in the baker's and went across to have it sorted out). She's got a lot of time for the local magistrates' court on Alexandra. Stares at them for at least five seconds doing 20mph.

'I've spent some time in there,' she says.

'Pleased to hear it.'

'Doing jury service.'

'What was the case?'

'Shoplifting.'

'Did you reach a verdict?'

'I think we found her not guilty.'

'What did she steal?'

'I believe it was sushi.'

She indicates the cemetery where Henry was laid to rest. 'Do you ever visit?'

'I can't say I do. Am I rotten?'

'Almost certainly.'

She points out her old flat on Church Road, and the doctor's old house, and the sycamore tree Stewart crashed his bike into, and I'm reminded as we go and as she points how rewarding and fruitful it can be to go somewhere with someone else, if only down to the local supermarket. Then a spot of rain causes a brief panic. For about ten seconds *everything* is on: the front and back wipers, the hazard lights, the radio, aircon. In her effort to see more, she succeeds in seeing less.

**30 April.** Kitchen. Morning. *Desert Island Discs.* The guest is Fay Weldon, author of umpteen novels, nearly 90 now. Weldon says she doesn't drive because she can't be sure what's around the corner. I ask Winnie if she sympathises. 'Fay Weldon has written many excellent novels with ordinary women as their heroines, and has therefore earned the right to not do what the hell she likes.'

# 1963

*Young Arthur Carter has chronic and severe lung congestion. As a result he struggles to sleep. His mother has taken to lying on the floor beside his bed at night-time, sleeping in snatches during those brief windows when Arthur's body is too exhausted even to wheeze and falter. The pair are in the second bedroom of a two-bedroom flat in Wimbledon – the first family home. Not a grand place by any means. (Henry may well be descended from aristocrats, but the aristocrats he's descended from weren't exactly frugal.) Winnie doesn't know that she is carrying her second child. Her situation on the floor, curled and alert, recalls in an odd way an occasion in Florence when she was eighteen or so. She went with a friend called Ellen – you may remember – who was a large girl with a bosom whose reputation preceded it. Ellen was soaking in the tub one evening when Winnie popped her head in to enquire about the Italian word for butterfly. The sight of Ellen's bosom in the bath brought Winnie to her knees, and then to the floor, where she lay for some minutes laughing like a child – like the child she was. Winnie thinks of Ellen now, of where she might be, of where she mightn't. She manages to smile, and notices that her son has fallen asleep. In six hours Arthur will have a fit that will last for two hours. He will be driven to Great Ormond Street Hospital and will be mistakenly diagnosed with epilepsy. But for now he sleeps, and so, gratefully, does his mother.*

# 8

## Things are never past their best; they just become best at something else

**1 May.** Winnie's diary entry for today reads: 'Ben bunked off!' By bunked off she means got home at 7.30pm, a few hours later than planned. I was delayed because a friend was having a bit of an emotional crisis in the wake of their partner's departure to Bulgaria. I met Ali at Waterloo and we sat and talked for some time. I phoned Winnie to let her know I was going to be late for dinner – about an hour or so – and told her not to wait for me, to get stuck in whenever she wanted and so on. 'Stuck into what?' she said. 'Whatever you fancy,' I said. 'Oh it's like that is it?' she said.

When I got home she was in what you might call a huff. Without much of a run-up, she launched into a stream of consciousness about how the whole thing was very irritating and how she had a mind to ground me for a fortnight. It amounted to a rollicking for being home an hour late for dinner. But – surprise, surprise – it turns out my lateness was merely the straw that broke the camel's back. She'd had a testing day. She couldn't start the car. The lock on the front door got jammed. She put a load of washing out and it rained. Every egg in the house was a floater. And she couldn't find the phone for several hours. Fair to say that her nose was well and truly out of joint even before I phoned up and tugged it even further to one side.

Given the above, I can understand why she reacted as

she did. But at the time I hadn't been given the above, and so when I got home and Winnie started letting rip I had to really bite my tongue. And I'm glad I did, because by the end of dinner she was laughing and waxing lyrical about what Kuba had done with the raspberry patch. And by the end of the washing up, she was quietly admitting that what had really got under her skin was simply the prospect of eating alone, of *being* alone. Sensing a truce, I took the opportunity to ask if she'd consider drawing a line through today's diary entry. 'I'd be happy to draw a line *under* it, if you like?'

**2 May.** The recent rain has moved things along a fair bit in the garden and so doing has extended my ignorance. When I ask Winnie if she can tell me something about the new flowers, her face lights up. 'I'd be delighted to!' she says. (Odd what questions make people happy. If we knew what they were, would we ask them all the time?) The flower I was most intrigued by turns out to be a tulip. It's red but the edge of its petals are white and jagged, almost serrated. We agree that it's funny how something so sweet can also appear so menacing. She whips out her secateurs and cuts me off one. 'I shall miss this garden,' she says, stepping into the kitchen. 'You might never have to,' I say.

**4 May.** At breakfast, I direct Winnie's attention to a NIB (news in brief) concerning a lady who died after a bum enlargement went wrong. She doesn't know what to say. A rare occurrence. Then I show her how to send voice notes through a popular social media application. We send one to Abigail, who sends a reply immediately. 'Lovely to hear that Granny is learning how to send voice notes. This is excellent news. I look forward to hearing from you more, Granny.' Then she sends a voice note to Stewart, explaining how Arthur can now come over and visit without having to isolate on his return, and asking whether she's paying council tax by direct debit. Then I set her a challenge. To send Victoria a voice note and then tell me what the temperature in Nairobi is. She looks at me as if I've asked her to switch the light off with her big toe.

**5 May.** *Gardeners' World.* Some of the horticultural adages are appealing. 'Head in the sun, feet in the shade.' That's what they say about clematis, but it's not a bad tip for human folk either. Winnie has neither head nor feet in the shade as it stands. Instead, she's fallen asleep drinking a cup of tea. Not easy to do that. I take the tea off her before it spills. The robbery causes her to stir during a piece on interplanting and reclaim her tea while giving me a look that would deter slugs.

**8 May.** She's in the kitchen stewing apricots, one eye on the paper, one eye on the television, no eye on the apricots.

'Morning, Winnie.'

'Bald men are more affected by coronavirus.'

'Is that so?'

'Better not tell the postman. He won't sleep at night. He'll start going around in a wig. I'm afraid if you want toast it's rye bread only. I'm rationing the granary.'

Then she reads an advert in the paper: "'We invite you to slow down the signs of ageing.' Well thank you very much, Boots.'

I suggest she might want to go down to Boots and ask if they have anything to *speed up* the signs of ageing, and perhaps point out while she's down there that ageing isn't as repulsive and tragic as they seem to think. 'I would,' she says, 'but I tend to think that ageing is rather tragic, and in any case my bus pass is currently spinning around the washing machine, and you've more chance of getting me on a charabanc to Blackpool than paying what they charge for parking down there.'[1]

I make myself a cup of tea and then make a start on a book by a shepherd. I've not read the first page (about the noun *heft*, meaning something tied by choice/tradition to a particular piece of land) before Winnie has sent me up the shop for potatoes that 'fluff well'. Good job one of us isn't as hefted as the other, I can't help but feel, walking to Tesco. On my

---

[1] We're rarely encouraged to be proud of our age, or at least content with it, at peace with it, as we're encouraged to be proud of other elements of our identity. It's as if the consensus remains, 'Old is bad and must therefore be defied and dodged and delayed at all costs.' If you grow up receiving such messages, and thinking such things about elderliness, what are you likely to think of yourself when you reach the latter chapters of your life? At best you might be uneasy. At worst you might hate yourself. Imagine if the situation was reversed and all the messaging, instead of denigrating old age, strove to highlight the virtues of seniority. Why, you might end up with the ripest section of society feeling valued and involved, rather than rotten and beside the point. Just a thought.

return, for the fun of it, I share with Winnie my thoughts about irritation. 'I don't get irritated often, Winnie. But when I do, it's always because I'm in conflict. It's always when my desire to do one thing is challenged by an obligation to do something else. My desire might well be modest (to read), and the obligation might well be fair and reasonable (to source some potatoes that fluff well), but nonetheless the result of the desire-obligation conflict is usually irritation. One way to avoid irritation, therefore, is to never desire anything.' To this Winnie says, 'In what are we going to poach the haddock?'

**9 May.** She takes a cautious approach to toasting bread. She does it by degrees, nervous of burning it. But the trouble is, by popping it up and down five times to check on its progress, she provides herself with plenty of opportunities to forget about the toast entirely and burn it to a crisp. Her cautious approach to toasting, I fancy, actually has the unintended consequence of making it more likely she'll burn her break-fast. Is there a life lesson in this, I wonder?[2]

Something about the sight of Winnie treating her toast in this way prompts me to invite her to Derby. I've got a gig there at the end of the month and will be going up with Megan by coach and staying in a hotel. Frankly, I didn't think Winnie would be interested in the slightest, but she appears to be taking the idea quite seriously.

'I used to do that sort of thing a lot,' she says.

'And do you fancy doing that sort of thing again?'

---

[2] No, there isn't.

'I do, but – in Derby?'

'There's some nice paintings in Derby.'

'But what would Megan think?'

'Oh she wouldn't mind.'[3]

**10 May.** Winnie's on the phone to Rebecca and I swear her tone is kinder and softer than normal. Her words aren't much different, but the tone is. She's saying things about cow parsley and compost, but the subtext is: you're my daughter, and you're dear to me. That's what I hear anyway. Then she shouts, 'There's a goldfish in the bird bath!' She quickly spots her mistake (it's a goldfinch), and laughs loudly and at length. There's joy in that laughter. Then she hangs up on Rebecca unceremoniously and asks me to fill up one of the bird feeders. 'Not both?' 'No. Just one. Mustn't give them ideas.'

**11 May.** I do dinner earlier than normal, at Winnie's behest. I fashion a kedgeree with Winnie breathing down my neck rather than relaxing as she said she was going to do. It's not often you get wound up with someone for not sitting down with a cup of tea and reading their book. It's not that I prefer cooking alone, but rather that she seems to get as worked up watching me cook as she would cooking herself. As much as I'm fond of Winnie, I don't need her on my shoulder counting my peas (to coin a phrase). Whilst monitoring my

---

[3] That wasn't entirely accurate. Megan had been looking forward to a romantic weekend away, and worried that Winnie coming along might alter the quality of the occasion. She didn't find it funny when I suggested we could economise by all sharing a room.

performance, she has one and a half bits of marmalade on toast. When I put dinner on the table at 6.30, as per her request, she takes one look at it and then goes into the garden, where she remains for about half an hour. At several moments during her absence, I imagine putting Winnie's dinner in various places where she wouldn't expect to find it. By the time she reappears, I've sufficiently reordered my thoughts and deflected my dark imaginings to ask, 'Are you alright, Winnie? Are you not hungry?' She looks at me and then at her dinner. 'I am sorry,' she says, her hand on my shoulder, 'but a table really must have flowers.' She samples the kedgeree on her feet, says that it 'cannot boast of being flavoursome', then adds mango chutney and yoghurt until the dish is all but unrecognisable. Winsome Delores Lovelock Carter: incorrigible.

The news. Government anxiety regarding the potentially more transmissible Indian variant is followed by a piece about fresh conflict between Israel and Palestine. 'You can understand their frustration,' says Winnie. 'I'm not sure I'd want someone coming onto my patch and bossing me around, no matter their excuse.' Saying goodnight, Winnie calls me sweetheart, and I'm left with the curious feeling that perhaps she should watch footage of the Israel-Palestine conflict more often, if one of the outcomes is affection.

**14 May.** Breakfast. A bright day. The front page carries news of cases doubling in a week and the threat of fresh lockdowns. I turn to the crossword.

THINGS ARE NEVER PAST THEIR BEST

'Mail sack, seven letters,' I say.

'Scrotum,' she says.

'Household tool, again seven letters. Utensil?'

'Husband,' she says.

I proceed privately until *Desert Island Discs* comes on. The guest is Brian Greene, theoretical physicist and asker of big questions. At the end of the programme, I ask Winnie why she thinks we're here.

'Because Henry managed to knock the previous owner down ten percent.'

'No but seriously.'

'Seriously?'

'Yes.'

'Why are we here?'

'Yes.'

She thinks about it. For a long time. A *surprisingly* long time. And then says, 'Are there speed cameras on Worple Road, do you think?'

I don't like it when I'm on my way out and realise she's feeling low or bothered. Like now, for example. I try and work out what's got her down. I reckon it's the afternoon ahead of her. The prospect of it. I reckon it appears long and empty. I would invite her with me but I'm going to get a tattoo. When I tell her to use the afternoon to enjoy herself, she looks at me sceptically, as if I've just advised her to nip up to the shop in the buff. She looks out at the garden, then to the heavy clouds, and then back at me. 'But how?' she says.

When I get back, she's in her bathroom cleaning Arthur's razor. 'I've practically been at it since you left,' she says. 'Just finished, I'm pleased to say. Some bits were tremendously tricky. Had the good idea to go at them with an electric toothbrush.' Given this information, my first thought is: *whose toothbrush?*

**15 May.** We go to the farmers' market. She buys some goose eggs and then considers a young dahlia. The florist shows Winnie a picture on his phone of the plant in full bloom. Winnie takes the phone from the man, peruses the picture, says some polite things, peruses some more pictures (of the man's children swimming in Portugal, for example), and then pockets the phone. The florist is almost too polite to ask for it back. By the time he does, the phone's been in Winnie's pocket for about ten seconds and she's now of the opinion it's hers. As a result, she's not at all sure about giving it back. It occurs to me that women such as Winnie could, if they wanted, be prolific petty criminals. The florist says the dahlia needs a bit of support but will flower time and time again. She doesn't buy it.

**16 May.** She passes me the marmalade. By way of thanks, I tell her I'm going to Wakefield on Saturday. She asks where that is and I say, 'Near Leeds.' She looks at me, then out the window, then back at me, then back out the window, then back at me, and says, 'The Middle East?' She does another round of toast while paraphrasing an article about Barbara Hepworth. 'Everyone thought she was an awful mother.

THINGS ARE NEVER PAST THEIR BEST

But now they've got hold of some letters and basically they make clear that raising triplets on next to no money and practically alone while also trying to answer one's vocational calling and chip away at a phallocentric institution wasn't, simply put, always terrifically easy. Are you having another slice?'

She's discovered an old leek at the back of the cupboard. God knows how long it's been there. She's adamant it's a leek, but to be honest I'm not sure. Could be anything. I tell her to bin it. She tells me that things are never past their best, they just become best at something else, which is a sweet maxim but hardly applicable to a six-month-old leek.

**17 May.** A quiet dance as we move around the floor to boil the kettle, reach the muesli, fetch a teaspoon, load the toaster, throw out crumbs and so on. The silence doesn't signify anything – not animosity, not awkwardness. It's the comfortable type one hears about. Normally she'd vocalise her offer of toast, but this morning she just points to the toaster (in part because her mouth's full). The silence is broken when a pigeon flies into the kitchen window.

I'm interviewed by Rose Hartson for *Positive News*, who is keen to celebrate intergenerational home sharing in no more than 500 words. I say some positive things about Winnie (that she's cheerful, entertaining, informative, and so on), then pass the phone over and make myself scarce. Well, not completely scarce. I sit at the bottom of the stairs and eavesdrop.

I immediately wish I hadn't because Winnie reviews me as though I were a bowl of pasta. Asked what motivated her to get me in as a lodger, she says that I was delivered to her on a plate. Asked what she likes about me, she draws a resounding blank. Asked what she's learned from me, she prevaricates. With some skill, Rose manages to coax a morsel of positive news out of Winnie: she gets her to say that I'm good for security and know 'how to break into the internet'. Momentarily, sat at the bottom of the stairs, I feel really quite sad. I boil the kettle, make a pot of tea, listen to Winnie tell Rose at some length about the challenges of having a large garden. She hangs up. I go through with the tea.

'Did it go alright, Winnie?'

'I don't think I enlightened her ever so much.'

'No?'

'I said we respect each other's space and that's the most important thing.'

'So you didn't tell her I sometimes try to get into bed with you?'

She laughs. I offer her a cup.

I take advantage of my newly restored freedom to go to the cinema. The film is called *Nomadland*. After months of lockdown, I was drawn to its premise. I buy my ticket, my popcorn, take my seat in row W, and there wonder (later than I might have done) how exactly I'm going to eat popcorn with a mask on. The lights go up. A member of staff enters. They make an announcement: the film is cancelled; it was sent to a different cinema by mistake and they've just realised. So no *Nomadland* for me therefore. I eat my pop-corn outside the cinema under my umbrella. I recognise the strange feeling of being knocked off course. That feeling you get when you thought you were going to be doing something and then aren't. I thought I was going to be occupied and diverted for two hours, and the abrupt cancellation of that plan is jolting, disorienting and slightly saddening. I imagine the feeling scaled up. I imagine it multiplied by a hundred. How must it feel for your husband and best friend of 60 years to be alive one moment and then not? How profoundly and lastingly jolting and disorienting and saddening must that be? I imagine Winnie being turned away from the cinema, kicked out of screen 1, eating popcorn sadly under an umbrella, and not knowing what to do.

I go to a place where the filter coffee is a pound. Sit in the window and watch a different screen: station, road, tree, bus, people, pigeons. It is a typical urban scene. No part of it is emotive and nor is the sum. And then something happens of interest. A woman of late years walks left to right across the screen. She spots someone she knows, potentially her husband, on the other side of the road, going in the other direction. She stops. Calls out to him. But she's wearing a mask and the traffic is haring past, and so he doesn't hear. She turns on her heel, starts going in his direction, then stops and turns again and continues the way she was going, only faster, towards the crossing point. She'll have to lose more ground, she realises, before she can make any up. She waits impatiently to cross, then does so, then walks from right to left across the screen as fast as she can, until she disappears. I half expect to see her husband go by on this side of the road in the opposite direction of his wife, but instead, about five minutes later, I see the pair of them, holding hands, on the other side of the road, heading towards the station.

18 May. It says in the paper that the World Health Organization is warning that 800,000 deaths a year are caused by *overworking*. Shouldn't we be more aware of that? More worried about that? More active in preventing that? Winnie tells me to calm down. Says I don't need to worry about dying of that in the slightest.

She's locked me out. I was in the garden and she's locked the back door. I sit on the step and read the sport pages. Half an hour later, the door opens behind me. She's laughing her head off. 'The next time I offend you, Winnie, just jot down a note and leave it on the kitchen table, OK? No need to lock me outside.' She carries on laughing for a good twenty seconds, and I think: *See? You could have mentioned that yesterday. You could have said, 'Yeah it's really nice living with Ben. I get to lock him out and then laugh my head off.'*

I drive us to the Škoda garage. To get her wing mirror sorted. She points out a restaurant called The Kindness where she ate with Henry once but only once because the food was lousy. She tells me to slow down when she realises we're in front of a taxi. 'One of life's little pleasures,' she explains.

**21 May.** She's in the garden, in the rain, trying to plant some yellow daisies in what she's previously referred to as 'inauspicious soil'. I go out with an umbrella, hold it over her, as a caddy might shelter a golfer lining up a putt during a downpour. There's a robin, watching, from the belly of a fir.

I got a big laugh out of her just then. Biggest yet, I'd say. I told her I went to buy some clothes this afternoon for my mate's twins. I picked out a couple of T-shirts (size twelve months) and took them up to the counter, where I explained to the young cashier that I was a bit worried the garments wouldn't fit me. The cashier didn't blink, simply said matter-of-factly that if they didn't fit me then I could bring them back so long as I kept the receipt. When Winnie stops laughing she says quite seriously that the cashier might have been a robot.

We're watching *Later with Jools Holland*. They're showing bits from previous shows. Lou Reed comes on, does a lovely version of 'Perfect Day'. Winnie watches politely for a couple of minutes, takes in the subtitles, and then announces, 'I can't say the rhymes are very good.'

**22 May.** Off to Wakefield to see a friend (Russell) and his new twins (Evelyn and Zachary). The mother (Rachel) is elsewhere for the day (searching for scraps of her sanity, etc), so it's just the pair of us, which means one each really. Three-hour cycles of milk, wind, gobbledegook, sleep – and that's just me and Russ. Lovely moment when Russell soothes

Evelyn with a really quite impressive rendition of 'Ain't No Mountain High Enough'. Less lovely moment when Zachary, during a change, wees in my face. Awful Chinese takeaway, Eurovision on the telly, and then back to the hotel around 10. At which point Winnie calls.

'Hello, Winnie.'

'It could be you up there waving your hair around.'

I do that thing where you take the phone away from your ear and look at it disbelievingly. '*What?*'

'You could be one of the Danish ones, waving it all about.'

'Are you alright, Winnie?'

'Though I don't suppose you'd want to climb into one of those pink leotards.'

'What are you watching, Winnie?'

'Eurovision.'

'Right. I'm with you. I watched some of that too.'

'Where are you anyway? Are you in?'

'I'm in Wakefield, Winnie.'

'So you are. Silly me. I'm afraid she's going a bit potty, the poor girl. Can you credit some of the *hairstyles*? And I don't fancy Israel's chances if I'm candid.'

**23 May.** I unload some pistachio nuts and marinated artichokes onto the kitchen table. She quickly samples both, despite not having fond memories of either. 'The nuts remind me of going round after parties picking shells off the floor, and the artichokes remind me of artichoke soup, which made Henry and I fart, if you don't mind me putting it like that. We were practically in sync.' It makes me smile. Not the thought or image of Winnie and Henry farting in sync, but the way just about everything carries a connection for Winnie, even pistachios and artichokes. I'm confident I could have put just about anything on the table this evening – peanut butter, fluoride toothpaste, a pair of nail clippers – and something would have been stirred. 'Ah, now, I'm afraid I haven't been near lemon curd since I was forced to eat an entire jar against the clock.' As one goes through life, associations gather and amass at the back of our minds, on the tips of our tongues, where they lie snug and pointless and dormant for days or years until summoned forth by the sudden appearance of some artichokes on the kitchen table. More time, more memories. Life gets thicker as it goes on. It gains texture, weight, *matter*. And by gaining matter, it matters more. I look forward to the occasion, many years from now, when somebody presents a jar of homemade marmalade and I'm prompted to recall the time I lived with a woman who pleased and amused and inspired and baffled and angered in equal measure. When I lived with Winnie Carter.

**24 May.** Winnie's on her feet, toast in hand, leaning over the news. She points to a picture of a young Bob Dylan. 'I'm intrigued by this picture of Bob Dylan. He looks like one of Henry's cousins who was a lesbian.' She phones the care home to plead for Arthur's release. She leaves a message. 'Winnie Carter here. I'd like to take Arthur *out of jail*. If I may. I'd like to *bring him home*.' (You can somehow hear her underlining certain things.) Someone phones back and says, quite kindly, that, far from being in jail, Arthur can come and go as he pleases – subject to Winnie testing negative.

There's a downpour the second Arthur steps out of the care home. Not ideal when you're uneasy on your feet and use a wheelie. He's in a good mood – chatty. Tells me the road we're on meanders the way it does because it was designed with cows in mind. When we get home, and make our way through to the kitchen, he asks, 'Is there a cup of tea somewhere?' A chip off the old block, this one. A telling sideways stab at directness. Winnie is less worried about tea and more worried about where she put what was left of yesterday's fish pie. She's practically having a panic attack. And she's practically having a panic attack because it's Arthur who stands to suffer if the pie can't be located. If it were anyone else on the brink of going without fish pie her disquiet would be far less acute. In the event, I find the pie in the back kitchen and immediately crack on with getting a chunk of it ready, thinking that if I get on with lunch then Winnie can focus on Arthur. On the one other occasion Arthur was over (after a hospital visit a few months ago), Winnie spent most of the time preparing a four-course lunch for him, rather than sitting down and having a chat with the lad. Of course, Winnie can do what the hell she wants. Though I can't help but think it's a shame if she spends his visits with eleven pots on the go and the extractor fan on full blast.

I tell Winnie that I'm off to the theatre and ask if she wants to come. Her answer, somewhat surprisingly, is yes. She

THINGS ARE NEVER PAST THEIR BEST

puts on new shoes for the occasion – black sneakers, bought two years ago, hitherto unfilled. We get to the theatre early so go to the pub next door, where we share a fancy scotch egg (lamb, rhubarb and chervil) and half a bottle of white wine. She says she feels like she's getting back to normal. Says there were a couple of moments over the last year when she genuinely thought about going mad before deciding against it. The drama – when it comes – is two short plays by Bernard Shaw (an up and coming Irish writer). Both feature couples acting badly. Winnie drops off early, has a power nap, then attends the remainder keenly and laughs more than anyone else, especially when one character declaims that satisfaction is death. When it's over and we stand to leave, I see that our cushions are decorated with motivational statements. Mine says: 'Aspire, but don't forget to be.' 'Be what?' says Winnie. 'Just *be*,' I say. She looks at me and the cushion as if we were mad. When we get home, the first thing she does is take off her new shoes and put the kettle on. The second thing she does is phone Rebecca to tell her that Kuba is coming tomorrow to trim the wisteria back.

**25 May.** Front page of the paper shows a family on a Spanish beach ignoring the government's request for Britons not to travel to Spain. 'So that's what people are desperate for,' she says. 'To do things on their phone in front of a vast ocean under an umbrella.' She looks closer at the picture. 'See. He's got one. And she's on hers. And even this chap having a paddle is on his phone. Wouldn't catch me on a beach. In

Spain or otherwise. I've loathed sand ever since I ate some to see what it tasted like.'

I notice a photo album under a lamp in the sitting room. It's a small album, just twenty pictures or so. I ask Winnie if she'll throw some light on them. At first she says she can't because she's dipping the silver, but eventually she relents and comes and stands at my shoulder. There's a black and white picture of Stewart as a baby, mouth agape. Arthur as a toddler in *very* baggy underpants. Rebecca as a baby in a thick woollen jumper. Winnie outside a hotel in Devon wearing what seems to be a tablecloth. Arthur on the same holiday, sat on a rock, a sheer cliff face behind him, knees together and feet apart, a triangular effect mirrored by the open book in his lap. Henry alongside the River Thames, frozen in time but presumably in the process of running the London marathon. A family scene around the dining table, Arthur with a moustache you could sweep a chimney with, Winnie in red dress and apron, Henry in shirt and tie, Stewart with two drinks on the go and looking *beyond* bored. Arthur stood in a carpark wearing arguably the worst pullover ever fabricated. Henry and Winnie skiing. ('Cross-country skiing,' clarifies Winnie. 'Which is much better. Harder to fall over going uphill.') Stewart upon graduating, outside a soot-blackened Bristol building, his expression (to my eye) a combination of confidence and nonchalance and worldly indifference. Stewart on a gondola in Venice, his expression (to my eye) a combination of confidence and nonchalance and worldly indifference. Henry in a restaurant, eyes closed, laughing over his chicken. Rebecca in the sitting room of this house, packing or unpacking, Winnie at her side looking like a fearful assistant. Henry in a chair that's too small for him, holding an empty champagne glass with both hands, a framed portrait of his father in uniform on the windowsill behind. And last but not least a group shot on the terrace, on the occasion of somebody's birthday, Winnie using a hand as a visor, Arthur raising his glass, Henry smiling and leaning back in his chair, Rebecca unwrapping a present with a bowl of cereal in her lap, Stewart laughing at something said or imagined. Winnie (here, now) takes the final photo from me. Examines it closely. Says, 'Look at the state of that flowerbed. Not good news at all.'

**29 May.** She's nervous about our scheduled city break to Derby. About going. About 'abandoning' Arthur. About the recycling. About hotels *per se* and about the hotel I've picked in particular. About the bank holiday traffic. About the fact that Megan is no longer coming and what that means about our relationship. About being 150 miles from her home, her roof, her garden, her patch. I give her the chance to pull out. Say I'm happy to go alone. She puts a piece of bread in the toaster and says, 'Oh let's go. What's the worst that can happen?' I tell her we could be involved in a fatal accident and the house could get stolen.

**30 May.** 11.15. Twenty minutes after she said she was just coming and I said I would wait in the car, I find her in the kitchen stewing fruit. She ends up bringing three coats on the hottest day of the year.

11.30. At first she's restless – lots of shouted instructions, largely unhelpful – but by the time we reach the North Circular she seems happy to be on the road. For someone so entrenched and rooted and domiciled, she's astonishingly curious about what's beyond the pale. She enjoys the sight of a seagull miles inland, pecking at something speculatively outside Brentford.

12.00. We hit heavy traffic a couple of miles shy of the M1. Searing heat outside. You could cook an egg on the hard shoulder. Winnie wonders if she 'went to toilet enough before we left'.

1.20. We've hardly moved for an hour. Silence in the car except my huffing and the aircon. Winnie quite content, ogling the mise en scène, all lit up by a thick, unexpected sun. She's at ease, perhaps, because she's accepted that there's absolutely *nothing* she can do.

2.20. Two motorbikes collided a few hundred metres ahead. The news is delivered by a lorry driver who's going up and down the aisles, playing the town crier. Winnie has a decent chat with him, says she doesn't expect his wife minds him being away a lot.

2.40. Motorised purgatory.
  'I think we're going to miss the event, Winnie.'
  'That woman's got out of the car and is walking the dog.'
  'I need the loo.'

THINGS ARE NEVER PAST THEIR BEST

'I was wondering who'd need it first.'

'What a thing to wonder, Winnie.'

3.15. I'm due on stage in less than two hours. I phone one of the organisers of the book festival to let them know it's unlikely I'll make it. 'I am sorry, Ben,' Winnie says, tapping my arm consolingly.

3.40. We've inched forward to a junction, where we're turned around by the police. We've got a clear road ahead of us for a couple of minutes and then – crunch: back in a jam. 'A case of oven to the frying pan,' she says. 'Yeah. And what comes after the frying pan?' 'Probably another oven.'

5.00. I pull over the first chance I get – a parade of shops in Ealing, west London. We stretch our legs, use the loo in a Turkish restaurant. I'm tempted to cut our losses and go home.

6.00. Motorway services, somewhere on the M1. I decided we might as well have a night in Derby – given the effort we'd invested so far. And I worried that if the adventure was aborted Winnie would never attempt to leave London again.

6.30. On the outskirts of Nottingham she says, 'Nottingham? I think we're off course.'

'No. Nottingham's near Derby.'

'Derby? Are we going to Derby?'

*WTF?*

8.00. Park in a multi-storey carpark, walk to the hotel. Pass a statue of Florence Nightingale, who was a local girl. Apparently she lived to 90. When I suggest that living to 90 back then was a decent effort, Winnie says, 'Well, she knew how to look after herself.'

8.30. She's not happy with the hotel. Not one bit. Last time she stayed in a hotel was the night before she sailed to America in 1952. On that occasion, when she reached the characterful Regency hotel in Southampton she was carried from her car to her room on a sedan made of tulips and grapes. The Premier Inn chain – somewhat of a misnomer – is the short-back-and-sides of the hotel world. You're lucky if you get carpet, to say nothing of a red one. And she's not happy with her key card. She wants a proper key. An old-fashioned key. Does not trust a plastic card to keep a draught out, let alone an assailant. She says that somebody's *bound* to come in during the night – 'on at least one occasion'. When I suggest that it's very unlikely that there's somebody in Derby harbouring an earnest and irresistible desire to explore the interior of Winnie Carter's hotel room, she simply looks at me and says, 'You know nothing of mankind.'

9.15. She's not exactly hungry but reckons we should go and get some supper, if only to escape the hotel. I suggest a Wetherspoon pub for a bit of culture, but Winnie, with uncharacteristic decisiveness, walks straight into a branch of Pizza Express.

10.00. During her second glass of Pinot Grigio, she enjoys the sight of a young woman sauntering past with 'more bottom than she can possibly have use for'. When it comes to pudding, Winnie orders a chocolate mousse, eats two thirds of it, then sends the rest back on account of it being too rich. It's taken off the bill.

10.30. Back to the hotel. Before I leave her to it, I remind her that I'm just next door and that she can give me a shout or a knock at any time, and that in any case I intend to stand guard outside her door and fend off whosoever turns up with a view to relieving Winnie of her valuables. 'You are sweet, Ben,' she says, then shuts the door in my face.

**31 May**. 7.15. A phone call. 'Ben. Winnie. I'm trapped in my room.'

7.20. She's having issues with the handle. I ask her to slide her key under the door. 'You want me to get on the floor?'

7.25. When I open the door, Winnie seems surprised to see me. She says she was starting to panic. Says she tried to contact reception. Shows me all the buttons she pressed, including 'HOME'. Turns out she was trying to organise her escape via the remote control.

8.30. We go to a café for breakfast. It's fair to say Winnie has something to say about the experience. The furniture is too low. The bread is too thin. The marmalade is too sweet.

Connecting her complaints is that none of this is *hers*, that none of this is *home*. We watch the people passing outside. 'She hasn't been home since last night,' says Winnie. 'And nor has she. And nor has she. I suppose there can't be much else to do in Derby.'

9.15. We go for a walk around town. I point out that the taxis are yellow and the benches are blue. Winnie isn't exactly impressed with my observations. 'And that's what travel writing amounts to is it? "The taxis were yellow and the benches were blue!" If the bar's that low, I might chance my arm.'

9.45. We find the art gallery but it's closed, so we have to enjoy the one or two paintings of Joseph Wright we can see through the windows.

'Local, was he?' I say.

'He was called Joseph Wright *of Derby*,' she says.

'And what was he known for? Artistically I mean.'

'Chiaroscuro.'

'Is that a marinade?'

'The dramatic use of darkness and light – you great twit.'

10.00. We pop into a branch of Waterstones. When Winnie says quite loudly that they had at least one copy of *Mein Kampf* at the cottage in Dartmoor, I pretend I'm not with her. Elsewhere in the shop, she gives a decent amount of time to Monty Don's latest book ('Now is he slightly gay, do you think?'), but very little to *The Art of Rest*, which I hand to her goadingly. 'I don't need to be told to lie in a hot bath,' she says, handing the book back to me. 'That never solved a thing.'

12.00. We're on our way home. Winnie is absorbed in the road atlas, trying to extract from the chaos of lines and colours and numbers a calming sense of direction. She's been searching for the M25, the bit that meets the M1. 'It's simply not *there*,' she concludes outside St Albans. I have some uncharitable thoughts about Winnie's map reading ability.[4]

1.00. Near Woking, she tells me that when she cleared out her brother's flat after his death, she was pleased to discover evidence of a bachelor lifestyle.

'What do you mean by evidence?'

'I mean equipment.'

'What do you mean by equipment?'

'I mean caps.'

'Caps?'

'You know, for collecting the results.'

'Sorry, what?'

She attempts to demonstrate what she's getting at. It's quickly obvious she means condoms.

1.30. 'Here!' she cries. 'Turn off here!' I turn off here and it turns out I should've turned off there. For the first time since setting off yesterday morning we are indisputably lost. Is it

---

[4] It's little wonder she couldn't find it. It wasn't built by 1973, when the road atlas was published.

meaningful that it's not until we're all but home that we lose our way? Probably not.

1.50. The house smells dusty. A period away resets the senses – you can smell what a stranger smells. She goes out to the garden, checks on the daisies, tidies up some weeds, and then sets about watering the whole thing. I lie on the lawn, in a late and declining patch of sun, and half read a magazine supplement. She spots me. Sprawled on the grass. No doubt thinks about giving me a dosing. She says, 'Can you imagine a better garden?'

3.20. Winnie's still in the garden. She must have done nearly two hours' gardening without a break, which is unprecedented. And there's been an appreciable uptick in her mood. Perhaps one good thing about going somewhere is that you get to come back.

4.00. She calls Arthur and leaves a meandering message about how much she disliked Derby. Then she does the same for Stewart, and then she does the same for Rebecca – long happy messages for each, bemoaning middle England. Clearly for some people gaining cause for complaint is a genuinely uplifting experience. She hangs up the phone then asks which of us is going to 'sashay to the shop for milk', and when she says 'sashay' she tries, without a fantastic amount of success, to approximate somebody sashaying.

# 1973

*The British Prime Minister is inspiring no confidence in Winnie Carter whatsoever. And don't get her started on the trade unions. It's because of the trade unions that Winnie has to light candles at dusk each evening. Dinner by candlelight, she's told herself more than once, is supposed to be romantic, whereas this is just ever so slightly danger- ous. (She's stockpiled 400 candles in any case, because they're already proving hard to come by – even in broad daylight.) Her mood on this particular evening is also dim. When Stewart feeds the dog a hand- ful of peas under the table, she reprimands him with uncharacteristic gruffness (Stewart, not the dog). And yet when Arthur performs a simi- lar trick, she merely ruffles his hair and says sweetly that he oughtn't pay his brother the respect of imitation. In about five minutes, Henry will phone to say he's working late, and that he crossed paths with the Labour leader today and it wasn't as unpleasant as he'd assumed it would be. Winnie can't match Henry's light-hearted air, can't meet his levity with some of her own. It's been a long day. Frankly, it's been a long week. And if you really want to know, it's been a long month, a long time. She asks Rebecca if she'd be a good girl and run Arthur a bath, but Rebecca isn't listening. She's transfixed by a robin on the terrace. Rebecca knows it's rare to see them at night-time.*

# 9

## What stops us saying to people we love that we love them?

1 June. I go to the pond. Sit on my regular bench. Almost cliché summer scene – its splendour more pronounced after six weeks of rain. A patch of the pond is sparkling white: sunlight bursting into a billion bits upon impact. The atmosphere is the opposite of valedictory. Everything seems at the start of something. A schoolboy swaggering along swigging a drink. Someone cycling in a suit – off to a wedding perhaps. But the mood won't last. Give us a week of such weather and the earth will be turning arid and the mood newly tinged with complaint. But for now it feels close to ideal – speaking for myself. This bench beneath the tree – I've not counted its shade a virtue before. I suppose virtues are conditional, revealing themselves in certain scenarios.

I go to Megan's. It's the first time I've seen her since her grandad died. There's a framed picture of Dave when he was in his twenties. For some reason, I touch the picture with the back of a forefinger. The gesture feels, I guess, more tender. Megan says it was her grandad's face she liked the most. I say it was his left leg I preferred. She smiles. She's coping. She's not coping. She watches episodes of *Call the Midwife*. I read Samuel Pepys' diary. Apparently Sam had a genius for happiness, which must have been a nice thing to have.

In bed, we lie closer for longer. No two experiences of grief are the same: a recurring thought before sleep.

**2 June.** A voicemail. 'Ben. Winnie. Have you moved house?' Megan wants me to stay longer. I say I need to get back for Winnie. She doesn't look convinced. 'But I can stay for a few more hours?' I say. She says, 'If you're going to leave then leave.'

When I get home, Winnie is dressed for the Bronx. Baggy jeans, headscarf, chunky sneakers, bling, a loose T-shirt under a puffer waistcoat. She greets me with a bulletin direct from her prefrontal cortex regarding Arthur's benefits. Then she asks if I'm alright. She asks because I've not responded to her bulletin, or because my eyes are telling her something. I remind her I've been with Megan because she lost her grandad. 'Ah, yes. How is she?'

I do an impromptu barbecue. She thinks it's a bit of a shame doing it for two people but isn't going to stand in my way. It's nice sitting outside. The cooing of a pigeon. The swooping of parakeets and magpies – their undulant paths. Winnie says she always fancied a stint as a bird. 'Just a stint?' I say. 'Well someone's got to keep this house in order,' she says. (So even in her dreams there's housework to be done ...) I ask what spice she put in the salad dressing. It's on the edge of her tongue. She's searching for the word. But it's no good. She can't find it. And so she stands, in anger almost, and goes to the kitchen, to the spice cupboard presumably, and then returns saying cayenne pepper again and again until the words are made senseless by repetition. Then there's silence. And then she says the minted lamb kebabs taste of shower gel.

**4 June.** Breakfast. She draws my attention to a neologism in the paper.

'Feelgood,' she says.

'What about it?'

'One word.'

'Yeah …'

'Now just what is that about?'

'It's an adjective.'

'I'm seeing it everywhere. Feelgood films. Feelgood trousers. Feelgood loo roll.'

'Loo roll?'

'And I wonder how far it will go. When I expire, will my children plump for a feelgood funeral?'

**5 June.** Arthur has a hospital appointment at 1. We're picking him up at 12.30, so need to be at the care home at 12 in order to be tested for the virus. At 11.15 she announces – more or less going out the door – that she's off to the farmers' market for eggs. There's no way she'll be back in half an hour – no way. Winnie's sudden departure provides an insight into her mind. The need for fresh eggs is felt to be acute enough to risk Arthur being late for his appointment. But the thing is, it's not the eggs *per se* that Winnie's bothered about, but rather putting a fresh pair of them in front of Arthur. Accordingly, one is forced to reach the conclusion that Winnie can sometimes put providing for Arthur ahead of Arthur in the pecking order, if that makes sense. Anyway, she's back. From the market. Says the following coming through the door, 'Damned cement mixer in the middle of Leopold Road. Try one of these strawberries. What time is it? Yikes. Good aren't they? And the nice girl gave me some chicken sausages for free. She wants an honest opinion – which is bad news for the sausages I think. They look *ghostly*.'

We arrive at the care home. Get tested for Covid-19. I can't say Winnie's doing a good job of swabbing her throat and nose. I offer some encouragement.

'You can go further up than that,' I say.

'Says who?'

'On paper you can go all the way up your nose and out your mouth. I've seen someone do that with a bit of string.'

'Well I don't visit such entertainments.'

Half an hour later, Arthur emerges. I watch him progress slowly to the car, and must say that when the man's on his feet it's not easy to relax – a feeling, I would hazard, that Winnie's more familiar with than any other. I drop them outside the hospital entrance then park up. They're going to be about an hour, so I wander to Tooting High Street to kill some time. Doing so, I pass a leisure centre which is familiar. It comes to me: I played football here on a bright winter's day many moons ago. I couldn't have guessed then that ten years later I'd be dropping a couple of people off at the neighbouring hospital, but so it goes: the afternoons of our futures are largely unknowable. The thought – that we cannot know the ways life will take us – elicits a feeling of nostalgia for a time when the future was just an idea, a feeling of nostalgia for the past *per se*, for the past alone. At root, it is a feeling of shock: that everything in life is uncertain; that all will come to pass. But maybe I'm over-egging the pudding. Maybe the feeling was simply one of curiosity that during the present we cannot know what echoes of the past our future will contain. It's hard to describe a feeling. That's why we use shorthand. I was sad, it felt weird, we were shocked. I don't think I understand one tenth of what I feel, to be honest. How do I feel about Winnie? The answer isn't neat. I care about her. I like her. I respect her. I occasionally want to throw her out the window.

I continue walking. Continue walking until I'm drawn to a Kurdish café. I sit outside to be near the energy of the street. The movement. The heat. The noise. The flow. The scenario is manic and harsh, and yet it retains an uncouth beauty. A pigeon is trying to get up onto the ledge above the café's window. It can't do so because a barrier of spikes has been established to stop this from happening. I'm told the pigeon used to have a nest up there; that the nest was removed; that the barrier was erected; that the pigeon has been trying to return ever since. It's a sorry spectacle. I turn my back on it, return to the hospital, gather my friends. Drive them back the long way so Arthur can see things he hasn't seen for a while. The common looks idyllic: shiny bikes lying on their sides, picnic rugs, various games. Arthur spots someone who cut his hair once many years ago. 'At a very reasonable price, I seem to recall,' says Winnie, her first utterance since Tooting.

*8 June.* I take some photos of the garden. Might make them into a calendar for Winnie's birthday.[1] A butterfly making a meal of a leaf. The frame of the old swing amid longish green grass. The shadow of a young flower against a sunlit brick wall. The house seen from a distance through a thicket of hedge and shrub and flower and tree. A close-up of holly. An outstanding pink rose. Winnie in sunglasses and sandals (and nothing else) watering her borders. Winnie five minutes later looking accusingly at the lip of a flowerbed after almost losing her footing. The various straps and buckles that are currently holding the mulberry tree together. I take half-a-dozen more then go upstairs to consider what I've got. It's the mulberry tree that wins. It's not a beautiful image, but it's suggestive. That's its virtue. It suggests the tree's eventual demise and its knock-on effects. Without the tree, no silkworms. Without silkworms, no silk. I make a note: *Not easy for a photograph to convey consequence.*

Winnie gets back from dinner with Rebecca and the girls. She says they went to the Wiggly Pig. I ask if she means the Giggly Squid. 'It was good fun in any case,' she says. 'The girls went for rosé, which baffled me. Rosé has always struck me as nothing but the outcome of indecision. It did

---

[1] That never happened. Instead she got a T-shirt that says I LOVE PEANUTS.

the job though. Tight as drums they were by the end. Tried to deposit me in the wrong house. I had to put them straight. "Pardon me but I happen to live *here*." Of all the things that I might respond to, I opt for Winnie's malapropism. I tell her I bought the same two bits of fruit from the same greengrocer four days in a row, and on the fourth day, when you'd expect me to be on top of things, I asked for a pink banana and a lady. She finds this really quite amusing. Disproportionately so. Maybe because it involves somebody else's confusion and the purchase of food.

**9 June.** It's Winnie's birthday. I stand on the threshold of the kitchen. Channel my inner Pavarotti. Sing my heart out. She indulges my performance without managing to warm to it. 'Oh I'd forgotten about that,' she says. I give Winnie her card. On the front it says: 'Everything Gets Better As It Gets Older Unless You Are A Banana'. And inside it says: 'Dear Winnie. So far it's been a pleasure living with you. Happy birthday.' Then I give Winnie her present, which is a T-shirt that says: 'I LOVE PEANUTS'. She regards the T-shirt sceptically, as if it were trying to sell her something. I know what she's thinking: *Would Arthur fit in this?*

I order us an Indian takeaway. It's hot enough to eat outside on the terrace (the weather, I mean, not the Indian). I ask what Winnie was doing last year on her birthday.

'You know, I *cannot* remember.'

'And do you think you'll be saying the same thing next year, Winnie?'

'With any luck, yes.'

'Charming.'

'Oh I'm teasing. It's been a very nice day. And I hope I remember it.'

I count to five in my head, waiting for the final remark that undermines the preceding one. Something like: 'Apart from that T-shirt.' But it doesn't come. Instead she says, 'No, it's been a very happy occasion.'

**10 June.** When I get up in the morning, I discover the PEANUTS T-shirt folded up outside my bedroom door. I go down to the kitchen.

'Morning, Winnie.'

'We need some sour cream. Urgently.'

'T-shirt officially returned, is it?'

'I'm afraid it doesn't fit my sense of humour.'

She goes outside to replenish the bird feeder only to discover it's already full. She asks if I did it. I say I didn't. She says in which case it must have been the ghost. I laugh and she says she's not joking, says she's increasingly convinced there's a phantom going around doing things that by rights she ought to be doing – like locking the back door, filling the bird feeder, paying the gardener. 'Not good news,' she says in summary. I privately agree.

**11 June.** I come down in the morning with the book I'm reading – the diary of Samuel Pepys. Winnie asks how it is. I tell her she's mentioned a few times. She doesn't acknowledge this remark, tells me instead that the recent death of

William Shakespeare from Warwickshire is being misreported in Argentina. The William Shakespeare from Warwickshire who died last week (she explains) was one of the first people to be vaccinated for Covid. Wires were crossed as the news travelled to South America, where one news bigwig, evidently unaware that *the* William Shakespeare perished unvaccinated roughly 400 years ago, started reporting the untimely death of Britain's greatest writer. 'In other news,' says Winnie, 'a new poll has revealed that the British public [i.e. 52 per cent of the 1,300 people questioned] want freedom day [21st June] postponed. So I'm off to Boots for cake mixture.'[2]

Ten minutes later. She's not yet off to Boots. She's lost her handbag. Is calm in pursuit thereof.

Ten minutes later. She's still lost her handbag. Isn't yet blaming a ghost. Less calm in pursuit thereof.

Five minutes later. I locate the lost item in her bathroom, sat happily on a stool behind the door, meaning that anybody who just popped their head in wouldn't have spotted it. Granted, her memory isn't what it was – she would be a genetic freak if it were what it was – but it's not so leaky as to be worrying or dangerous. She 'lost' her bag not because her brain is falling to bits but because she started panicking when trying to think where she last had it (her bag, not her brain). And it's also worth bearing in mind that Winnie pretty

---

[2] I believe by cake mixture she meant make-up.

much takes her handbag around with her *everywhere*, with the result that it can come to rest in some unlikely places – like behind the door in the bathroom. What I'm trying to say, I guess, is that it would be easy to mistake a character trait Winnie's had all her life for senility. But what do I know? I've only known the girl eight months. I'm not the best judge of whether she's waxing or waning, going this way or that.

**12 June.** She comes into the sitting room.

'Do I have time to go to the farmers' market?'

'I don't know if you've got time, Winnie.'

'Don't get clever.'

'Did you get out of the wrong side of bed this morning?'

She answers with a smile, but a sarcastic sort that seems to be telling me to sod off. 'I don't suppose you want to come, do you?'

'I'm kind of in the midst of something.'

'Fine. Fine.'

She goes into the kitchen, returns with her handbag, starts rummaging through it, saying under her breath, 'Wouldn't mind the company, to be honest, but hey-ho, on with the war.'

We go to the farmers' market, but she drives, because my lower left side is playing up and has been since Derby. We run into Pam Strange, an old acquaintance of Winnie's. She sizes me up, doesn't look thrilled, then turns to Winnie and asks who drove. Pam's pleased it wasn't me. 'They try and stop us, Winnie. Tell us we're dangerous. It's nonsense. I'm a better driver now than I've ever been.' Pam sizes me up again, over her sunglasses, which she has pushed down to the end of her nose. 'Does he cook?' she says.

**15 June.** Megan's been in contact with two people who have Covid. She's worried about missing her grandad's funeral. She's giving a eulogy for heaven's sake. Rapid test is negative (meaning *unlikely* to be infectious *now*, which is good news for Winnie and me). She goes for a PCR test (polymerase chain reaction, which is more sensitive, and therefore more accurate), but won't get the results back for 24 hours. Her knickers are in a twist. I try to untwist them. 'There's nothing you can do, Meg. Keep yourself to yourself. Get tested every two days. Worst case scenario you'll be delivering the eulogy from the pulpit in a hazmat suit.'

Arthur phones during dinner to thank Winnie for the strawberries. They both struggle to hang up.

'Alright then.'
'See you.'
'OK.'
'Night-night.'
'See you.'
'OK?'
'God bless.'
'See you.'
'Take care.'
'Alright.'
'God bless.'

'Bye.'

'Bye-bye.'

'Take care.'

'OK then?'

'Alright.'

What stops us saying to people we love that we love them?

**16 June.** I open the fridge and notice that an egg has been written on with a felt tip pen. It says: 'Am I cooked or not?' My first question of the egg is: to whom are you addressed? My second question is: WTF? Are you cooked or not? I'm left feeling genuinely baffled. Can only think that Winnie boiled some eggs, didn't use them all, put one back in the fridge, and now can't be sure whether she did that or not. I suppose there's a chance she's just having a laugh: that the question is rhetorical, a sort of puzzle, designed to get people thinking. I pick up the egg. It doesn't *feel* cooked. But nor can you hear its liquidity. In short: I haven't got a clue. I close the fridge and try to forget about it.

I sit on the bench opposite the house and think how hard it is to see the largeness of things from inside them. I see Winnie's blurred silhouette in the hallway and think how every moment alters your past and changes your future – if only slightly, if only lightly. The past months have altered and changed me, no doubt about it, and largely for the better. I've got a new friend, for a start. I can defrost a freezer now. I've learned how difficult it can be to say certain things. And I've seen how a simple absence can strike a life like a meteor. I send a message to my younger sister. 'When I'm 85 and living alone and can never find my handbag, will you keep an eye on me?' She sends a message back. 'Sure. But only if you return the favour.' The light comes on in my bedroom. What the fuck is she doing up there?

**17 June.** As I'm reading that Freedom Day has definitely been cancelled, she comes through the front door saying that tinned tomatoes are holding their price well. I meet her in the hall, help her unburden herself, say, 'You know, Winnie, I doubt there's another person in the whole world who would come through the door making such an announcement to potentially no one.'

A parcel from Nan. It's a hand massager for my injured leg. There's a note with it: 'I wish you could see yourself through my eyes. Love Nan.' Intriguingly, my nan doesn't hint what I might encounter if I did see myself through her eyes. An absolute plonker perhaps. Winnie looks at the note. She's not convinced. 'I'm not sure I'd want to see myself,' she says. 'It's more than enough having to look at everyone else.'

We talk about feelings at dinner. I suggest that something like love is shorthand for so much – respect, care, worry, pride – and that the *feeling* of love, therefore, is the occasional collision of all of the above.

'And there's sex of course,' she says.

'Yes, I suppose there is.'

'Mustn't forget about that.'

'Quite right.'

'For a long time I thought boys were pointless.'

'With good reason, I'm sure.'

'Then I met Henry and it was almost immediately passionate.'

'Immediately?'

'Almost.'

'Parked on double yellow lines, was he?'

'I had no preconceptions at all.'

'Which was probably to his advantage.'

'Yes, I suppose it was.'

'He could tell you it was tiptop no matter what.'

'No need for such sophistry, I can assure you.'

'Were you ones for public displays of affection?'

'Occasionally. If nobody was around.'


**19 June.** I'm in Ramsgate. Weekend away. Voicemail from Winnie. 'Ben. Winnie. Where are you? The tap could do with a new washer. Would appreciate your reappearance.'


**20 June.** Still in Ramsgate. Voicemail from Winnie. 'Ben. Winnie. Are you upstairs? Arthur's calves are as hard as iron. Could you lend a hand? Do let me know if you're dead.'


**21 June.** Lunch. I've a funeral tomorrow, and she has one on Friday (via Zoom), so our talk is funeral themed. Henry's was a celebration really, she tells me, rather than a deeply sad occasion. But then again, when you celebrate you underline what will be missed. No headstone as yet, she says. Just a patch of land. She had an inscription in mind – 'It was the time of roses. We plucked them as we passed.'[3] – but says she's not so sure anymore, not since she got ensnared in a bush the other day. I ask what inscription she'd have on her headstone. She gives it some thought, then says, 'Was meant to be enjoying herself but polished the doorknob instead.'

She doesn't go to the cemetery much. Doesn't go at all if she's honest. Some people need to be practically stood on the deceased in order to remember them. She doesn't. She only has to open her eyes. He's the anorak in the downstairs loo. He's the shoes under the bed. He's the washing machine that's been playing up for 25 years. He's the car in the drive, the bike in the garage, the shirts in the cupboard. He's the space in bed. Winnie wouldn't be surprised if Henry had actually altered the material character of her brain – or soul if you prefer. She prefers brain. She has him on the brain, and always will.

After dinner, she sits down next to me with her mobile phone, asks if I could help her with a spot of admin. There's one email about a 'Swift Awareness Walk' next week. Winnie's interested in the event. I can tell she's interested because she hasn't said something dismissive or cutting about it. 'I used to want to be a swift,' she says, emulating their topsy-turvy flight pattern with her hand, 'but not anymore because I fancy I'd be sick.' She doesn't want to commit to the walk but wants it to remain a possibility. So I stick the date in her diary. As I

---

[3] Thomas Hood. From 'Time of Roses'.

do so she says, more to her inbox than me, 'No, it would be good to make an appearance at one of these things. If only to see who's dead.'

She brings down some photos from the Philippines. There's one of Winnie sat formally in a row next to Henry and the Filipino chief of police, Winnie with a bob cut and stripy dress and heels, Henry looking boyish and dapper and sun-tanned and happy with one leg over the other, the chief of police looking deadly serious, hands on his knees. Other pho-tos of note include: somebody cleaning a floor with coconuts on their feet; Winnie dancing with the chief of police (who still looks deadly serious); and Arthur in an incubator being fed through his nose. ('The nurse said as we were leaving the hospital, almost as an afterthought, "He'll be damaged for life, Mrs Carter," and then just left us to it.') But my favourite photo is a portrait of mother and child in the garden of their house in Cebu.[4] Winnie and Arthur are in the centre of the photo, on a rug. They are small. They don't take up much room. Henry must be stood at least twenty or 30 metres away from them, at the bottom of the garden. The top half of the picture is dominated by the family's home, while the bottom half is almost entirely garden, which tapers as it hones in on the subjects of the image. Most of Henry's shadow is in the shot. He's waving. Or trying to get their attention. Hard to tell which. I pass the image to her.

---

[4] Cebu is the country's oldest city; it was the first Spanish settlement and the first capital of the Philippines.

'Yes, quite right,' she says. 'I'm sure that's all you can bear. It's awful imposing family snaps on someone. That's why I keep them—'

'I find them beautiful and interesting, Winnie.'

'Do you?'

'Yes. And educational. Now I know that I ought to be cleaning with coconuts.'

'I'll pick some up at Lidl.'

'Have you shown Arthur? Or Abigail? Or Mango?'

'No, I don't think I have.'

'You *must*, Winnie. Don't keep them locked away upstairs in a cupboard. This is their family. This is who they are.'

She gives this some thought. Exhales through pursed lips. 'I suppose I could keep them in a *downstairs* cupboard.'

We have dinner – mushroom risotto *and* spaghetti bolognaise – while watching the Denmark–Russia match. I mention England are playing again tomorrow. 'Are they entitled to?' she says.

**22 June.** Dave's funeral. Terry (Megan's nan) copes really well – tearful throughout, but able to appreciate those gathered, and the feelings and memories expressed. I cry a lot, because Dave was such a good bloke, and I know how deeply he will be missed. I got Terry a card. With a big sunflower on the front. I wrote inside: 'Your sunflower has lost a significant and irreplaceable petal, but remains beautiful.' A bit saccharine perhaps, but true nonetheless.

I'm stood at my bedroom window. Watch a young girl going down the alley with an adult. I overhear the following. I'll let you guess who says what.

'I wish my hand was banana.'

'Why?'

'Because then I could eat it.'

'Short-term thinking, my love.'


Winnie says Hannah called and she wants to bring the kids over this weekend.

'Great,' I say. 'When are they coming?'

'Oh. Well. I'm afraid I gave rather a vague answer. What with all that's going on.'

'What's going on?'

'On Saturday I should prioritise Arthur.'

'The occasion being?'

'And Sunday doesn't work because I rather think there should be some *space* between such things.'

I look at her. The look is a question. And the question is: *Really?*

She looks at me. The look is an answer. And the answer is: *Yes, really.*

'It's a matter of *provisions*,' she says. 'There isn't enough food in. Hannah's children are no doubt accustomed to constant snacks.'

'Needless to say, Winnie, you can do or not do what the hell you want.'

'How generous of you.'

'But I happen to think it would be a great shame if the

reason Hannah didn't visit was due to a shortage of snacks and a lack of space between Saturday and Sunday.'

Later. She phones Hannah. '*Do* come over on Sunday. I'll send Ben out for provisions. If I can find him.'

**23 June.** We go and have a look at a garden up the road. A private garden that's open to visitors for a few days. Something the RHS organises. When we get to the house, we're asked for a fiver to get in. She looks at me and I look at her. There's no point her looking at me because I didn't even bring my wallet, made the mistake of thinking an open garden was what it said on the tin. She gives an exasperated, not-this-again sigh. Poor dear, she's only getting fourteen pensions. She has to dig to the bottom of her purse for the entrance fee – makes a fair meal of doing so. Says an emotional farewell to each coin before handing it over. Once inside, we do a slow lap of the garden. Doing so, we get talking with a lady called Daisy, who has the appearance and manner of a school governess in the British Cayman Islands circa 1932. Daisy says (or whispers rather) that the garden's a bit *fussy*. This encourages Winnie to say (rather than whisper) that it's frankly off-putting. Daisy says it's fiddly and dark. Winnie says it's bland and aloof. Both commend the cake. On our way out, we meet the householder. When she asks where we live and I say that we live on Hill Rise, she says, 'Oh, are the Carters still on Hill Rise?' To which Winnie says, 'I *am* the Carters, dear.' Walking to the bus stop, Winnie says, 'You know, I cannot *believe* it's the middle of the week.

It feels like a summer holiday.' By the time we get to the bus stop she's had second thoughts and wants to keep on going.

**25 June.** Come home and she's sat unusually by the window in the sitting room in one of the swivel chairs with a book open on her lap and a plate bearing cake crumbs to her side on a stool. She says she likes how the light at this time of the evening seems to pick out certain things; how it seems to pay certain trees or flowers special attention before calling it a day. I respond by asking if she's feeling at all inspired in relation to dinner. She says she's feeling inspired to continue sitting where she is, before consenting to bangers and mash.

Watch *Countryfile* and then the news. It's not looking good for the Health Secretary. He's been caught on CCTV ignoring his own regulations with his hands on the bottom of an aide. Winnie's surprisingly sympathetic, 'Oh, we've all done it.'

**26 June.** Front page shows the hand, the bottom, the aide, the Health Sec. Front page also gives news of a new super-charged variant of the coronavirus – Delta Plus – which Winnie reckons sounds like a type of toothpaste.

Voicemail. 'Ben. Winnie. The children *are* coming tomorrow. Hannah's children. And they'll need something. Else they'll start chewing the furniture. There's always peanuts, but you can't very well entrust children with peanuts. We do have a variety of biscuits, and I bought some apple juice, but if you spot anything that looks attractive (and I mean in the way of food), do pick it up. Arthur had a roast lunch today and most of it went on his trousers. And I discovered to my horror that the bird feeder closest to the kitchen has had its bottom chewed off by squirrels, meaning the seed is raining down at speed. Interested to see what plants come through in the wake of this disaster.'

**27 June.** I don't have a huge amount of experience buying food for children, which is probably why I buy them Pringles, Jaffa Cakes, ice lollies, microwavable chicken curry, a cheese and tomato pizza and some bubblegum. Hannah doesn't think much of my selection, but Winnie is quite amused. In the end the children have cheese sandwiches. They don't even have an ice lolly afterwards. What is this new world we live in? Nice to see Winnie playing with them (the children, not the ice lollies). She's brought down a box of building blocks and is supervising the children's construction of what appears to be an outdoor toilet. Winnie wonders if the walls shouldn't be two bricks thick, and whether a moat is out of the question.

**28 June.** Walking home through the village, I give Winnie a call to see if she needs anything. She says she's thought better of a fish pie for Arthur's birthday and wants a chicken instead, a good one, enough for six or seven, plant-based. No, not plant-based. That's not right. *Organic* – that's it, that's the word. Perhaps Sainsbury's might be the best shout?

'I'll give Sainsbury's a go,' I say.

'Then we need to work out who's coming.'

'To what Winnie?'

'To Arthur's *birthday*.'

'Well who have you invited?'

'Well, that's the thing.'

She hasn't invited anyone. That's the thing. She hasn't phoned Rebecca, or Abigail, or Stewart, or even Arthur himself. She knows the politics are tricky, so she's loathe to go near them, is clinging on to the *idea* of a successful family gathering in its purest form. I tell her to pick up the phone and make some calls. Tell her that pleasant and meaningful family gatherings (as far as I'm aware) aren't readily available in the afterlife. 'You're quite right,' she says. 'No I see your point perfectly. It *is* a large house. Does need filling. By the way, what are your thoughts re a trip to M&S to get Arthur some socks?'

We're watching the football. I ask her if she made some calls. She says nothing, just carries on watching the football. Which is interesting when you consider that she couldn't care less about it.

'Winnie?'

'Hm?'

'Have you phoned Stewart?'

'No.'

'Are you apprehensive about phoning him?'

'Yes.'

'Because of Jane?'

'It's hard to bear the idea of having her in the house again.'

'Ah.'

'Yes, ah.'

'Would you agree that life is too short?'

She gives this some serious thought. I reckon she's tempted to say no. 'Yes,' she says. 'At a push I'd say it was.'

'Then perhaps—'

'She took everything. She went into Arthur's bedroom and erased all traces of him.'

Someone scores an own goal. We watch the replay in silence.


I'm preparing dinner.

'Are you cooking that sordid pork?' she says.

'I am.'

'How are you doing it?'

'I'm poaching it.'

'Really?'

'And then pulling it.'

She looks at me like I've just told her that the Queen has started identifying as a king. '*Pulling* it?'[5]


Doing the washing up, I ask what she loves about Arthur. She looks at the plate she's drying.

'I know what I *like* about Arthur.'

'Right …'

'His fondness for historical events.'

---

[5] She would later describe the pulled pork as 'fractious', 'intimidating' and 'seemingly already eaten'.

'Anything else?'

'His appetite.'

'His appetite?'

'Yes.'

'Good lord, Winnie.'

'I like his courage.'

'That's better.'

'And I like that he likes me.'

'That's nice.'

'At least I think he does.'

'He loves you, Winnie.'

'Does he?'

'Any child that phones their mother three times a week must love them. There's no other explanation.'

She asks if I can run a yoghurt and a birthday card round to Arthur so he's got something in the morning. She applies a label to the yoghurt and three more to the bag I'm to carry it in. One label identifies the contents, another carries the yoghurt's provenance, and the third one carries Arthur's full address, presumably in case I'm in an accident and somebody chances upon the yoghurt and wants to complete the delivery. Can you measure a mother's love by the number of labels they put on a yoghurt?

When I get back she asks if I wouldn't mind running a yoghurt round to Arthur.

'Another one?'

'What?'

'I just took one.'

'Did you?'

'Yeah. With the card.'

'No of course you did, of course you did. It's my brain – it's addled. Short-term memory syndrome. Not fun in the least. *Stupid* woman.'

She enters the sitting room in her huge dressing gown. ('Are you planning to grow into that, Winnie?' 'Shut up.') She addresses the television, principally because it doesn't have emotions. 'Thank you for dinner. I'm very grateful. Bit weird, but thank you. It feels like I'm turning into a kid, having it all done for me – not good really, not when you think about it. But I am lucky, getting to try new things, like strangled pork. Anyway, lots of love. And thanks again. For everything. We'll get there in the end.' And she turns, and leaves, and climbs the stairs, and you can't help but love her.

**29 June.** Kitchen. Morning. I ask her where she was when England won the world cup in 1966. 'No idea,' she says. I ask where she was for the moon landing. 'No idea,' she says. I ask where she was when there was an attempt on Thatcher's life in Brighton. 'Are you trying to pin something on me?' she says. Then she says that she might not be able to say where she was throughout *history* but she can say where she was for the raising of her family – at *home*. She says she knows where she was for Stewart's christening – trying to park the car. She says she knows where she was when Rebecca's first tooth was yanked out by a so-called friend – at the dentist having root canal surgery (the irony made the coincidence memorable). She says she knows where she was when Mango started breaking out in measles before her very eyes – in front of the poor girl. And she says she knows where she was when Henry died (upstairs in their bed by his side), and where she'll be when she dies if she's got anything to do with it (upstairs in their bed). Those are the big events, from where she's standing. That's what history's made of, as far as she's concerned. The rest is largely background noise. (With the exception of the UK butter crisis of 1973.) Home is where history is. That's what she's getting at. 'Having said all that,' she says. 'I do know where I was when Diana died.' 'Where?' 'Ipswich.'

She's had enough football, so I'm sent upstairs to watch it. England come out on top. I go down after the match, pumping my arms up and down in celebration. She deliberately misunderstands. 'No, I've had my exercise today, thank you. Did some Pilates this morning. But I would like some supper if you can bring yourself to stop doing that.'

**30 June.** Off to a pub for a bit of lunch and to look at an exhibition of photography the pub is hosting in its dining room. The taxi journey across London proceeds smoothly, which comes as a relief when you consider that Winnie said it wouldn't do so in a million years. Unsurprisingly, certain things catch Winnie's eye along the way.

'There's Putney church.'

'Didn't Cromwell and his mates gather there to thrash things out during the Civil War?'

'That's it. Before popping over to Wagamama. I was bed-bound in that hospital for two weeks.'

'When you had your knee done?'

'I can't remember what it was exactly. But I can tell you the custard was miserable. That's Bishop's Park. Rebecca used to go blackberrying there.'

'Bit far from home.'

'I used to be up and down this road most days, running her to school. She started off getting the tube, but then she saw a man injecting himself at Earl's Court station, and reasoned that she'd see less of that sort of thing if I took her in the car.'

'By the way, when will the raspberries come out in the garden?'

'They already have come out.'

'You kept that to yourself.'

'Of course I did. I'm not daft. Besides, there was only two.'

'There are two of us, Winnie.'

'Yes, but you can't just try one. There's Portobello Road.'

'Where you got your special fork.'

'Got a pair in fact. And that's all we had for a long time. All we needed. This was before all sorts of strange people began moving into the house.'

'Your children you mean?'

'Now this is a nice part of town. A friend had a place around here. Terrific parties. You want to go right here, driver. Right here, I said. RIGHT HERE!'

We have a look around the pictures first. She approves of the introductory text, is taken by the artist's stated intention to capture the distinct beauty of ordinary moments during a time of crisis. We move around the photographs in opposite directions, she from the end to the start, I from the start to the end. Inevitably (well, perhaps not inevitably), we meet in the middle: before a photograph that shows in the foreground the enviable backside of an ancient sculpture, and in the background a curious museum-goer inspecting the other side of the bottom while wearing a face mask and sunglasses. 'It's life writ small,' says Winnie. 'At once ridiculous and sweet.'[6]

We go through to the pub to eat. She rejects three generous samples of wine before plumping for a small glass of the house white. She has the gnocchi and is more than happy to tell the waitress that it was 'too squidgy by half'. She's also happy to tell the waitress that she couldn't possibly consider a portion of bread-and-butter pudding with crème anglaise, before doing far more than consider a decent amount of mine. In short, she behaves precisely as she would in her own home, at her own dining table, including not thinking for a second about paying for any of the above. When the bill comes she looks at it incredulously, not quite sure what it is. I tell her it's my treat. She says she'll get out in the garden when we get back and find me a couple of raspberries. I ask if she's got anything for a tip. 'Oh I've got a tip, alright. "If at first you don't succeed, skydiving is not for you." Are we taxiing?'

---

[6] The photographer is Richard Morgan, who's certainly worth a peek.

# 1979

*Waterloo train station. Late summer. Early evening. Arthur Carter is off to Exeter to study theology. The wheels of his suitcase (which was both his father's and grandfather's before him) are more square than round, so the sound of him moving along the platform – 'ba-dum, ba-dum, ba-dum …' can be heard as far away as Covent Garden. Watching him go, Winnie Carter feels something she can't put her finger on. It's not a swelling of pride or a spasm of fear, and nor is it indigestion. In the end, she puts it down to a combination of the three. More important than what she's feeling is when Arthur is going to turn around and wave. He's had ample opportunity by now; why, he's almost walked past the entire train. When he doesn't turn around at all, opting instead to board the train without so much as a glance in her direction (which is fair enough really, for as far as Arthur is concerned, his mother is by now on the tube heading south on the Northern Line), a fourth thing is added to the trio of feelings being felt by Mrs Carter, the addition of which causes her to reject the protestations of the ticket inspector and hurry down the platform towards Arthur's carriage. When she gets there, and gets on board, and sees Arthur taking off the outermost of the several coats Winnie insisted he went off in, she doesn't know what to say, or what to do. Eventually she says, 'Hello, darling.' To which Arthur says, 'Hello, Mum.' And then the sound of a whistle and the shout of a platform attendant provide Winnie with a reasonable excuse to get off the train without saying anything else. She stands on the platform. The doors close. The train moves off. Some moments later, a gentleman on his way to Reading will turn to Arthur and say, 'She's gonna miss you, mate,' and Arthur will immediately turn and look out the window, back towards Waterloo, as if the statement — and the idea it contained — had come from that direction.*

# 10

## Deep breaths please

**1 July.** Winnie's had a haircut. She looks a bit like Grayson Perry.

**2 July.** My dad comes, bearing gifts: a jar of marmalade and the bird temple he's been working on. Bit of lunch in the village, then tea and biscuits in the garden. Later on, Winnie sits down next to me to watch the tennis.

'Won't be here long. Need to get back into the garden.'

'It's alright to sit down, Winnie.'

'I've been sat down watching tennis a lot lately. It's not good.'

'It's only two weeks a year. You can indulge.'

'Yes, but it takes everything out of my head.'

'That's called relaxing.'

'But I don't like it. It takes me off track. And I just end up looking at the players and thinking about their anxieties.'

'Do you actually?'

'Yes.'

'Then you're beyond help, Winnie.'

'Thanks for the update.'

'It was nice to see my dad.'

'Yes I expect it was. He seems a very civilised man. Just like his son.' She gives me a quick look, a quick smile. 'I'll say that quickly.'

'You can take as long as you want saying things like that.'

'Things to be done, I'm afraid.'

'Good news that he brought us some marmalade.'

'Yes, but it's impure.'

'Sorry?'

'It's three-fruit marmalade.'

'Still, it was a nice thought.'

'Oh I can't knock the thought.'

'Pleased to hear it.'

'It's just you can't put thoughts on toast, can you?'

**3 July.** I bust the blind in my room when I go to raise it. Too forceful. Now it's permanently (or semi-permanently) neither up nor down. When I enter the kitchen she's staring sceptically at the three-fruit marmalade. I take some food scraps out to the compost, and then take some flowers from the garden (forget-me-nots) and put them in the middle of the kitchen table. Winnie enters a question in her diary – 'Booster jab for Arthur?' – and then underlines it. She eats her muesli and stewed fruit on her feet looking out the window. 'There is something deeply comforting about a garden,' she says. Her mood is unusual. At once sweeter and sadder. She goes to the bread bin. It's all but empty. Just a lonely half-slice remains. 'It seems the birds have been in during the night,' she says in my direction. She toasts the half-slice, retrieves it with a pair of scissors, then spreads on butter and the impure marmalade. She wipes the knife clean with her finger, licks it, then cuts the half in half and gives me one of the quarters. 'And before I forget,' she says, 'I've got something for you.' She goes into the garage (ominous). The alarm goes off ('Oh blast!'). She turns off the alarm ('Now you be quiet'), enters the garage ('Now where was it …'), returns to the kitchen bearing a dusty piece of treasure (a hot-water bottle). 'It's a good one,' she says. 'It used to be Arthur's but he's assured me he's not in the habit anymore, so it's fine.' I'm touched. Disproportionately so. Absurdly (though I suppose no expression of emotion is actually absurd), there's the start of a tear in my eye, because at the end of the day it's the thought that counts, it's *this* thought that counts. 'But there's no lid,' she says, 'so you might want to source one, else you'll be wetting the bed every night.'

It's half-past six. I've just ordered a taxi. It's arriving in two minutes.

'Can you just help me pull up some weeds in the garden?'

'I can't, Winnie. Taxi's literally here in a minute.'

'Where are you escaping to?'

'Going to watch the football. The England match.'

'Oh yes that's right. Back for dinner?'

'No. As I said before. Back after the match.'

'It's no good saying things. I need them written down. In LARGE text.'

'But you've got that pie from the market in the fridge. And there's some cold chicken from yesterday if you fancy that.'

'I'll survive. Off you go. Good hunting.'

I get in about midnight. Front door is shut but not locked – flipping heck, Winnie. There's a pack of balloons on the kitchen table – for Arthur's party tomorrow, I presume. I heat up a frozen chilli con carne. Take it upstairs as quietly as possible. Open my window for a crafty cigarette. And that's when I hear her crying for help in the darkness. I rush down. She's on the paving stones between the conifer trees. It's her hip. She fell. It's agony. 'Stay still, Winnie.' 'Good plan,' she says. 'Are you in pain, Winnie?' 'Never felt better,' she says. I phone 999. 'Has she been vaccinated? Has she lost her sense of smell?' 'Forget Covid, she can't move and she's been out here for hours, for heaven's sake.' 'The ambulance will be there in three hours, sir.' 'Are you joking?' 'It's a global pandemic, sir.' 'Yes but she's 86 and she can't move and she's in agony and she's been out here for hours. How do I know her? I live with her. Where was I when she fell? Why the hell does that matter?' She screams. 'Ambulance on its way, Winnie.' 'Oh thank God you're here. I was scared. I was calling for help.' 'You're being very brave, Winnie. I'd be cursing and sobbing if I was in your position.' 'It hurts more if you cry,' she says. 'Do you want me to talk to you or do you want me to shut up?' 'No, it's a comfort. It's good to know you're here. How was the football?' 'They won,' I say. 'Let us rejoice,' she says. I'm on my knees. Holding her hand. Stroking her hair. 'The foxes came and had a look at me,' she says. 'I was scared they were going to have a nibble. Or even worse pee on me.' She laughs. We laugh. 'How did it happen, Winnie?' 'I fell. In the flowerbed. Made an impression on the daisies.' She lets out another cry. I'm still holding her hand. Still stroking her hair. 'Do you mind me doing that, Winnie?' 'No, it's nice.

Thank you. The flowers look funny from this angle.' Three hours, fuck me. 'Are you warm? Are you hungry? Do you want something to eat?' 'Steak and potatoes please,' she says, then screams.

I phone Rebecca.

'Did you mean to call, Ben?'

'I did. It's Winnie. She fell. She's in the garden. I came back. After the football.'

'Christ. Oh God. Oh my. Oh dear. Shall I come? I mean. I don't drive and— Maybe I can wake up one of the girls. Oh dear. Not good news for Arthur's party. Shall I bring the cake with me do you think?'

The doorbell rings. Penny and Steve. Paramedics. Two hours early, thank God. They question me: who am I, what happened, where was I? They're trying to ascertain if they need to phone the police. I lead them to Winnie. Steve kneels at her side. Just going to give you some gas and air, Mrs Carter. Deep breaths, please. Let's get these blankets off, shall we? Temperature's fine. Heart rate's fine. Mind if I take a look, Mrs Carter? Winnie screams. Could be hip *and* pelvis, says Penny. She won't be playing football for a while, says Steve.

Rebecca comes. Offers to hold the torch. I help Penny fetch the trolley from the ambulance. She asks about the football. Says she saw the first goal. I think: *With all due respect, Penny, but I don't give a toss if you saw the first goal.* Then I think: *They have to be like this. They do this ten times a night. They have to calm people down. They have to* be *calm. It wouldn't work if they were as scared as you.*

Hold this please, Mrs Carter. That's it, deep breaths. Going to turn you now, Mrs Carter. She screams. Going to lift you now, Mrs Carter. She screams. Deep breaths please. And onto the trolley. That's it. More deep breaths please. That stuff's your best friend, Mrs Carter. That's it. Good girl. Shall we take the gardening gloves off now?

She's loaded into the ambulance. I see her rise in profile, and then disappear by degrees. Rebecca goes with her. I tell her to call if she needs to switch, or needs anything. Open a bottle of wine. One of Henry's reds from the basement. Smoke on the back step. Bloody mad. Should have clocked it sooner. The front door unlocked. Shouldn't have gone out for that matter. Should have stayed in. But it could have happened anyway. Could have happened if I was here. But she wouldn't have been out there on her own. That's the thing. That's the difference. Just glad I opened that window. Couldn't see a thing. It was pitch black. And then her voice. She must have heard the taxi, the front door. I can't eat this (the chilli con carne). I'll have another glass of wine though. Christ almighty. Happy Independence Day. I raise my glass. To Winnie's health. Poor sod.

**4 July.** Text message from Rebecca. X-ray confirmed broken hip and pelvis. Operation sometime next week. Feels strongly that Arthur's party should go ahead. She's got some quiche and some smoked salmon and the cake and will be round in a couple of hours. I don't argue. Not my place to. If she wants to have a party for her brother two hours after depositing her mother at the hospital following a traumatic injury, then who am I to object? And I mean that seriously. Part of me thinks she's mad, and another part thinks fair play, Arthur's wellbeing is important to you, crack on.

We're seven for lunch. Myself, Arthur, Rebecca, Abigail and a few of Arthur's friends from church that he hasn't seen for over a year. Nick – one of the latter – pops open some champagne, hands me a glass. It goes down oddly easily. I give Arthur his card. Inside it says that I've subscribed him to a magazine called *Positive News*, which is pretty ironic given that his razor keeps breaking and his calves are as hard as brass and his freedom has been significantly squeezed for the last fifteen months and his mother spent five hours outside on the floor with a broken hip and pelvis last night. Someone called Richard plays 'Happy Birthday' on the guitar, which makes Arthur laugh. (His laugh is hilarious, by the way. It's really deep and sort of grows in confidence, as if the thing or notion that initially tickled him is getting funnier and funnier the more he thinks about it.) We eat the quiche and the salmon and the cake. I take photos, thinking Winnie would appreciate evidence that we all had a cracking time behind her back. Someone tells a story about Andy Murray. Nick apologises for being a lawyer. Richard apologises for being an accountant. Rachel says her youngest daughter seems determined to never leave home. Rebecca says she can't relate to such determination, says she was practically climbing down the drainpipe aged fourteen. They are so alike, Rebecca and Winnie, which is good for them both when all things are considered. Abigail picks raspberries and flowers to take to the hospital. I tell the story of the egg in the fridge that had 'Am I cooked or not?' written on it. It's enjoyed. Goes down well. Gets a laugh. When the titters and comments die down to silence, someone says, 'Oh, Winnie', which prompts Rebecca to get up and start clearing the table.

I'm watching *Countryfile*. In the recliner. Odd to be in the house alone. You don't realise what the presence of another does, what it brings, until they are gone. I phone the hospital. Am put through by a nurse.

'Ben?'

'Hello, Winnie.'

'What's troubling me is I can't walk.'

'I can imagine.'

'This is meant to be the modern age, but they've got my leg hoisted up with recourse to a bucket full of stones. It's a medieval contraption.'

'How's the food?'

'Abigail brought some raspberries, which were very nice.'

'Yes I know. She cleared the bush. I'm quite cross about that.'

'It was roast beef for lunch, apparently. Disgusting. Tasted like the heel of a boot.'

'Are there many people on the ward?'

'There was quite a group but I managed to get rid of them and now it's just me. Don't ask about my methods.'

'I won't.'

'I keep thinking I should be *doing* something. But I can't. I'm stuck here.'

'Time to put your feet up for a bit, Winnie.'

'And poor Arthur. I went and wrecked his party.'

'The party went ahead. I've got evidence. We were thinking about you. He had a good time.'

'Oh that is good. And he got home alright?'

'He did. I dropped him off.'

'And what about his razor?'

'I managed to get it back together.'

'Good. Though it's only going to break again. That's the real problem. It's the wrong *design*.'

'He said that if his razor keeps playing up he's going to start using it to shave parmesan on his pasta.'

'No he didn't. You said that.'

'True.'

'He wouldn't say that.'

'You know, it's a bit ridiculous but I went out to the garden, to where you ended up, and lied down where you were, to see what it was like.'

'You *lay* down.'

'Lay down.'

'Speak English, man.'

'So anyway, I lay down where you'd been and I'd had enough after a minute.'

'I bet you had. It was torture. I came down like a ton of

bricks. Lucky I didn't thwack my head. That's what I keep thinking.'

'At least you got to see the garden from a new angle.'

'Some perspectives one can do without.'

'True.'

'I'm going to be in here for a while they tell me.'

'I'm just glad I heard you.'

'Well I'm more glad, believe me.'

'Would have been rather inconvenient if you'd perished out there.'

'Oh I wouldn't have taken it that far. Too much to do.'

'You're very croaky.'

'They assumed I was a chain smoker. But it was all the screaming.'

'If it hurts to speak I should let you go.'

'Alright.'

'OK.'

'Alright then.'

'The foxes miss you.'

'I should think they do. It's not every evening they encounter a crazy old woman on the floor, ordering them to retreat.'

'Alright then.'

'When's Kuba coming? Is it Monday? No today's Monday.'

'Today's Sunday.'

'Is it?'

'4th July.'

'Of course it is.'

'Independence Day.'

'How meet.'

'Meat?'

*'Meet.'*

'Meat?'

'M-e-e-t.'

'Meet?'

'Meet. It means appropriate.'

'Does it?'

'The opposite of much of your behaviour.'

'Got it.'

'Wakey-wakey.'

'See you, Winnie.'

'God bless.'

'Bye.'

'Bye.'

My phone pings. I've been in contact with a positive case. I'm told not to go anywhere for ten days.

6 July. Send a postcard to Winnie. One of Don McCullin's photographs, bought at an exhibition yonks ago. It shows an older lady being carried away by the police in 1972. My message reads: 'Dear Winnie. Have been pinged so can't visit. Hope the food is OK. Couldn't resist this postcard. Brought to mind your departure from the garden on Saturday night. Sending love. Ben.'

Later. Text message from Winnie. It reads: 'I'm in hospital.'

**10 July.** I use what's left of the granary. Sticking to the impure marmalade for now. Illegally run the Saturday papers and some raspberries round to Rebecca, who's visiting Winnie later.

**Later.** Phone Rebecca to see how Winnie was. She says Winnie couldn't remember having the operation but could remember every scandalous supper she's had thus far.

**11 July.** In Winnie's absence, things happen. There's more light hitting the dining table. There are dying flowers in the hall. There's out of date milk in the fridge. Overripe raspberries are coming off their stems and staining the flagstones and earth. These things evoke her presence as much as her absence. They make me realise the daily things she did to make the house tick, to make it turn, to make it a home. I haven't been honouring her example. I make do with black coffee when the milk runs out. Go without breakfast when the loaf is done. Keep the hall and landing in darkness after dusk. And other things are different, too. Arthur doesn't call. I'm careless about portion sizes. I use unfiltered water in the kettle. I don't heat my plate. Eggs don't ask questions. The paper isn't read. Crumbs aren't gathered and flung into the garden. Parakeets aren't warned off. The robin isn't spoken to. In short, the house is less of a home.

I phone Rebecca. She says they're still none the wiser about how long she's going to be in, and what the next steps are. Might be relocated for a stint of rehab, as part of the NHS experience. I say that I've tried to phone the ward a few times but nobody picks up, and that I've tried Winnie's mobile but the same applies.

**12 July.**  When it rains it pours. Black water comes down the chimney and onto the fireplace. It spills onto the carpet, adding a stain to a burn. The TV aerial on the roof is doing a mad dance. The leak in the ceiling of my bedroom is getting worse. The alarm is playing up. The microwave has gone kaput. And my blind is still bust.

**13 July.**  Winnie phones.

'Ben?'

'Winnie.'

'I've moved beds.'

'Oh right.'

'She picked me up like a parcel.'

'Sharing with someone else now, are you?'

'What?'

'Sharing with somebody else now are— Don't worry.'

'It was nice to be briefly aloft and in someone's arms, I can tell you.'

'That's good to hear.'

'It's been quite scary. This whole thing. I've been hallucinating pretty much full-time.'

'Crikey.'

'I've been all over the world. I thought I was in Malaysia this morning. Or last night. Or whenever it was. I was asking the nurse when I'd be returning to London.'

'Crikey.'

'And what's more, I was trying to ask her in *Malay*.'

'Didn't know you spoke—'

'I've been periodically screaming and crying. Can't recommend it.'

'You poor thing.'

'They put so many needles in me I felt like a pin cushion.'

'And are you through the worst of the hallucinations?'

'What information?'

'ARE YOU THROUGH THE WORST OF THE HALLUCINATIONS?'

'I couldn't say. I don't know what's going to happen in five minutes. I might be back in Malaysia.'

'I've spoken to Arthur.'

'Who?'

'ARTHUR.'

'Oh good.'

'And taken him round some soap and his magazine.'

'I had a blood transfusion yesterday.'

'Really?'

'I was anaemic by all accounts. Now I'm all wired up. Part woman, part tube.'

'I would come and visit, Winnie, but I'm self-isolating because—'

'It's been a revelation. I just said yes to anything offered.'

'You're very much missed, Winnie.'

'And I think I'll keep saying yes, to be honest.'

'It's not the same without you.'

'That's diplomatically put.'

'No really. It's better when you're here.'

'Well, I cross my fingers.'

'I do the same.'

'Anyway.'

'OK speak soon, Winnie.'

'Lots of love.'

'Lots of love. Bye.'

I empty two vases, add the old flowers to the compost, cut new ones from the garden, which I arrange as well as I can and place in the hall and sitting room. Then I pick some raspberries. It's quite satisfying getting down on my haunches, finding the fruit behind the foliage (which is abundant), spying the right shades of red, minding the small thorns, gently pulling at the berries. I wash my haul in the kitchen, watching the news. Catch a headline along the lines of: summer Covid wave could see up to 5,000 hospital admissions a day. When will this not-so-fresh hell end?[1]

**14 July.** I go down to Mr Spinnici the baker. Order a loaf of wholemeal. 'Wholemeal? Where is the lady?'

**15 July.** Blazing hot day. Kuba comes. He needs two keys. One for the shed, one for the garden gate. We have a job finding them. Winnie probably keeps them under her pillow. He asks how she is. I explain as best I can. '*Nic nie zrobisz,*'

---

[1] Summer Covid wave peaked at roughly 700 admissions a day. Out by a factor of seven.

he says. What can you do? I get some cash out to pay him, put it out under a plate with a coffee and some biscuits and a can of beer. '*Jest tradycja*,' I call across the garden. He smiles, shakes his head, says, 'The tradition is three biscuits!' His cancer is in remission.

Push bike home from gym – tyres getting flat. Slow puncture, if that's a thing. Not excited to get home. The evening looms large. Daft and unreasonable, but true. Days don't loom large. Days take care of themselves. But evenings (when on paper we're entitled to some leisure, some company, some small reward for the day's endeavour), evenings can loom large. Black holes, even at the height of summer. They can almost terrify, and certainly sadden. And that's why wine is inviting, why beer appeals – they partly fill the hole. But by partly filling the hole, they partly stretch it. Such are my thoughts, pushing my bike up the hill.

Dinner is salmon and rice and leeks and broccoli. Noticeable lack of complaints. I eat at the kitchen table, with *The Times* for a placemat. Just a fuel stop really. When it's over I don't know what to do. I just sit there. Then I go out to the garden and just sit there instead. Nan rings. Asks what I'm doing.

'Just looking at the flowers. Wondering what they are. I've lost my interpreter. You?'

'Grandad's just got back with the shopping.'

'Do you know much about cherries?'

'Cherries? A bit.'

'Morello. We've got loads in the garden.'

'I wouldn't.'

'No?'

'Even the ripest are sour.'

'I'll give some a go.'

'I better help Grandad.'

'OK.'

'Love you lots.'

'Bye Nan.'

*Love you too. Thank you for loving me.*


**20 July.** St George's Hospital. Nip into M&S to buy Winnie some pork pies, some fruit, and a copy of *The Week*, then proceed to Gunning Ward, bay 5, bed 3. Winnie's awake and says she's pleased to see me. I don't take this to heart because she might be hallucinating. She looks … OK. Better than I expected. Frail certainly, but very much alive. She isn't drinking much: confesses that she's not inclined to on account of the catheter. She's happy with the fruit but doesn't think she'll be able to manage the pork pies. I ask if she got my postcard. She says she's got all her cards stowed away for safekeeping. Reckons someone will help themselves if they're on display. Good old Winnie. Always on her guard. A nurse brings her a cup of tea. Unreasonably, I'm momentarily annoyed not to be offered one. I raise the top of the bed so she's more upright, so she can get at the tea. But she doesn't touch it.

'I feel pulverised.'

'I bet you do.'

'Very noble of you to come.'

'It's alright.'

'Not much in it for you.'

'I'm sure you'll do it for me one day.'

'Don't count on it.'

'I would have come sooner but—'

'I look like I've been run over by a tank.'

'But how do you feel?'

'Like I've been run over by a tank.'

'And how does that feel?'

'How do you think?'

'I'm joking.'

'I could do with a hairbrush.'

'You look alright, Winnie.'

'That's sweet of you to say, but I caught a glimpse of myself and I look like Donald Trump.'

'Donald Trump?'

'Aged 216.'

'You look a million dollars in comparison to some in here.'

'Don't be so hard on yourself.'

'Touché.'

'You're covered in fuzz.'

'True.'

'And you need to get Liz round to look at your hair.'

'Put some colour in.'

'I really don't think I could manage the pork pies, Ben.'

'Shall I take them with me then?'

'I didn't say that, did I?'

I'm pleased. That we're chatting. That she's taking the piss out of me. Bloody relieved to be honest. She closes her eyes. Not to sleep, she says. Just to rest. I tell her a few things as she's resting. That Kuba's been round and is on top of things. That I've spoken to Arthur a few times and he seems to be doing OK. Tell her that Rebecca is on holiday in Wales for her birthday. That Abigail is in Italy with her fella, somewhere in the north.

'Italy?'

'Yeah. Shall we give her a call?'

'Could we?'

'We can give it a go. Where's your phone?'

'Christ knows.'

Her phone is dead and beneath the *Financial Times*. I plug it in and get through to Abigail. Winnie's face is a picture as Abigail recounts her journey so far. The food. The people. The lakes. Florence! Winnie leans in closer to the phone. Wants to stress something, to underline something. 'You must take it all in, Abigail. Anything beautiful. Anything at all. Because one day – and I promise you this – you'll fall over in the garden and that'll be it.'

She nods off holding a strawberry. I relieve her of it gently, clean her fingers with a tissue. I make some enquiries of a nurse – Trish. She gives me a few minutes she doesn't have. Tells me Winnie's been up and down but is steady now. I ask if she's eating. Trish raises her eyebrows, half smiles. 'She could be a judge on *MasterChef*, couldn't she?'


**22 July.** Clean Arthur's razor. Not sure what he's been doing with the thing. Getting all the muck out takes some doing, and requires a variety of instruments. Never sworn so much in my life at something inanimate. No wonder it used to take

Winnie a couple of hours. No wonder she moaned to high heaven about it. I used to think she was milking it. Didn't know what she was going through.

**23 July.** St George's Hospital. Gunning Ward. Winnie's not in her bed. Unless her condition has altered dramatically and she's now a man in his forties. Won't lie – sharp moment of panic upon not seeing Winnie. The moment lasts until it's explained by a nurse that she's been moved to an NHS rehab facility.

I cycle to the rehab facility (Marshland Court) only to learn that Winnie won't be able to receive any visitors for the next ten days because a member of staff tested positive for Covid this morning. I'm told that staff members get tested every morning and that the staff member in question came in this morning without symptoms and tested positive. 'I'm sorry,' I say, 'but can you explain why everyone in your care has to self-isolate because a member of staff tested positive this morning? Surely the member of staff self-isolates and that's it? Who are you protecting? The visitors? It doesn't make sense. I know you don't make the rules, but I'm just worried that ten days without any visitors might not do Winnie the world of good. At all. To say the least.' I'm told that everything happens for a reason.

**26 July.** Watch highlights of the Olympics. Adam Peaty doing the breaststroke – Christ almighty. If Adam saw me doing the breaststroke he'd be in stitches. Winnie can do the breaststroke quicker than I can, even in her present condition. Then it's the triathlon. Georgia Taylor-Brown has a flat tyre for five kilometres but still manages to battle back to finish second. We can all take heart from that. Genuinely inspiring stuff. Though I can't say as yet what it's inspired me to do. Certainly not what they're doing. I call Winnie. No answer. Call Arthur. No answer. I call Kuba to check he's still coming over next Tuesday. No answer. I pick some blackberries and run them round to Carlotta. She's not in. Lord, even Carlotta's got more going on socially than me. I end up passing the evening listening to golf on the radio. A new low.

**27 July.** Have a proper breakfast. The whole routine. Set it all out. Bowl, spoon, plate, knife, marmalade, butter, muesli, some raspberries from the garden, paper on the table, a coffee, the radio on. Toast a slice in stages, retrieve with scissors, whack on the marmalade shamelessly – and not the three-fruit stuff my dad brought up. Crunch. Yum. I've missed that. Not sure why I stopped with the daily toast. Odd and slightly worrying how behaviour changes when alone. Front page of the paper causes the usual cognitive dissonance. A member of the WHO says Britain's approach to the pandemic (easing restrictions despite rising cases) is 'epidemiological stupidity'. While elsewhere on the front page a professor of medicine is saying we're on the right track and urges readers to ignore the naysayers. And just to clear the whole matter up, another boffin is reported as being 'utterly unsure' about the whole thing. After just one page, I'm reminded why I stopped reading the paper. I do like the phrase 'epidemiological stupidity'

DEEP BREATHS PLEASE

however. It's got an oxymoronic quality, epidemiological being one of the least stupid words in the world, and stupidity being one of the most. This is the sort of pointless observation I'd share with Winnie. Who'd invariably give the remark all the attention and enthusiasm it deserved, before finishing her toast and telling herself to stop having so much fun and get on with the day.

I phone Winnie. Or rather, I phone her and she phones me back.

'Hello, Winnie.'

'What these girls can do on a beam beggars belief. I have no idea how they land on their feet.'

'Are you watching the Olympics?'

'I would like to regain some fitness but not that much I can tell you. How are you?'

'I'm fine. Fine. How's the hip?'

'It's getting better. *Slowly*. I have a wheelie. Like Arthur's.'

'Are you compus mentus?'

'Compos mentis? Yes, I am. For the time being.'

'Are you comfortable?'

'The view is certainly better. I can see some wild flowers and a portable toilet. But the food remains satanic.'

'Ah.'

'Speak of the devil. Here comes lunch. I've got some cauliflower that looks worse than I do. They don't use salt. Don't think they've heard of the stuff.' She eats something. 'Oh my God I'm going to vomit.'

'Do you want anything, Winnie?'

'Yes, a bucket. Nurse!'

'I can't visit, I'm afraid.'

'I know. I've been told. They're terrified of Covid.'

'But I can drop things off.'

'One of your home-cooked meals would be nice.'

Blimey. The food *can't* be good. 'How about Saturday's paper?'

'Yes. If you would. Pick out the relevant bits. I don't wish to drown in it. I must say that the armchair I have is *very* good. It just makes me feel so *lazy*.'

'But you have to rest, Winnie.'

'I miss *tidying*.'

'They do say tidying releases endorphins.'

'Nurse! And I really must say thank you to everyone. I've had so many cards. They really have been a comfort. Some have had the most beautiful flowers on the front. They've made me want to look out of the window.'

'At the portable toilet?'

'Perhaps we can hang a sign in front of the house saying thank you.'

'Let's deal with the thank yous when you get back.'

'Or you can stand outside and clap. Nurse! I promise you, Ben, I can't eat this cauliflower.'

'I cleaned Arthur's razor by the way.'

'Oh good.'

'Nightmare. I swear he mows the lawn with it. Took me an hour.'

'Not surprised.'

'Be glad when you're back to reclaim your duties.'

'Might be a while, I fear.'

'It's a trial of patience and hip, Winnie.'

'Nicely put. Nurse!'

I hook out certain sections – Life & Art, Review, House & Home – and then go round the garden with a pair of secateurs and snip one of everything I can find. Quite a pleasant undertaking, and quite a motley bunch in the end. Maybe a dozen different flowers. Don't know the name of any of them, I'm embarrassed to say. Bind them with a tiny elastic band. Put the bunch in a paper bag and stow carefully in my backpack, alongside the bits of the paper. Cycle up to the village, nip into Bayley & Sage, pick up a fish pie, a cottage pie, a tomato soup, a pasta salad and a scotch egg. Up to Marshland, where Winnie's on the fifth floor. I buzz up wearing a mask. I'm told to leave it all in the porch.

I'm in the Co-op. Winnie calls. The gist of it is this: 'Ben. Winnie. You mustn't spend money in Bayley & Sage. Mustn't. Though I am excited about the fish pie. The flowers. Oh my. So beautiful. Such a clever selection. Couldn't be bettered. You've got a hyacinth, and a snow pea, and the red one I forget the name of. I've got them in a glass here. They put a film on this afternoon. Rather good. Most of us saw it when it first came out in the sixteenth century. *The 39 Steps.* Rather inappropriate when you think about it. Anyway, off you go.'

When I get home there's a message on the answerphone. It's Winnie. She must have called here before she got me on the mobile, because it's the same content. Ben. Winnie. Flowers. Couldn't be bettered, etc. I'm genuinely not sure if I've ever given someone something that's been so well received. Must do it again sometime. Make a habit of it. But that wouldn't work because it's the context that's crucial, isn't it? And it's hard to replicate contexts, isn't it? They're too complicated. Change too quickly. Though I could make a bunch for Carlotta. And one for Megan. Neither are in rehab but still. In short, pick flowers. Preferably in your own garden, but if you don't have one someone else's will do. And then give the flowers to someone. Simple as that. It won't hurt. It *can't* hurt. End of note to self.

**31 July.** Take Winnie some cards that have arrived plus an individual quiche and a fruit medley. Nurse who collects the items from me is wearing disposable apron and gloves and transfers the individual quiche into a vast, 40-litre transparent plastic bag, which is tragicomic to observe.

'No knickers?' says the nurse.

'Sorry?'

'She needs knickers.'

'Oh right. I wasn't aware.'

'I phoned you.'

'Did you?'

'We spoke this morning.'

'Did we?'

'I told you to bring knickers.'

'Did you?'

'You're Stewart?'

'No, I'm Ben.'

'Ah. OK. Bye.'

'Er – one thing. Just quickly. Winnie said her nails need cutting.'

'We can't do that.'

'But neither can anyone else because she's not allowed visitors.'

'If you bring some clippers I will give them to her. That's the best I can do.'

'OK.'

'And some knickers, please.'

'Sure.'


Later. Winnie calls.

'How are you?' she says.

'I'm OK. Did you get the quiche?'

'Yes. It looks terrific.'

'Good.'

'It came in a huge plastic bag.'

'Yeah I saw that.'

'It's just so *boring*.'

'What, cheese and bacon?'

'They're saying no visitors until Monday. What's so special about Monday?'

'Ten days since the cleaner tested positive.'

'Not that you'd appreciate seeing me.'

'True.'

'It's not going to be as simple as just going back to the pad, I'm afraid.'

'So I hear.'

'The window is a solace. I can see some bilious plants.'

*Bilious?*

'Rhododendrons, I think.'

*Bulbous maybe?*

'And there's a tall conifer tree.'

*I suppose they could be bilious.*

'And somebody's house. And a big aerial or antenna for communicating with outer space. Which is where I might as well be.'

'You're at odds and at sea, Winnie.'

'I am indeed.'

'Kuba was here today.'

'Who was?'

'Kuba. Trimming the hedges.'

'Where was he putting it all?'

'Tarpaulin sacks.'

'Californian tracks?'

'TARPAULIN SACKS.'

'Ah. Tarpaulin sacks.'

'That's it.'

'Thank you for what you're doing.'

'It's a pleasure manning the fort.'

'Can't think of anyone nicer to be there.'

'Went to Arthur's this morning.'

'Haven't seen Arthur for ages. He hasn't called.'

'Dropped off a *Spectator* and a box of tissues.'

'A *Spectator* and what?'

'A box of tissues.'

'Unlikely combination.'

'That's what I thought.'

'Potentially unprecedented.'

'I suppose these are unprecedented times.'

'As they keep telling us.'

'Just the weekend and then it's Monday, Winnie.'

'That is consoling.'

'Hang in there.'

# 11

## Almost got to I love you

**1 August.** A lot of new things come as a nice surprise. Others don't. Living alone doesn't. I used to think doing dinner each evening and sitting down to eat with Winnie was something I mostly did for her, but now I see that I was doing it as much for myself as for anyone else. I also used to think that her habit of always having something plugged in making a noise – the radio, the TV, the washing machine, the kettle – was a bad one. Now I know why she did it: because silence amplifies solitude. I also used to think that her habit of *keeping busy* didn't do her any favours. Now I find myself picking blackberries despite having a few kilos in the freezer, and hoovering two days in a row. Hey-ho.

**2 August.** I cycle up to Marshland Court. In my bag is a small loaf of granary, a small jar of marmalade, and a novel called *Love* (Roddy Doyle's latest). I'm shown through to a waiting lounge, where the women's pole vault final is being shown on various screens. I'm tested for Covid. The nurse is a character. Jovial. Cynical. Temperamental. Wonders how much the inventor of the test is making. Wonders if the tests even work. Tells me about a man – now in prison – who sold bomb detectors for millions that were nothing of the sort. I'm taken up to Winnie's room on the fifth floor. She's in bed. The fact that she's lost a lot of weight is obvious and alarming. Her bed's alongside the window. So here's the strange antenna, the portable toilet, the wild flowers. Dominating the view is a huge conifer. If the window were open you could touch it. 'That's my escape route,' she says. Curious how she keeps ending up next to conifers.

Also curious is what's on the telly. We watch elite humans do unthinkable things with their bodies. The athleticism on display accentuates Winnie's immobility. Not that she sees it like that. She just can't believe how huge some of the weight-lifters are. My attention is taken by the whiteboard facing her bed, used by the nurses and physios to chalk up news and targets. I read that today's target is 'exercise!' and that her provisional release date is 21st August – three weeks hence. I present the bread. She holds it, weighs it up, smells it. I present the marmalade. She wants to know where it's from. I tell her I transferred some of hers into a smaller jar I found in the back kitchen, which satisfies her. I present *Love*. She wants to know if it's real or made up. 'Made up,' I say. 'In which case take it home,' she says.

I cut her nails. Catch the clippings in a section of the *Financial Times*. She says again and again how thankful she is, but I don't mind doing it, not a bit, feels utterly normal. Holding her fingers, her thumbs. She's not pleased when some clippings go flying and hide among her bedclothes mind you. I nip her finger. 'Ouch!' I can't help but laugh. 'Call an ambulance,' she says. Cutting her nails, I become conscious of my own: they need doing. I ask if she's spoken to Arthur. She attempts to shrug. 'He's got his own life. I don't want to intrude.'

She has a bite of the bread but no more. Can't get it

down. Doesn't have an appetite. It's plainly a vicious cycle: loses weight, does less exercise, has less appetite, loses more weight. She's meant to be recovering, and in a sense she is, but in another sense she isn't, in another sense she's getting worse. She shows me the large plasters running the length of her upper leg, where the surgeons went in. 'The pelvis was already weak,' she says. 'They had to chop it up to get Arthur's legs out. I really did fail him, the poor love.' I tell her that she emphatically did not fail him. That it was nobody's fault. That it couldn't be legislated for or guarded against. But it falls on deaf ears. Or seems to, anyway. Who knows which of our words make an impression?

My allotted hour is up. I want to give her a kiss on the cheek but I also want to just leave, so I meet myself in the middle and put my hand on her shoulder and say pointless, empty things. 'Take care. Take it easy. Don't jump out the window.' And if I could say what I wanted? I don't know. But it wouldn't be take care, take it easy, don't jump out the window. It would be deeper and more honest. But there you are. We say what we can. And what Winnie can say is, 'Yes, off you go. God bless. Put the kettle on.'

5 August. Normally when it comes to crumbles I just chance my arm, chuck it all in, see how it pans out. But this time I listen, I follow, I defer – to Raymond Blanc. Raymond's secret is preparation. The blackberries and apple get an initial five minutes in a pan with some butter and sugar, while the crumble gets ten minutes in the oven before being dumped on top of the fruit. It's a considered approach, a thoughtful

ALMOST GOT TO I LOVE YOU

approach, a *borrowed* approach – the type of approach I haven't tended to bother with up to now. And the results are excellent. I eat a large bowl of the crumble in front of *Gardeners' World*. Maxwell, aged eleven from West Yorkshire, has just shown 1.3 million people his garden, which although small sees a fair bit of action. The lad gets home from school and cracks on with the growing of courgettes (two types), potatoes, rhubarb, celery and plenty of cannabis. Towards the end (of the bowl of crumble), I realise that something's missing. And it's not Winnie. I'm not *that* sentimental. It's the ice cream Raymond recommended.

**9 August.** Take Winnie a bag of goodies Carlotta put together and some cards from various people. One's from my niece, Annabelle, aged seven, who knocked it out in about five minutes. On the front of the card is a drawing of Winnie wearing a jumper with the letter M on it. (M for marmalade.) She's also wearing a stripy skirt and some dangly earrings. To be frank she's not looking too bad. When I give it to her, Winnie asks if it's meant to be me or her.

She's been on her feet more. Has even been getting told off for walking around too much, for leaving her room. She's not allowed to leave her room because she could be a vector of disease. But the physio is happy, and the nurses are happy – with her progress, I mean. She wants to know about the house. I tell her about the rain, and the roof, and the alarm, and the fireplace, and the fox I caught sunbathing, and the Bramley apples, and the raspberries, and a newspaper clipping I found in the basement, which alleges that

80,000 salmon went missing on Henry's watch in October 1992. She remembers the latter incident. Henry was chairman of a seafood company at the time. 'Can't keep a good salmon down,' she says. 'That's the trouble.'

She's been asked to think about her options going forward. Put another way, she's been asked to consider the idea of not going home. She's been warned it's not practical, not realistic, not safe enough, and who is she to disagree, after what happened? But that's down the road, and this is now, and for now she's just bored, bored, bored. Though she can't complain. The staff are good. And she's secure. And there's always the window.

She shows me her 'cupboard'. It's a sturdy purple bag from Liberty – the department store – that she keeps down the side of her bed. She's got all her valuables in it. Cards, make-up, hairbrush, phone charger, face masks. She doesn't let it out of her sight. Insists on carrying it around with her when she's doing her exercise, which she admits is probably a bit over the top.

Also over the top is Abigail's new hairdo. Apparently she's dyed it practically orange. We give her a call. She tells us she's in Venice. Winnie speaks warmly of the place. Says Henry once dropped his ice cream on the Ponte Vecchio.[1] Says she won't be going back any time soon. Not because Henry dropped his ice cream. Because she can't. No chance. She'll just have to remember. To travel that way. Which isn't a bad thing. Not really. It's much cheaper for a start.

---

[1] Which is in Florence.

'Anyway, darling. God bless.'

'Bye, Granny.'

'It was Henry's grandmother who used to say God bless.'

'Was it?'

'It's a warm thing to say, I think. It's loving. A loving way to sign off.'

'It is.'

'That's why I picked it up, I suppose. That's why I always say it.'

'Hm. I guess.'

'So God bless, darling. Carry on. Off you go. Lots of love. God bless. See? I've said it again.'

'Bye, Granny.'

'Bye, darling. Bye. Bye.'

She almost got there, didn't she? Almost got to I love you.


**10 August.** The occupational therapist comes to the house. Kirsty. Stewart and Rebecca turn up for the occasion. It's curious watching and hearing someone survey the house with only one thing in mind – risk. By the sound of it, the house is jam-packed full of the stuff. Kirsty tests the reclining chair. Measures the height of Winnie's bed. Scrutinises the front steps. Sizes up the downstairs loo. In short, the outlook isn't promising. Winnie would need assistance up the stairs, and into the house, and around the house, and with bathing. And several zones would be off-limits entirely, including the garden and the basement. (The roof is fine apparently.) In effect, what Kirsty's saying is that Winnie couldn't be herself here. She couldn't do those things she feels utterly compelled to do. What's more, Kirsty's also worried about Winnie's confusion, her post-op delirium, her mental health. She says Winnie has on several occasions got out of bed in the night to get on with the day, and is often adamant it's Saturday on a Tuesday. (Nothing new there then.) Rebecca says there was a time she left the gas on. Stew says there was a time she lost control going down Arterberry Road. I say there was also a time *I* left the gas on and lost control going down Arterberry Road, but my interjection is laughed off. Both children are keen to know about the options *outside* of Winnie's home. And I don't blame them. As much as I want Winnie to go where she wants, I also want her to go where she's least likely to come to harm. The two might be at odds. Indeed, I think the two *are* at odds. If she moved back here – Stewart is saying – there's no *way* she wouldn't go outside unassisted, or down to the basement, or mount a stool to wind up a clock. And if she fell again it wouldn't be good news. At all.

**11 August.** Up early to get petrol for the lawnmower. Deliver said to Kuba, who's having a coffee in the shed. Pick various apples, two types of plum, blackberries. There's loads of the latter down in the jungle, where the tennis court used to be. Blackberries don't come off their stem like raspberries do. They *retain* their stem for some reason, won't give it up, and are much less fun to pick therefore. The figs aren't ready – are figs *ever* ready? – and nor are the quinces. Spend the evening researching approaches to freezing blackberries.

**12 August.** Voicemail. 'Ben. Winnie. Where are you? I've not seen anybody for ages. Have you seen my family?'

**13 August.** Nazir Afzal (lawyer) on *Desert Island Discs*. Speaks of his mother. Says she was a mountain. (One assumes he's talking figuratively.) Says he massaged her legs as she died. Couldn't believe how small her feet were. Regrets that he didn't show her the love she deserved. Picks a Kate Bush song, 'This Woman's Work'. Here's a lyric: 'I can't stop thinking of all the things I should've said that I never said.' Note to self.

**14 August.** Winnie calls complaining about her hair, wonders if I could bring myself to locate some clips or similar. I go up to the pharmacy in the village. Similar to clips are grips (it transpires), so I get those as well. Also get a hairband, or headband, or Alice band – one of those horseshoe-shaped things. I reason that if she wears all three – a clip, a grip and a band – and still can't see then it's something *she's* doing wrong. Continue up to Marshland. Locking my bike, I notice that the building isn't dissimilar to Windy Ridge. The same brick, the same classical style. It's just larger and full of people you wouldn't normally catch at Winnie's place. I sanitise, don my mask, ring the buzzer. Clark comes down. Says I can't come up because they've reached their quota of visitors for the week, but he'll take up what I've brought. I hand over the hair stuff then cycle round to the southside of the building. Identify the tall conifer that Winnie plans to climb down should she run out of better ideas. But her curtains are drawn against the sun, so she wouldn't spot me if I stayed here all day.

**15 August.** Happen upon an album of photos under some CDs. There's one of Winnie and Arthur after the latter's graduation in Exeter, Arthur in his gown and mortarboard, Winnie in a dress that brings rhubarb to my mind, daylight between them despite the key occasion.

**16 August.** The children are talking of Winnie going into a care home. Of now being the time to change, to sell, to move on. Should the house be sold, it's likely it would go to a developer, and Windy Ridge levelled to make way for several up-to-date properties. The house – and the home it has been – is on borrowed time, sure as eggs is eggs. As a result I spend longer going upstairs, moving along the hallway, taking my bike out of the garage, picking fruit, hanging sheets. More curious, more watchful. More tender. Like I'm paying my respects.

**17 August.** Stew and entire family (wife and three kids) come round for the afternoon. Stew does some paperwork, the others roam around, play in the garden, pick raspberries and blackberries. (They leave me a decent amount of each which is nice.) Nice kids. I've met Mango before but the others are new to me. Jane says the house depresses the kids, and depresses her, which makes me think they really can't have had the best of times when they all lived here for six months last year. Jane gives a potted version of what happened.

ALMOST GOT TO I LOVE YOU

Winnie had made clear that she wanted to move to a much smaller house. Stew and Jane moved in to 1) provide support during the pandemic, and 2) help facilitate Winnie's move by sorting through the tons of stuff lying around doing nothing. When they made a start on the sorting – and this will come as news to no one – Winnie freaked out. She couldn't let anything go. She insisted on checking *everything*. She took the clearance *personally*, as if every old bed frame, every old bike pump, were being taken directly from her heart, from who she was. The rest is history. Relations soured, Winnie's plan to move out was parked, and I was brought in. So it goes. From my perspective, there's no villain of the piece. Just a family being human. Which is often all it takes for things to go haywire. There's a nice moment in the sitting room when I ask all the kids what their favourite subject at school is and Mango (aged eight) says philosophy. I ask what the most philosophical thing she can say is. She gives it some thought and then says that the meaning of life is to avoid suffering.

**18 August.** Winnie has requested: some books from the pile beside her bed; a pair of tweezers; and the radio from the kitchen. Browsing the pile of books throws up a surprise. Namely, a copy of the *Kama Sutra* on top of *The Holy Bible*. When I get to Marshland, I find her in her room, engrossed in a programme about rationing. You wouldn't say I'm given an enthusiastic welcome – she tells me where to put the radio and that's about it – but I suppose that's not entirely unusual. I know from experience that if you catch her when she's engrossed in something, don't expect the red-carpet treatment. During an ad break, I tell her a few things that have been going on, but she's not interested. A nurse delivers two types of medication. Winnie thinks they're paracetamol but can't be sure.

**19 August.** The leak in the roof isn't getting any better. The old slate tiles have given an inch, and now the bad weather gets through. I know this because when it gets through it gets on me. Roger the roofer turns up. I could hear him coming – all the way from Staines. Talks to the trees this one. Winnie warned me about him. She said, 'You might not care for the information but you'll know Roger inside and out before he's been there five minutes. The man's got what you'd call an overdeveloped personality. But he doesn't bother with scaffolding, which saves us a fortune.' By the time Roger's been here five minutes I know the following: he had breakfast at the Bridge Café in Raynes Park; that the Bridge Café does a good steak, salad and chips for seven quid; that one time when Winnie broke her arm she got Roger to drive her down to the bakery on Kingston Road; that Windy Ridge is too much for Winnie, too much by half, so perhaps it's time for her to move on; that wherever Winnie ends up, he hopes she's got a roof and that he gets to come round and fix it now and again; that he thinks the door knocker is actually a sturgeon rather than a mythical fish; that, speaking of fish, he drinks like one himself these days because he almost dies three times a week; that he'll have a quick cup of tea if there's one going and then he'd better make a start fixing that hole.

**21 August.** Winnie's GP drops in during my visit. He's doing his weekly round. Winnie doesn't recognise him. Doesn't want to by the look of it either. Her focus is on an interior design programme on the television. 'This is not good,' the doctor says to me. 'I've been her GP for twelve years. I was in and out of her house every week. I'd like to test Winnie for dementia. Get a diagnosis. She's had three significant relocations and such events tend to unmask problems that were already there.' He rounds off his appraisal by saying that Winnie falling over was the worst thing she could have done, which is pretty insightful of him. That's churlish of me. I know it is. But to be frank I'm not entirely convinced by his take on things. I'm tempted to offer an alternative report, something along the lines of: 'I hear what you're saying, Doctor, but Winnie could really do with some hearing aids, so don't necessarily think that the reason she's irresponsive is because she's got dementia, and she's also knackered, so that needs to be factored in, and this interior design programme has well and truly caught her attention, so there's that to be considered as well, and although you're right to say she's been going into other people's rooms, she's been going into other people's rooms *to help* the people in them, so surely it would be amiss to consider such behaviour unhinged or offbeat when it is in fact entirely in keeping with her character, but then again I've only known Winnie ten months whereas you've known her for twelve years, and you are, after all, the doctor, so I *do* hear what you're saying, it's just that, it's just that I guess I don't want to; I guess I want instead to think it's her hearing, it's fatigue, it's boredom, it's a bit of depression, and I maintain it *could* be a combination of those things, and besides, the reason she doesn't recognise you might be because you're wearing a mask. Mightn't it?'

**23 August.** I bump into someone I know outside Marshland Court. She tells me her dad died this morning, aged 92. He was in his own home until a week ago. Carers used to pop round twice a day, but he was never nice to them. Never wanted them there. They were too close to the bone. He had a fall and then came here and lasted a week. She says she read to him as he was dying. I ask what she was reading. *Around Ireland with a Fridge*, she says. She's got a tear in her eye. A tear in both. Just occurs to me now that tear and tear are homonyms.

**31 August.** Winnie has been relegated. From the fifth floor to the ground floor. From NHS rehab to private care home. One good thing about her relegation is a change to the visiting policy. Now more than one person can visit at the same time. Which is why I'm sat in the car outside Arthur's place. Indeed, that's why Arthur's just got in the car. 'You negative, mate?' I say. 'No I'm alright,' he says.

We find Winnie in the lounge with some other residents. Bit of a party going on by the look of it – there's a bottle of whisky on the coffee table. She spots us out of the corner of her eye. Stands. Walks. It's bloody good to see. Before she reaches us she's being told off by a nurse for neglecting her

Zimmer. 'That's your best friend, Winnie. Your *best* friend.' You wouldn't think it was her best friend the look Winnie gives it. She says to the nurse, 'With all due respect, Caroline, but I'll decide who my friends are.' She makes a beeline for Arthur. Gives him a hug, a kiss. There's a look in Arthur's eyes – *crikey*. She puts her hand on my arm and says thank you. Thank you for Arthur. For bringing him. Then she spots the state of Arthur's wheelie.

'Oh, Arthur …'

'What?'

'Look at your wheelie.'

Arthur looks at it. 'Yeah. And now what?'

She takes Arthur through to the lounge. Addresses the crowd. 'Everyone, this is my son.'

I give them some time. Invent a pretext: just getting a few things from the car, Winnie. Have a moment outside, sat on a bench, facing the care home. My first impression is that it doesn't suit her. That it's not right. Stew reckons she's 'settling in', but I'm not so sure. Just watching her for a minute with the other residents was telling. She's behaving like one of the staff. Facilitating. Organising. Introducing. Caring. Explaining.

I go back in. Winnie's cleaning Arthur's wheelie with a napkin. She asks how I'm getting on and I tell her it's only when you're alone that you realise how big things are. She wonders if we can get someone else in, to give me a bit of company, to perk the place up a bit. She suggests Megan as I suggest Carlotta, which has us laughing. She turns to Arthur. Puts her hand on his. Just smiles at him. 'It's a nice lounge,' he says. 'Don't be fooled, Arthur. This whole place is insufferably boring. Not a brain cell in the joint.'

There's a lady sat alone. I go over and ask if she wants to join us for a chat. She checks her watch, says alright then. Her name's Joy and it's her first day. Says she can't wait for her son to come. Says he was meant to be here already. Joy's from Northern Ireland. Had polio as a child. They said she wouldn't be able to walk again but they got that wrong. Can't walk now though because her knee has had it – hence the wheelchair. She keeps being put places and just left there and it's getting on her tits. When she calls out to be put somewhere more lively ('the middle of the road for example'), they just give her a gardening magazine. But her son's coming soon. Was meant to be here already. Is probably stuck in traffic. Which can be a nightmare around here she's been told. Then Joy leans into Winnie and says, 'I'm miserable, Winnie.' To which Winnie says, 'Wait until you try the food.' Joy shakes her head. Winnie laughs quietly. Joy smiles. And then Arthur laughs too – more and more, as per his fashion.

Then our time runs out. She's not meant to, but Winnie comes outside to bid us farewell. As we drive away, I see her in the rear-view mirror waving, and then being ushered inside.

# 1999

*Stewart and Jane's wedding day. The reception is in the garden of Windy Ridge. A marquee has been erected on the lawn to accommodate a hundred guests plus the walnut and mulberry trees. (The former, incidentally, has found itself behind the top table, where it is liable to appear in a lot of wedding photos.) Children divert themselves by hiding under the bride's dress or playing on the tennis court at the bottom of the garden, which will have hosted its last encounter (a straight-sets win for Henry) within a year. Winnie Carter is in the kitchen, briefing the young team of caterers contracted for the occasion on certain key matters, including the utmost importance of the plates going out hot. There's a nice moment (that goes some way to puncturing the generally stressful atmosphere) when a teenage waiter asks if the rule about the plates extends to the pâté.*

*Between the third and final courses, Winnie goes around the tables. She puts her hands on the backs of chairs and shares some words with the seated – dry remarks, mordant quips, wry asides: the stuff she's known and celebrated and occasionally feared for. 'I'm afraid the chicken hasn't exactly risen to the occasion.' 'It was good of the walnut tree to join us.' 'If Joan keeps drinking at this rate she'll soon lose sight of her fiancé.' She's wearing a matching skirt and collarless jacket, the fabric for which – a light blue silk – she bought in the East End of London on a rare trip into town. (She'd like to get into town more, if she's honest, whether for plays or suppers, or the parks or the galleries, or to meet old friends or Henry on his lunch break, but there just never appears to be enough time.) Handling the silk for the first time, some six months ago now, she gave a silent nod to the mulberry tree in her garden, and took some comfort in the thought that somehow all things are woven. She's been saying to a few of the guests that the fabric was intended for curtains, which provides an old friend of Henry's with occasion to wonder if Winnie's hoping to get pulled at some point. It's obvious to most that she's in her element – at home, in her garden, surrounded by people who are content with short exchanges that lack unsettling quantities of sentiment. Not that she isn't emotional. It's not that. It's just that when it comes to emotion she's developed a preference and / or a habit for not sharing it, certainly not its deeper hues in any case. (Hey-ho.)*

*At Winnie's behest, everyone is wearing a flower from the garden. One such flower has found its way to the ground (one always will), where it was spotted and rescued by Winnie's first grandchild, who is presently at Winnie's feet pulling on her grandmother's skirt. Winnie thoughtlessly puts a hand on the top of her head (Victoria's, not her own) and strokes her hair while continuing to share a reminiscence with a friend about the time Arthur fell off a horse. Henry is now tapping his knife against his glass (Winnie wishes he wouldn't), so she excuses herself and returns to her place by his side. During his speech, she adopts a broad, closed-mouth smile and casts her eyes half-down at the small vase of flowers on the table before her, and can't help but notice that the primrose is on the turn. At the end of Henry's official contribution to proceedings (he'll continue to contribute unofficially for some time yet), she laughs sincerely, claps once (keeping her hands together as if in prayer after completing the gesture), and then gives the vase a drink of sparkling water (the provision of which she considers a mad indulgence). Next to offer an address is the best man. As he speaks, Winnie can't take her eyes off him – for fear, for support, for love. When Arthur is done, she's on the brink of tears. To the surprise of few, Winnie is the last on the dance floor and the first off it, citing as an alibi the need to oversee some of the tidying in the kitchen, and perchance rescue one or two things that might be unduly got rid of – the asparagus spears, for example. But Henry does get one slow dance out of his wife: when he adds his rose to hers and tells her he loves her she almost misses a step. When the song comes to an end, Henry wants to keep going, but Winnie explains (blushing so slightly) that as head of the house it's incumbent on her to see people off in taxis (which she will later describe, on more than occasion, as 'rather a fun part of the night'). She shares a longish embrace with June Mendoza on the driveway, who recently painted Henry's portrait. When at last she gets to bed, Winnie cannot sleep for fear the marquee will take off in the wind. She will finally drop off around dawn.*

# Acknowledgements

Everyone at Share and Care Homeshare, for matching me with Winnie and doing excellent work across the country arranging safe and suitable home-shares that allow people to live independently in their homes for longer. Everyone at Icon Books and especially my editor Ellen, who somehow manages to appear unfazed when presented with a first draft three times larger than anticipated. Ed Wilson, my agent, and everyone else at Johnson & Alcock. Winnie Carter, for putting a roof over my head. Her family, for being good, decent people. Everyone at Ruth Killick Publicity, not least for getting me a plum slot in the Waitrose magazine. And then there's everyone who has provided support and inspiration over the years – my family, for example, and my friends. I've already dedicated the book to my partner Megan Menzies (who's a painter by the way – look her up), so do I need to acknowledge her as well?

## ABOUT THE AUTHOR

Ben Aitken was born under Thatcher, grew to six foot then stopped, and is an Aquarius. He is the author of *Dear Bill Bryson: Footnotes from a Small Island* (2015, 2022), *A Chip Shop in Poznań: My Unlikely Year in Poland* (2019) and *The Gran Tour: Travels with my Elders* (2020).